All the Moves I Had

All the Moves I Had

A Football Life

Raymond Berry

with Wayne Stewart

Guilford, Connecticut

An imprint of Rowman & Littlefield

Distributed by NATIONAL BOOK NETWORK

British Library Cataloguing in Publication Information available

Library of Congress Cataloging-in-Publication Data available

ISBN 978-1-4930-1780-5 (hardcover)
ISBN 978-1-4930-1781-2 (e-book)

∞™ The paper used in this publication meets the minimum requirements of American National Standard for Information Sciences—Permanence of Paper for Printed Library Materials, ANSI/NISO Z39.48-1992.

To my father, Mark Raymond Berry, who was, without question, the biggest influence in my life, and to my mother, Bess, who also helped start me out right in life. Also to the man who was really responsible for my pro career, my head coach Weeb Ewbank. Without him I wouldn't have had a pro career.

—Raymond Berry

To the Stewart family: my wife Nancy, sons Sean and Scott, and their wives Rachel and Katie; and to my grandson Nathan.

—Wayne Stewart

Contents

Introduction

by Wayne Stewart

When I first interviewed Raymond Berry, it was for a book entitled *America's Cradle of Quarterbacks*, which covered the great signal callers from the Pittsburgh vicinity. Raymond graciously shared his myriad memories of Johnny Unitas. Together these two men set records, won NFL titles, and captured the hearts of football fans everywhere. Their names are forever linked with a sweet nostalgic tinge, from countless broadcasters joining their surnames as if they possessed a communal name, "Unitas-to-Berry."

After a while we strayed from the topic of Western Pennsylvania quarterbacks and Raymond regaled me with great stories about his life and career. I knew the basics about his journey in football, but here he was offering new on- and off-the-field insights. I was astonished when he said that no writer had ever approached him about putting together his autobiography. I knew right away the story of this all-time great, this legend, had to be preserved and shared.

Any fan would love, for example, Berry's great explanation of how, through thirteen grueling NFL seasons, he fumbled the ball just once, and, more important, the main reason behind *why* he became so skilled at protecting the football. His tales and take on Unitas and his Colt teammates are also priceless.

An autobiography also would give readers the opportunity to separate myth from reality—a chance to hear from the man himself, for example, whether, just from his football instinct, he sensed that a practice field he was coaching on was not of regulation size. The tale has it that the field wasn't off by much, yet Berry knew something wasn't right.

This book affords Berry the platform to share many of his insights and to relive the happiness and achievements of his childhood and high school and college days in Texas. From there his life story continues, chronicling the glory of winning back-to-back NFL championships with the Baltimore Colts and continuing through his days of coaching, including his leading the New England Patriots to a date in the Super Bowl.

Raymond Berry is a man who, by the end of his playing days, had taken a few basic skills and some basic physical attributes—none of which were especially overwhelming—and, with single-minded determination, diligence, and intelligence, transformed himself into the greatest receiver of his time.

Prologue

"Driving" for Treasure in 1958

The setting is venerable Yankee Stadium, the House That Ruth Built, three days after Christmas 1958. The Baltimore Colts and New York Giants square off under the scrutiny of 64,185 fans (about 3,000 spectators shy of a sellout) and under the looming triple-decked structure adorned by its classic scalloped frieze. At stake: the NFL championship. The field is bejeweled with future Hall of Famers such as Frank Gifford, Sam Huff, Lenny Moore, Giants coaches Tom Landry and Vince Lombardi, and two twenty-five-year-old men, born about two months apart. These players, who served as the Colts' main passing combo, are rifle-armed Johnny Unitas and stellar receiver Raymond Berry.

Berry scores a touchdown on the Colts final possession in the first half as he maneuvers to find a crease between two defensive backs, five-time Pro Bowler Jimmy Patton and Hall of Famer Emlen Tunnell; and Unitas hits him with a 15-yard strike with just 1:20 left on the clock. It is one of Berry's record-setting twelve catches for a title game to go along with his other championship game record of 178 receiving yards. The Colts take a 14–3 lead into the locker room.

Flash ahead to the fourth quarter. The clock ticks down to just 1:56, and the Giants now cling to a slim 17–14 lead. The Colts have the ball, but they are an astronomical 86 yards from a touchdown and only slightly less than that from field goal range. Determined to tally the first Colts score of the second half, Unitas, not yet the legend he would become, starts the two-minute drill, one Berry will years later call "the best drive Unitas ever conducted."

But Johnny U. misfires on two passes.

Then he hits Moore for a first down at the Colts 25-yard line.

Next he goes for broke, but it's another incompletion.

Then the most dramatic part of this monumental drive begins.

We got in the huddle, and I stared down the field. The goal posts looked like they were in Baltimore. On the drive to tie it, we didn't think specifically about field goal range or the end zone, we were just going to score whichever way time and position demanded. Unitas was terse, saying little more in the huddle than the play calls. It was just the way he was.

After we got to our 25-yard line, I caught three straight passes. None of these routes—there was a slant, a square-in, a hook pattern—were thrown to the outside, to the sidelines, which would have stopped the clock if I had stepped out of bounds. We didn't go to the boundary on any of the three passes. That was what was unusual about the sequence of plays. It was exactly the opposite of what teams usually do, and it wasn't by design. We weren't thinking at all. I don't think we were even aware of what we were doing.

It was catch-and-run, and our coach, Weeb Ewbank, had trained us in the no-huddle offense, so I don't think we were ever in the huddle but one time on this drive. Unitas hit me on the first one and we lined up and ran the second play, because Weeb taught Unitas and all of us to operate with two plays called in the huddle. So when we came on the field to begin that drive, Unitas had stepped in the huddle and called a one–two punch. We'd worked, of course, on this type of thing all year.

The exact procedure was this: In the huddle Unitas would say, "All right, first play is out left flank right 60. The second play will be out left flank right 68." So, when you went to the line of scrimmage, you ran the first play—if it was incomplete, the clock stopped, so you came back in the huddle and he'd call two plays again. The second play was always the one that, if you hit the first one in bounds, the clock runs, you get back on the line and you run it. You do not huddle.

Sometimes a third play, in effect, would be called—Unitas would audible a third one. If I remember right, that's exactly what happened in that game.

On Unitas's first pass to me, in a second-and-10 situation, we ran a slant pattern, good for 25 yards to midfield, but there's a famous story behind this play. It was supposed to be a 10-yard square-in, but we wound up running a slant. When I lined up, I saw Harland Svare, their veteran outside linebacker, on my side. From film study I knew he walked out on top of the split end, but just occasionally. Sure enough, he moved out on top of me to stop me, but Unitas and I had reviewed and rehearsed what we were to do on the slant pattern *if* the linebacker came out and stood right in my face. I told Unitas, "If he does that to me, we aren't going to run a 10-yard square-in or square-out. We have to come up with an adjustment. We'll go to a Plan B of some type, because I can't run my route with him right on me."

Our arrangement was to adjust a square-in to a slant. If the situation came up, I would make an outside fake, drive off the line real hard like I was trying to release outside of him, because I knew he would come after me and try to hit me and hold me up. Then I would slant underneath him. I'd get him overcommitted outside, and I'd jump up under him. I told Unitas, "We'll call it the linebacker slant."

But would it work game time in a tense situation? When I lined up and Svare walked out on me, I thought, "Does John remember what we agreed on?" And he was looking at me, thinking, "I wonder if Raymond remembers what we agreed on." We had talked about it, worked on it, agreed upon it, then forgot all about it. Forgot about it, that is, until the two-minute drive came up and Unitas called for the square-in and here came Svare. That was the first time the situation we had planned for happened in a game for us.

The film study and the preparation ahead of time and the communication with Unitas reached its proving point. When the ball was snapped, I did what we had planned—I took two quick steps outside and Svare came out there to knock my head off, hold me up, and keep me from getting into my pass route. I slanted underneath him clean as a whistle, and John backpedaled, watched me, waited, then drilled me with the ball. I caught it about 6 yards down field, then turned it up for a 19-yard gain before I was brought down.

Some writers have stated that after locking eyes for a second and realizing we were on the same page, he smiled. Now, I don't recall that for sure, but it certainly sounds like a Unitas deal—I would not disbelieve it at all. We didn't need any audible, that's definite. We just changed the play, and it was a key play. If we don't run that play, we may never have earned our championship ring.

Others have said we discussed the possibility of having to change a play to a linebacker slant several years earlier, making this moment a miraculous meeting of the minds honing in together on the long-distant past. Nope. It hadn't been that long, but it had been several months between the time we agreed on this play and the time it actually happened; and we had reviewed it the week of the championship game. We actually had two weeks off before we played the Giants, so we had a lot of time to prepare.

I will say that this play was the most important single play of my entire career, because that was the start of our three completions. We went on a roll—go to the line of scrimmage and hit one, go to the line and hit another one, and another one. The play ultimately led to the tie and the eventual win.

After that gain to the 50-yard line, the clock showed 1:04 left to play. We got back on the line of scrimmage, and we hit on a square-in pattern for 15 more yards—clock still running. I caught the ball behind Svare and in front of Carl Karilivacz's coverage, down to the 35-yard line.

And then we got back on the line of scrimmage, and John barked out the third play—there was still no huddle. He hit me on a hook pattern—again, all of these plays were inside routes, every one of them. So the clock was moving, and on the last one, I went down there 10 yards, hooked, and he drilled the ball into me.

Visualize what happened on that catch: I'm split out to the left and Karilivacz, the right defensive halfback, is covering me man-to-man. I drive down there 10 yards and hook *inside,* and John throws the ball to me. Well, Karilivacz comes up to tackle me, and he's coming at an inside angle because I'm leaning inside. But I had practiced catching that hook and making a little, quick inside fake then spinning back to the outside to elude the corner—and that's exactly what happened. I caught that hook, I made that little fake, he overran it, and I spun around and ran, picked up 22 yards on that play, to the 13. Jimmy Patton, the right safety, tackled me downfield.

Now, the New York Giants defensive coach was Tom Landry, who had played defensive corner in the NFL himself. He had a tough-as-nails mindset, and he believed that his two corners were out there to cover man-to-man. By having them do that, he got more support to stop the running game. His philosophy was, "We're going to stop that run and make them throw. And one reason we're going to stop the running game is we're going to have nine men up there who can tackle, including both safeties and three linebackers along with the four linemen."

That's exactly what he did, and that's why I had Karilivacz out there man-to-man all day. Patton cheated over at times, and he also played the deep middle so I couldn't run any deep post patterns against Karilivacz, but I could run everything else. Emlen Tunnell was the strong safety, always on the tight end, and Patton was always free in the middle, playing a deep middle.

After Patton tackled me, the clock was still running, down to about 20 seconds. Weeb had trained us on the hurry-up field goal when there are no time-outs left. So everybody rushed out there and got lined up, and we were all so aware that the clock was running. Steve Myhra got lined up and kicked it, and the clock didn't stop until 7 seconds were left, right after he nailed it through that upright. Tie game, 17–17.

Now, we weren't the first team to use the two-minute drill (even though Don Shula once said he felt as if Unitas had invented it), but I think we got the most fame for it because of the 1958 drive. You just don't see anything like that. Three or four plays in a row where you just keep on going, keep on going, keep on going. It was practically unheard of. And there was so much at stake and so big a payoff. You couldn't help but kind of shake your head and say, "Good grief, I've never seen anything like that."

Later, when I had reflected on it, maybe a year later, I talked to Unitas about our drive to tie the game. I said, "John, you kept coming to me. Explain why you came to me three times in a row." He said, "Oh, I figured you'd catch them." Once at a banquet he and I talked about these three straight passes again. I made the observation, "You kept throwing it to me," and he replied, "Well, you kept catching it." He kinda had a dry sense of humor.

As I started to understand football players more and what makes athletes tick, I realized that what I was looking at here was an instinctive player doing what he felt would succeed. I'm not really sure it was a thinking process as much as it was him knowing what to do. Why, he'd come to me *three times in a row*—that just never happens.

I told author Tom Callahan that in this contest maybe our game-tying march "came down just to how well John and I knew each other." I once wrote a story for *Sports Illustrated* stating how vital it is for a receiver and his quarterback to "speak the same language." "It's almost like a marriage," I wrote. "You got to make allowances and understand each other and get to where you know each other so well that you know instinctively what to expect in any situation." It was easy with John because he was so easy to talk to.

Such communication and such a figurative marriage paid off big time. Instinctively we knew what to expect from one another in any kind of situation. Three big Unitas-to-Berry plays for 62 yards, capped with the field goal to push this game into overtime. Sheer excitement.

It ended up being the biggest game of our careers, our first championship. In a later chapter I'll share the rest of what happened as we drove for "treasure" one more time in this classic game.

One thing is for sure—the best was yet to come.

Chapter One

An American in Paris

I was born on February 27, 1933, in Corpus Christi, Texas, and that was a fitting place to come into the world, given the fact that the town's name translates from the Spanish as "the body of Christ," and given the fact that religion became a huge part of my life in my adult years. But I actually spent the majority of my childhood in Paris, Texas, where, naturally, football was an enormous part of my life.

When I was growing up, Texas was a state not very far removed from the frontier. Texas was one of the late states to join the union, and Texans were (and still are) independent, hard-headed, and tough.

Football has been my world from the time I was in school. It dominated my interests and my life then, and it continued to do so all the way through my years in college, through my NFL days, and then into my coaching career. It's been quite a journey.

I come from Scotch-Irish-Welsh roots. My mother, Bess Hudgins, gave me the Welch part. She grew up in a little town outside of Fort Worth, Texas, called Hanley. She came from a family of nine—seven girls and two boys. She was right in the middle. Her father died when she was fairly young, so her mother ended up raising the children alone.

My mother was very musical. She played the piano and organ, and my sister—my only sibling—Peggy, three years older than me, grew up learning to play them, too. Growing up there was music in our home all the time.

My mother was one of the toughest individuals I've ever known. I didn't even realize this until I got out in the world and became exposed to people and started analyzing them, but she was someone who didn't suffer fools lightly.

And my mother made ours an ideal home for me and my sister. She was a stay-at-home mother and really was always there for us. Through all my years growing up, we always had lunch at home. My dad would drive home from teaching high school, which was only about five minutes away, and I was in elementary school about four blocks away, so we ate practically all our meals together. I didn't realize it then, but there's a lot of power in getting together as a family at a table three times a day. And we didn't eat in front of a television set, either. We bonded.

We had a home with a big garden, a chicken lot, a place for a cow, and a barn. That was also a big part of my adolescence.

I had some close friends in our neighborhood. I could walk to their house, or they'd come over to my house. We'd play football together. Because our elementary school was right there in our neighborhood, we had a big school ground that we could use to throw and kick and play.

Baseball wasn't a big part of the Paris scene in those days. I think when I got into high school there was a professional baseball team that came to Paris, so we started going to the games and a lot of the guys got into baseball after that.

I didn't play high school baseball or basketball, though. I followed baseball, got interested in the game. But let's just say that the thing that eliminated me from baseball was the curve ball.

In Texas you could play football pretty much year-round. When I got into high school, I started running track, too. I participated in the high jump and broad jump.

As kids, a lot of us played barefoot on grass and dirt during the Texas summers. It was just the norm—you might have tennis shoes on, or you might play barefoot.

I was a child of the Depression, but I don't remember being affected at all by it. I was probably too young to comprehend the economic conditions that were causing tremendous financial problems for a whole lot of people. My family wasn't hit hard by the Depression, and I think that's because my father was teaching and coaching. By the way, my father was named Mark Raymond Berry, but he went by Raymond Berry.

I grew up in a home where there was clear-cut, strong discipline—no fooling around. You did what you were told to do, or you'd get your butt whipped. Years after I grew up, I read a book by a psychologist who stated that what you'd like to have in a home for a child is love and discipline. As soon as I read that statement, I thought, "Good grief, he just described my home." You can take this one to the bank: My home was an absolute picture of the principle that a home should have an equal amount of love *and* discipline. I benefited a lot from that.

I learned that love without discipline does not work, and discipline without love does not work. When I became a head coach, that was something I told my football team every year when we started out.

I would share with my teams one of the most vivid memories I have of growing up. It was when I was about eight or nine years old and my dad suspected that I was starting to lie to him. Looking back on it, I realize what he did. He waited until he had a situation where he had me red-handed, where I couldn't squirm out of it one way or another. He took me out to the shed we had in back of our house, a razor strap in his hand, and he went after my ass with everything he had. I'm not even sure how many times he hit me, because I was jumping and leaping and dodging and so forth all over that shed. But he scared the living hell out of me. He got the message across. I can tell you that, for sure. And lying just fell off my list of options. I never even thought about lying again after that.

Looking back on it—and I'm not saying that physical punishment should be anyone's go-to disciplinary tool—that was an absolute picture of the power of love and discipline. My dad's motivation was this: He knew that if I became a liar, I would destroy myself, and he loved me enough to not stand by and let me go that route. There's nothing enjoyable about beating the hell out of a child. It was really one of the few times I was hit as a child, but he knew that if he didn't step in and do this, lying would destroy me. Going back to my grandparents, my relatives all handed down the idea of absolute honesty—they didn't know any other way.

I started cursing at a very early age, though. I was often around high school players when I was five or six years old and on up. So I started picking up curse words. My dad didn't really realize what was happening, but I developed a big vocabulary of curse words by the time I was around eight or nine years old. Then, as my temper began to surface, there was a great link between the two—once I lost my temper, the curse words would flow. (A temper and a tendency to swear: two problems I've had to deal with throughout my life.)

Most of my childhood memories are of my mom and dad. I grew up with a feeling of absolute security. And books were a huge part of our home—reading was going on all the time. This was the age before television, so I grew up reading books on a regular basis. I still have my dad's entire library, including an autographed book by Knute Rockne.

My father was a very successful football coach in Texas. He was coaching in Corpus Christi when I was born, five years before we moved to Paris, Texas. As is the case with all football coaches, the move was not voluntary, but you get fired every four, five years, so you move. He defied the odds—he coached in Paris for twenty-five years, then retired from coaching. In all he coached thirty-five years and only got fired once. He also taught math and physical education. After my dad retired, a building at the Paris High School was named after him, the Raymond Berry Athletic Complex.

He never coached anyone who went to the NFL except me, but he coached some All-State players. You have to remember that my dad's time span went through World War II, and so many of the players he coached went off to war. Some of them never came back.

My dad coached Gene Stallings, who had a fine college career at Texas A&M from 1954–1956 playing under Bear Bryant. He was a survivor of Bryant's grueling first training camp, which was depicted in the book *The Junction Boys*. As an assistant on Bryant's first coaching staff at Alabama in 1958, he went on to be a part of their 1961 and 1964 national championship seasons. Stallings later became the head coach at his alma mater, beginning that job at the age of twenty-nine, before becoming the head coach of the St. Louis Cardinals (1986–1989). From there he led the Alabama Crimson Tide (1990–1996), and his 13–0 team in 1992 won the Sugar Bowl to help them earn consensus national championship status. He was inducted into the College Football Hall of Fame as a coach in 2010.

Another one of my dad's players was a great runner, one of the greatest athletes my dad ever saw, whether it was high school, college, or professional football. He was a halfback named Charlie Haas. He was also a sprinter who ran a 9.8 100-yard dash, which—on the cinder tracks used in the day—was outstanding. All of the players who played for my dad heard about Charlie Haas.

There was another great runner, a big fullback who played for the Paris High School Wildcats named Bobby Jack Floyd. He ended up being my daddy's tailback in his junior and senior years. Then he went to Texas Christian University and had a good career there in the Southwest Conference. Those were the two most outstanding players I remember my father having.

I guess coaching a lot of good-to-great high school kids, including a future NFL Hall of Famer, over a career that spanned more than three decades more than validates the fine coaching job he did.

My dad came from a family of seven. His father died when my dad was eight years old. His mother raised the family as a widow, and those children grew up extremely independent. My dad said he was working from the very earliest age, and with his father gone, all of this shaped him into a man who didn't look for anybody else to do things for him. A part of his DNA was absolute confidence. The most important lesson I absorbed from my dad was his unshakable conviction that he never met an opponent he couldn't beat.

I've never understood exactly where this came from; I puzzled over it for years. But one of the biggest parts of my dad's makeup—which obviously I absorbed without realizing it—was that he never felt inferior to anybody. He could have sat down with Franklin Roosevelt or Winston Churchill—the great men of his day—and been *perfectly* at ease. He could have had a conversation with them and he wouldn't think they were any better than he was—or any smarter. That was the way he was, and he wasn't even aware of it, wasn't even conscious of it.

As I got older, I began to realize that he didn't even understand that part of his makeup. But when that lesson was communicated to a football team, it was the most powerful thing he brought to the job. When you played for my dad—and I didn't realize this until I played for other coaches who didn't feel like this—you never thought you were going to lose a game. That confidence absolutely became a part of my makeup. There was always a way to get it done, one way or another. My dad didn't always get it done, but he knew there was a way to do it.

That way of thinking was the greatest asset I had later as a head coach, one of the greatest things I inherited from my father. I spread that message to my players because I believed it, and you can't fool the boys—they know what you believe and what you don't.

My dad was the greatest influence in my life, and as I grew into maturity and went through life, I realized that having him for my father was one of the biggest breaks I ever got. His values and his discipline that he passed on to me meant that I couldn't have had a better home to grow up in.

Another tremendous influence on my life took place when I was eight to twelve years old, when America was locked up in the biggest conflict in its history, World War II. I was exposed to this more than most young boys were because my dad was a high school coach. Over and over again boys he had coached would come back from the war, from fighting all over the world, and visit him at our home. And two of my cousins from my dad's side of the family, who were much older than me, were killed in the war. So I was exposed to these tragedies, and the impact of the war and this time period in American history shaped me as much as anything else growing up. The war is still one of my chief interests today. I've got a lot of books on World War II. I read every one that comes out.

I mentioned this earlier, but there's more to it. As a kid I developed an explosive temper. My temper could trigger quickly, without my realizing what was happening. It has mellowed through the years, but it's a ticking time bomb even now—I'm not free of it. When I was about eleven, I was in a boys' summer camp for six weeks in south Texas. My dad couldn't afford to send me, but the owner knew him and had boys there who did work around the camp to pay for their camp experience.

I went there for two summers and it was a great experience. But during that time, I was working in the mess hall and there was a boy who was bigger and more mature than I was. I don't know what was motivating him, but he started after me verbally. I was just a young kid, and I didn't understand what he was doing. One day in the mess hall, for no reason, he attacked me. At that point I was just flailing around, trying to protect myself because I didn't know that much about fighting. But, when it was all over, he was a bloody mess and I didn't have a mark on me. You see, I had these big fists and though I hit him only about once for every four times he hit me, mine were doing damage and his weren't.

But there was something about that experience that left a tremendous imprint on me. It didn't come out until I got to junior college. The rooms there were in barracks, and there was a boy there who was a linebacker/fullback on our team, back in the days when I weighed about 155 pounds. I don't know what got into him, but he came to my room all agitated. He was getting ready to do me damage, and the memory of the situation at summer camp when I just stood there and took it at first was implanted in me.

So when the junior college guy came at me, I knocked the hell out of him right away. I had been practicing how to hit with a blocking dummy at home after that camp incident, because I was going to protect myself if it ever happened again. So when this guy came at me, in shooting range, I let him have it. I had learned how to hit straight shots, and I started beating him. When he got out of that room, he was a bloody mess, and it didn't even phase me because I had been taken advantage of once before, and it wasn't going to happen again.

I'm not trying to hide anything. If you're going to write a book, you'd better be real about it, so I'm not trying to paint a rosy picture. I'm just trying to paint it the way it is. Everybody's got flaws. One of them is my temper. Like I said, it can leap into action without me even realizing what's happening. It's off-the-board stupid, though. When you lose control of yourself to anger, you can be dangerous. As I got older, I lost control less often and not as drastically. But I do have experiences even now where all of a sudden my temper can flare up, so I realize I'm not free from it at all. It's still lurking there. It doesn't show itself very often, but it isn't going away.

Now back to my elementary school days. My dad continued to be a big influence on my life. One of the first things he did when he became head coach at Paris was to establish elementary school football. He saw the necessity for it, and the influence and positive results of getting boys started on football at an early age. His policy was that you could start playing in fifth grade. The school system provided uniforms for the six elementary schools in Paris. So, as soon as my dad got there, he made elementary school football a priority to get the kids started playing the game.

Playing high school football for my father also helped me learn other lessons. They were ones that would be of the utmost value to me as a head coach in the NFL. The number one thing I absorbed from him was the importance of looking on the positive side of things.

When my dad was a young football coach, he was an assistant under the guy who hired him, Pete Shotwell, a top football coach out in West Texas, which is tough football country. He was exposed to Shotwell for four or five years, and one of the things that he got from him was this: Shotwell always told his players what they *could* do. He did not deal with what they couldn't do. He stressed the positive. And he told them that they could win. Connect that to teaching fundamentals, and you're tapping into one of the most powerful forces on planet Earth, and that is a motivated man.

When you played under my dad, he always told you what you could achieve, what you were capable of doing. By telling you that, he was going to make doggone sure you were rising to your capabilities. And he wouldn't tolerate anything half-ass. I played for him on the varsity team for two years. We never thought we were going to lose a game. He believed in us.

When he turned ninety-three, as many as one hundred of his former players from a period of four decades showed up for his birthday party. To most of the players he was the most influential adult they'd had outside of their parents.

What was important to my dad was knowing that we had given it all we had—and he let us know it. We knew he was proud of us even in defeat. He was a person who may have been beaten on the field at times, but he wasn't beaten mentally.

His whole lifestyle was honest. He had only one woman in his life, my mother; and they were a team. He didn't know how to be tricky or manipulate or deal with smoke and mirrors. So we learned moral integrity from him without even realizing it.

I didn't really get into his starting lineup until I was a senior. I got to play very little on the varsity team in my junior year. I was very slow to develop physically. I probably weighed 135 pounds when I was a junior. The next year my weight was up, but only to 150, and I was about 5 feet 10½ inches. I was long, tall, and skinny, with real skinny legs and big feet—not a very imposing physical specimen.

Not playing much as a junior was fair. I couldn't meet the requirements to win a starting spot because of my physical limitations. However, by the time I was a senior, there was no question I was the best player, deserving to be in the starting lineup. I was still rather small, but I was an extremely good defensive player. I just had a knack for playing defense, and I had the ability to stay on my feet and take on blockers. As far as catching the ball goes, our team's tailback, Sammy Morrow, estimates I probably caught only twenty-eight passes in high school. Morrow also said my dad taught me the right way to catch the ball. He also recalled a saying my father had, "If you can touch it, you can catch it."

My dad had a policy he followed through most of his coaching career. It was to put the play calling in the hands of the boy he felt had the best instincts for the game and for directing the offense—the player who had the best grasp of leadership. It didn't make any difference what position he played.

In one of his best years, he had his center, Luke Abbett, call the plays. When I was a senior, he had me call the plays. We had only about twelve plays, so I guess he figured I could handle it. No signals from the sideline, either. My dad had a philosophy that the players had a better feel of what was happening. In that particular stage of the evolution of football, coaches weren't into calling plays so much.

In his first game he ever coached in Paris, he deliberately did not name the player he wanted to call the plays. They were a very young and inexperienced team, so you can imagine the scene the first time they got in the huddle that night. I'm sure it was the first time they realized that nobody had been put in charge of the play-calling responsibilities. After the game, my dad asked who wound up calling the plays. It was Barney White who had called the plays, a natural leader who had great football instincts. My dad had figured Barney would take charge, and Barney had done what needed to be done. This incident was typical of my dad—he had great confidence in his boys being able to think on their own, and he believed in doing things that encouraged it.

In my senior year I was a consensus All-District player and I made second team All-State, but I couldn't have cared less about that. What I was interested in was being All-District. When I was growing up and my dad was coaching in that district, it was just something that got locked into my head, "Man, I'd love to make All-District." It was a dream come true. I hadn't ever thought about making All-State. I thought that was out of my reach.

The Texas high school's football system, which was established somewhere in the late 1920s or early 1930s, had a playoff system in effect that resulted in teams from every division in the system playing for their division's state championship. I think it's still true to this day; the system is set up by enrollment.

In the time I was playing there, there was Class B, Class A, and Class Double-A. There were only three divisions with about fifteen districts spread all across Texas. Paris was in Double-A, which included schools with an enrollment of around five hundred up to fifteen hundred. We had an enrollment of just about five hundred.

Our biggest win happened when I was a senior and we had to beat Gainesville, a town about 100 miles from Paris, to win our district championship. They had advanced to the quarter-finals the year before, and most of those players had returned. We met them in the final game of the season in Gainesville and beat them, 13–7. It was the first district title in my school's history.

Believe it or not, I rank the thrill of winning that game as highly as winning my first championship in the NFL in 1958. To anyone who might say, "How can you possibly compare winning a high school game to winning the NFL title?" I'd say that for a sixteen-year-old, it really was in the same category as being a twenty-five-year-old and winning my first world championship in New York. You had to have been there to understand—you'd have to be from Texas to understand it. By my senior year in high school, I had been aiming to win our district championship for four years, and then we won it. Won it in a big game and a very close game, and it was just a mountaintop experience.

Incidentally, our school's colors were blue and white, the same as the team I would later play on when we won the NFL championship.

That season we had a 10–2 record and made it all the way to the bi-district playoff game, which meant two district champions played against each other. We had won our district, but got beat in the next round by Highland Park High School in Dallas, who got to move on to the quarter finals. They beat us by a score of something like 31–0.

Highland Park High School had about fifteen hundred students. This was something we had no control over—they had a whole lot more depth of talent than we had, and that disparity showed up in these playoff games. We just couldn't compete against them.

They also had a great football coach who knew what to do with talent. Their team probably averaged around 185 pounds per player. Our team averaged 150. The size differential was very much in evidence.

The significance of the Texas playoff system in my day was that at the end of the football season there would be only a few undefeated teams in the entire state. My dad said that meant you learned most of your football from getting beat. That stuck with me. He stressed that the lessons you really soak in are the ones that come from defeat. I applied all of the lessons that I absorbed from my dad throughout my career.

While it's true that to become a good football player I had to overcome some physical problems, there were some untrue stories, exaggerations about my physical condition, that were spread by the media. I did have a back condition that at times caused things to be out of place in my body. For example, at times one of my legs was a bit shorter than the other. But that wasn't a condition I had from birth, and it wasn't a permanent problem.

My condition started in high school, back when I was a real skinny kid. A great osteopath in Paris, Texas, Dr. Robert Spell, first looked into it for me. My sacroiliac joint on my right side was the offending area, it was weak. The place where the sacrum and the ilium come together in the back is what we're talking about. The groin and hamstring muscles have their origin in the lower back, they are attached there. So when the lower back, that sacroiliac joint, gets out of place, out of line, it causes a strain, and the groin and hamstring muscles are affected by it. If you weren't a football player, it might not happen, and it wouldn't make any difference to you if it did. But the stress of being a receiver, running routes, going high speed, making cuts, and all that puts these muscles under a strain. You can get pulled muscles in the groin and hamstring, which are debilitating for a receiver.

When my back got out of line during my high school years, I would go to Dr. Spell, who would put me on a table, flat on my back. He'd pick up my ankles and swing my legs in and out to relax them. Then he'd bring the ankles together. Using pressure and manipulation, he'd line it back up again. When things were out of whack, the ankle bones would be a quarter or half inch off. That's how the story about one leg being shorter than the other got started, but it wasn't really true; it was the alignment.

He told me, "What you need to understand is that if you get this misalignment here, then you put your hamstring and groin in a situation where you could get pulls." And that's exactly what happened to me when I got in college and got away from Dr. Spell. I got a groin pull my first two years over there, and it really set me back.

He gave me some exercises that I needed to do. One of the good results that came out of this problem was I realized that I had to work on conditioning and working out year-round. I couldn't let my muscle tone get out of shape, out of strength.

One year I had to go to Dr. Spell about five days a week for three or four weeks. Finally, the last several days I saw him he told me that everything was lined up right and I didn't have to go back to him anymore. He told me, "Raymond, you're going to have to keep these muscles in a high state of conditioning year-round." Manipulation and pressure would take the stretch off those muscles. I listened to him, and that ended up being a blessing because I was able to stay in good shape.

When I went to the NFL, there was also a misconception that I needed to wear a special shoe to rectify this problem. There was some truth to this, but it was mostly inaccurate. An overzealous sports information director with the Colts blew things out of proportion, looking for stuff to write. They're always looking for a story.

I think during training camp of my first year in Baltimore, where I didn't have an osteopath, this health issue cropped up again. I was desperate, trying to come up with something that would relieve the problem. It was a problem, and I didn't have an answer for it at the time. So I put something in my shoe to try to compensate for it. This public relations man—who got carried away with all kinds of stuff, always looking for something sensational to shout about—found out about it. So he got that started. And, as so often happens, the story got started and got a life of its own, and before long it went everywhere.

On Dr. Spell's advice, I got a back brace, a custom-made one about 4 inches wide that fit around my waist. It was made of canvas and had two little straps that went between my legs. I'd cinch it up real tight, and that caused my hips to be snug. That secured the problem area when I made a lot of violent movements playing football. That seemed to reduce the possibility of things getting out of line. I used the brace for thirteen years while playing professional football, and I wore it all the time. I very seldom had any more problems after that, but it was something I had to work through from my high school days on.

Nevertheless, I truly enjoyed my days playing high school football in Texas for my dad. But after that senior year season, it was time to move on. My college days were ahead.

Chapter Two

Mustang Berry

I spent one year at a junior college, Schreiner Institute in Kerrville, Texas. Going there and playing football for them was a really good transition from high school to college. It was the only school that offered me a scholarship.

For the first time I was playing football only as a receiver. I had never been in an offense that really threw the ball before. We ran the straight T formation, basic football all the way. We didn't have flankers or split ends, nothing like that, but our coach had a very balanced attack—run and throw—and we did complete a lot of passes. I had a real good year catching the ball, and I led our junior college Pioneer Conference in pass receiving with sixty-seven receptions.

I left Schreiner Institute to play under Rusty Russell, who was the head coach at SMU. I was interested in him because he was throwing the football. Coach Russell had seen me in junior college. I only weighed 155 pounds coming out of Schreiner, and I was about 5 foot, 11 inches. I had a basic skeleton, but very little else.

Still, Russell had interest in me because I had led my junior college conference in pass receiving, so that got his attention. That and the fact that I could catch a football, and they were doing nothing but throwing under Russell. His offense featured the passing game. He liked to throw the ball with spread formations—he had double wings, triple wings, motion—he had everything. I think he was throwing 75 percent of the time, and that played to my strengths.

I talked to him about wanting to come to SMU. Earlier he had asked me to come up and talk to him in Dallas. That's only 100 miles from Paris, so I went over there and he said, "I don't know if you're going to be big enough to play in the Southwest Conference or not, but I'd like for you to come here and I'll look at you this fall. You're going to play on our redshirt team, working against our varsity every day. I'll watch you this fall during practice, and if I think you can play in this conference, I'll give you a full scholarship at that point."

He explained that I would be ineligible to play on varsity for one year because under Texas rules in those days a junior college transfer who had only played one year had to "lay out a year," as they called it. So the first year I was at SMU, they put me on what they called their "T team," which was a redshirt team.

Our redshirt team worked against the varsity pass defense every day, running our opponents' pass plays to help Russell's pass defense prepare for each upcoming game. It was full-speed pass scrimmage. We ran plays off cards showing us what to do, and the defense went all out, trying to knock your butt off if you got in their way, and I was on trial.

The guy who was throwing to me three times a week for thirty minutes was Fred Benners, the greatest passer in the Southwest Conference, maybe in America. He was a senior tailback who was a throwing specialist—he couldn't run a lick, but he could throw like hell. So I had the best thrower in Texas throwing to me while I was under scrutiny to see if I was going to get to play at SMU for three more years or not, and we pretty well lit up the practice field, to tell you the truth.

Coach Russell had competed against my dad in Texas high school football, and Russell was a big proponent of the passing game. He believed in a wide-open, spread formation offense, with four or five guys out on every pass play and throwing the ball forty to forty-five times a game, back in a time when that was not what people did. It was almost like a West Coast offense years before that scheme came along. Russell coached players like Doak Walker, Forrest Gregg, Kyle Rote, and Bobby Layne.

Around midseason he gathered the team together after practice, before we went in, for a few announcements like he usually did. That day his announcement was this: "If you varsity receivers went after that ball like this little broomstick receiver," he was referring to me, of course, "we wouldn't have any problem out there on Saturday afternoons." That's when I knew I had my full scholarship. And even though he called me a broomstick, it was exactly what I looked like!

So I had a chance to play from my sophomore year on. However, I was only a starting receiver one season and scored just one touchdown.

I also ran track at SMU. The head track coach there was McAdoo Keaton, who was also the chief assistant football coach, so he knew why I was out for track—because I wanted to be a better football player. He said, "Raymond, you work with the sprinters. Whatever they do, you do."

I continued running track the entire time I was there, because I started realizing that working on my running, learning to become a sprinter, and developing my speed and my legs were important. In fact, that was one of the most important things that happened to me at the college level, because I was in the process of growing as a young physical specimen, and I was running year-round.

I think running track helped me create a particular gait or stride that was deceptive. A defensive back told me one time that he was deceived—that I was moving a whole lot faster than he thought.

On the days of track meets I'd do the high jump and broad jump at first. Then, in my junior and senior years, Keaton put me on the sprint relay, the 4-by-110 deal, and I ran the second leg of that. I learned a lot about sprinting. The coach told me, "Relax in your upper body when you're running. Keep your hands and your arms and your chest and shoulders relaxed. Don't tense up and get tight when you're sprinting." That was a huge help as a football receiver. It was a case of sprint full speed, but stay relaxed in the upper body.

Also critical was this: Psychologically I realized that I could run with those guys who were fast. We'd have those sprints and I could stay there with them. That did a whole lot for my mind and my confidence in my ability to run. That was a huge, huge benefit I reaped from running track at SMU.

They didn't time us at SMU, but later in Baltimore we would run the 40 every year. The way they did it, we ran in shorts and football shoes. The coaches with the clocks would stand down at the 40-yard finish, and we would line up and put our hands down in the three-point stance, and they'd watch our hands. As soon as the hand moved, they started the watch. Based on that method of timing, I ran 4.8 40s every year in Baltimore.

Back then the *real* fast people would be running the 40 in 4.5 or around 4.6—those great sprinters. On our team Lenny Moore was probably the fastest player, and I'm sure that when he ran a 40, he could probably clip off a 4.5 without any problem.

But one thing about football speed is that when you're talking about a 40-yard dash, the start is a huge part of being able to run it in a very low time. Now, I don't think that was the biggest part of my speed. I'm long-legged. Once you're past 10 yards and you're in the running mode, I think there's a different speed level. All I know is that I never really had any inferiority complex about running against NFL defensive backs, because I knew I could beat them. I knew I could beat them deep, and the 40-yard dash times had absolutely nothing to do with it.

Once into a pass route, making a break, and sprinting with the football, I think I could probably run as fast as anybody. Well, almost anybody. When I went to the Dallas Cowboys as an assistant coach, I worked with Bob Hayes, who was billed as the world's fastest human being—more on him later. Anyway, knowing I could beat defensive backs helped my football career.

On the negative side of my college playing days, Coach Russell got fired after my sophomore year. I really enjoyed playing under him.

We had two future Hall of Famers in Forrest Gregg and me, and six or seven future NFL players. At my position alone there were three future NFL players: Doyle Nix, Ed Bernet, and me. Nix went on to play mainly for the Green Bay Packers and Washington, and Bernet for the Pittsburgh Steelers. Bernet was one of the great natural catchers—his hands were among the most outstanding, the best of any receiver I've ever seen. In 1953 his seventeen catches for 227 yards led all SMU receivers.

Frank Eidom was our tailback, and he was the number one draft pick of the Baltimore Colts. But before he went to the Colts, he had two years of military service that he had to fulfill. Tragically, he was killed outside of San Antonio, Texas, in a car wreck, so he never got the opportunity to report to Baltimore. At SMU he had led the team in rushing in both 1953 and 1954, when he averaged 5.4 yards per carry. In 1954 he also led the team in receptions with nineteen, good for 246 yards.

Don McIlhenny was one of our halfbacks. He led the team in rushing in 1955 (5.2 yards per carry). He ended up playing mainly for the Detroit Lions, the Green Bay Packers, and the Cowboys.

We had such a concentration of talent on that SMU team, we could have competed against any college squad in America and won. One of the reasons SMU was so deep in talent in those particular years was because of Doak Walker, a 5-foot-11-inch, 170-pound tailback and defensive back. He had played there in the years just before all of the talent that I was a part of got recruited. We'd all grown up as Walker fans.

Walker was a World War II veteran who had played six games at SMU as a freshman in 1945, then came back from the war and played in thirty-three total games over his last three years of college from 1947 through 1949. He ran for 1,954 yards, passed for 1,638, returned kicks, and handled kicking duties. The last time I looked, he was tied with Eric Dickerson for career points at SMU with 288, and he still led all Mustang players for yards gained on punt returns with 750.

Walker was so popular that a second deck had to be added to the Cotton Bowl to handle the crowds who flocked there to see him. He graduated from SMU after the 1949 football season, in June 1950. Walker, a three-time All-American and the Heisman Trophy winner in 1948, was the most acclaimed, most famous college football player in America. He is in an elite group of men to be in both the college and pro hall of fame. He even led the Detroit Lions to two NFL championships.

So SMU was riding high—Walker was a high-profile name that attracted Texas high school boys. Anyone playing high school football in Texas knew who Walker was and wanted to go where Doak went.

When I got to SMU, I studied every film of Walker's games, close to forty of them. I was fascinated to understand what made him tick. It was one of the most thorough studies I've ever done. I probably knew more about Walker than he did. He was an incredible athlete. At SMU he played an average of around fifty-eight minutes a game. He was a safety on defense, and they used him as a tailback, a slotback, and a flanker—he was a runner, blocker, passer, and pass receiver and he did the punting and kicking. And Coach Rusty Russell, an offensive genius, knew how to use him.

Now, in both my high school and college football playing days, defense was where I made my name. The passing game of Paris High School was practically nonexistent. We played defense and ran the football out of the single wing. You can't always get a passer in high school football, and we didn't have one, so we didn't throw the ball. I played the left end in the single-wing offense, and all I did was block. We ran a little hook pattern once in a while, but again, we hardly ever threw the ball.

When I reported to SMU, the college rules of the day included free substitution, so teams had an offensive unit and a defensive unit. But then the NCAA made a huge mistake. Due to a rule that began in my junior season of 1953, with few exceptions that were included in that rule, putting substitutes into a game was highly discouraged. They decided to reduce scholarships, so in essence they went back to having players play both ways. Players just about *had* to play both ways, because while a player could be removed from a game, if that substitution took place in the first or third quarter, the player who left the game could not reenter during that quarter. Furthermore, a player taken out *before* the final four minutes of the second or fourth quarter could return only during the last four minutes of the first half or of the game.

So, if you weren't a good defensive player, you didn't get to play much. They picked players based on defensive ability. They couldn't have a hotshot offensive guy who gave up more points than he scored. The coaches learned that having some great offensive talent on the field who couldn't play defense meant getting your butt beat. That was the nature of the game.

Playing both ways is something virtually unheard of nowadays—from 1990 through 2008, only four NFL players started a game playing on both sides of the ball, with Deion Sanders getting the most attention for it.

In my time at SMU, players could be on the field for only two hours for practice sessions, so when players went both ways, we spent an hour working on offense and an hour on defense. Coaches had to simplify things, because they had to teach players to play both ways. Specialization is the norm today, but in those days players had to learn both offense and defense.

In my third year at SMU, as a sophomore, I had grown to about 160 pounds. I weighed about 175 by my junior year and 182 my senior year, and I topped out at 6 foot, 2 inches. As a sophomore I didn't even play enough to earn a letter. I played about fifty minutes that year. In my junior year I was on the second unit. I was pleased in my senior year when my teammates selected me to be a co-captain even though that was the first season I was a starter.

In my junior and senior years at SMU, we ran a straight T formation, where we ran the ball and threw a few times. On a good day, maybe three or four passes came my way, but usually fewer passes were thrown to me. I was a good blocker in the NFL because I learned that skill in college while in that T formation. I had to block defensive ends and linebackers who were head up on me or inside of me.

Later, in our offense under Weeb Ewbank at Baltimore, for about the first five or six years I was in the league, there were a couple of formations where I was in close, again blocking defensive ends and linebackers.

It sounds strange today that you could put a 185-pounder in there to block those guys, but in those days they didn't think that much of it. I knew, though, that I had to study everything I could about blocking and techniques, and look for tricks in order to get the job done. I also studied the guys I was blocking so I knew everything they were doing. I did all of this to get the edge on them one way or another, because it was a formidable assignment to block those big guys—so much bigger than I was. I didn't get beat up too much from blocking, though.

Defensively, I played the end/outside linebacker position, but when I first got to SMU I didn't play defense, not before the 1953 rule in my junior year that led to players going both ways. I hadn't even played defense in junior college. Defense was the strongest part of my game. I hardly caught anything in high school or college. They called me a defensive end, but I was actually, in today's terminology, an outside linebacker in both high school and college. Sometimes I'd be rushing the quarterback, and sometimes I'd be dropping into pass coverage. I was at my best pass rushing.

In my junior and senior years I was on the varsity squad and playing a lot, primarily as an outstanding defensive player like I had in high school—one who knew how to stay on his feet and take on blockers. I can't even remember getting knocked down. It helped to have quick feet, big hands, great balance, and jumping ability. I was very difficult to block.

I started understanding angles and how to play them. I was outside, down the line of scrimmage, so one of my jobs was to not let them get around me. On the other hand, you don't want to allow them to open any big holes on the inside, either. I was able to do both. Other teams began to run to the other side, away from me.

That happened when we played Frank Leahy's powerful Notre Dame team at South Bend, Indiana, in 1953, a season in which they were predicted to be the national champions in several polls. Forrest Gregg and I played together side-by-side for two years, my last two years and his sophomore and junior seasons. He was the left tackle and I was the left end. I don't know how much meat he had on his bones back then, but he was the epitome of a rawboned player. We were talented, but we couldn't upset the Irish.

Forrest wound up being Vince Lombardi's favorite player of all time at Green Bay. Forrest was the kind of guy who, when that whistle blew, gave 100 percent on every play, every time. He had the heart of a lion and a great competitive spirit. He was personable and had this big smile, but you didn't know you were really looking at a tiger. I actually played against him in high school—he went to a Texas school, Sulphur Springs, just 40 miles from Paris. We beat them twice when I played; both games were pretty close.

In 1954 SMU went 6–3–1, with road wins over teams such as Arkansas and Rice, where I played in front of 63,500 fans. That was the largest crowd I had ever performed for at that point. After that year, my senior season, I earned All-Southwest Conference honors, despite catching just sixteen passes, and was named an Academic All-American. I also got to play in the East-West game in San Francisco. I have a lot of great memories about that experience. I got to see the San Francisco area and the

Stanford University campus, where we practiced. It was also the first time I had ever been around other players from other teams.

The game was played at Kezar Stadium, where the 49ers played their home games. We played against the East team, and I had a heckuva day defensively. They had the Notre Dame quarterback, Ralph Guglielmi, an All-American who is now a member of the college football Hall of Fame. At SMU I had already played against Notre Dame, so I was familiar with their signal system. Early in the game, as I lined up and Guglielmi got under center, I heard him say the signals and realized the East team was using the Irish signal system—so I knew when he was coming my way and when he was going the other way. When he snapped the ball, I went where he had already told me.

I was lined up on the left side, but when I knew he was going to go away from me, as soon as he snapped the ball, I took off to the other side of the field, not concerned about anything like a reverse play.

So, by the time I was a senior playing defense, I was all over the field. If you could watch some of the films from that year, you'd see me all over that field. When the ball was snapped, I didn't stop until the whistle blew.

That attitude carried over for the rest of my playing days, and I knew I'd need to continue to display such diligence very soon to some critical eyes. My next stop: the NFL.

Chapter Three

From a Mustang to a Colt—
The Early Colt Years

At SMU I caught just eleven passes as a junior for 144 yards and one touchdown. I added sixteen receptions in my senior season for 217 yards. Add those from my first season at SMU and I had a mere thirty-two pass receptions as a collegian. I intercepted a pass and ran back a punt and one kickoff. I didn't even earn a letter as a sophomore. Those are hardly the statistics and feats of a future NFL star receiver.

I wasn't even selected to be in the College All-Star Game, a contest that was played every year by standout college seniors versus the NFL champs from the previous season. It was fortunate that I didn't get picked because I was going to struggle to make the Colts as a rookie in training camp anyway. Missing the first two weeks of practices to go to the All-Star camp and game could have been my death knell.

I remember that George Shaw, who was the Colts' number one draft pick quarterback, played in that game, so he reported late to camp. For a rookie, being selected was a good news–bad news deal. The good news was you got to play in the College All-Star Game. The bad news was you were two weeks late getting to training camp and your competition got a big start on you.

Some people said I was too slow and too small to play pro football, and that my vision was too poor to allow me to do well as a receiver. I wasn't too concerned because I was just trying to make it in the league.

I was concentrating on learning the game, how to be a receiver in pro football, and how to survive.

As a matter of fact, I didn't read anything in the media after a little while. I got my mind completely out of that track to keep from being distracted. A lot of it was negative, and that affected me, so I thought I'd be crazy to keep reading that stuff.

From the start I never had the attitude of, "Wow, I'm in the NFL," because the Colts weren't an established team when I went there. I was a 1954 20th-round "future draft pick" and the 232nd pick overall. I was drafted in my junior year at SMU, my fourth year at the college level. This meant that while the Colts did draft me, they would have to wait a year for me to join the team.

The Baltimore fans were great, but you had to earn their loyalty and affection. They didn't know anything about any of us at first. It was a very young team, really, with no veteran group of players. In fact, in my first season I was one of thirteen rookies to make the squad. It was a team that hadn't even been an NFL franchise until 1953, so they had no real established team.

Looking back on it, I couldn't have gone to a better place, because they didn't have any great veteran receivers, and that opened the door for me because, again, I didn't know anything about being a pro receiver. Also, the Colts used their ends to block more than other pro teams, and that helped me, but they only carried three ends and brought about ninety rookies into camp. They would wind up keeping a dozen of us.

The reputation I had at SMU, though, was that I was catching the football unbelievably, with all kinds of great catches—low, high, on balls thrown too far, whatever. That caught the eye of scouts to the degree of, "He's worth a twentieth round pick." Back then they drafted for thirty rounds. They didn't draft me for playing defense. They wanted me as a receiver, even though, as mentioned, I caught only one touchdown pass at SMU and had started just one year.

Somebody wrote a book in the 1990s and said if I had played college ball during that decade, no NFL team would have picked me in the draft. I think that's probably true, but they may have drafted me to be a defensive back. I was too light to be a linebacker, even though, as I mentioned, at SMU I was basically a defensive end and linebacker; but in pro football I wasn't big enough to play those positions.

I was fortunate that Weeb Ewbank saw something in me that he liked. He knew I'd been a defensive terror in college, and he knew what kind of a competitor I was. He also saw that I had the ability to catch a football even though, back then, I dropped some. So he felt I was worth keeping around.

I went to training camp with no idea about anything involving professional football. When I came to Baltimore, I came out of a total defensive era. I didn't know my butt from first base about being an NFL wide receiver. I was coming off playing in a college system that was straight T formation, nothing split. We ran the ball all the time, and I played defense.

Coming into the NFL, I had to learn the split-receiver position from the ground up, and it was a long process. Going to a pro-type passing offense, where you had to have great balance, with great running and great throwing, was new to me. But I didn't know anything about running routes against man-to-man coverage, simply because I had no background to prepare me for the professional game where you absolutely had to beat man-to-man coverage. That was the dominant characteristic of the NFL defenses in those days. Zone defenses were not a part of the scene. You had to beat a man to catch a pass, and those people who were playing corners knew what they were doing, and I didn't.

Plus, I was small—by the time I entered the NFL, I weighed around 185 pounds—but I played with a lot of heart. That was the biggest part of my game. I had a competitive spirit like a roaring furnace. A lot of that came from my dad.

On many teams in different sports, rookies are expected to shut up, listen and learn, and respect the veterans. There wasn't a lot of that type of atmosphere on the Colt teams. That was, at a minimum, not a part of the Colt culture when I was there.

Remarkably, I got the starting job for all twelve games in 1955, my rookie year. Had I not gone to the Colts, an expansion team with no veteran receivers, I would never have had an NFL career. I wasn't qualified, but I got the job because they had nobody else. If I had gone to any other team in the NFL as a rookie, I would have reported to camp and been cut in the first three or four weeks. I would have gone home and gone into teaching or coaching. They didn't have anybody else, so I got to play.

My rookie season wasn't exactly a blockbuster one. I really didn't catch anything because, again, I hardly knew anything about being a receiver. I didn't even score a touchdown. I played twelve games and caught thirteen passes from Shaw—you can do the math. On the positive side, I did average 15.8 yards per catch.

After being introduced to the league, however, and after seeing what was going on with the defenses, I spent the rest of my off-seasons studying every film I could get my hands on, watching every pass receiver in the NFL, watching to see how these guys did it. And I studied myself to see what I was doing. Back then, film wasn't as available to players as it is now. In the off-season I wrote to the Colts and asked them to send me game film of every game we played. They also had opponents' film from a mandatory film-exchange program. Say the Chicago Bears were coming up on our schedule. Well, they had to send at least three films of their previous games before they played us, and we'd do the same for them. So if I really wanted to study somebody, such as a player from the Bears, I could watch the films the Colts owned from, say, the two games we had played them each year over the last several seasons.

Back then studying film was not common at all. I don't think there was anybody else doing it when I started doing it. I don't know if the average player has the motivation to do extracurricular film study now. But coaches definitely put film on during team meetings.

From my study I began to adopt a fake here and there—I saw somebody else do something I could duplicate, so I copied that. That's how it all began.

And I started studying the defensive backs, as to their weaknesses and how to get open on them. So I kept improving. And, of course, Unitas would soon join the team, and with him, I didn't have to be real wide open. He could get that ball in a crack. That was a big help, too.

Still, when I came back for my second year, I was due to be replaced, and I knew it. The Colts had drafted one All-American receiver out of the Big Ten, Bernie Flowers from Purdue, and another end named Frank McDonald. They had to do something to get the production from that position, because I hadn't produced anything worthy of anything but being replaced.

When Unitas came to the Colts in 1956, we really hit it off in training camp. We started working together a lot, but we had a very simple pass offense. I didn't have any moves or fakes at that time.

Like me, John had been a rookie in 1955, but he got cut by the Pittsburgh Steelers and went home to play semipro ball for the Bloomfield Rams at a reported $6 per game. Had the Colts not taken a chance on this cast-off quarterback, and had they not seen something and stuck with me, the football world would have been deprived of one of the best pass–catch duos ever—if I do say so myself. Don't think I haven't puzzled about that over the years—I wish somebody would have explained that one to me.

Weeb Ewbank is the key to the careers of one Baltimore Colt after another. Number one on his list is John Unitas. Number two on his list is Raymond Berry. If it hadn't been for Weeb Ewbank, neither one of us would have had a pro career. John and I would have been gone.

Before I met John, I knew nothing about him. Somebody in camp told me, "We have a new quarterback from the University of Louisville." John was still a long way from being the new starting quarterback, but at least he was in a pro camp again. I think Weeb might have been the only one who knew much about him.

When we went to training camp in 1956, he was a free agent and I was due to get cut. We hit it off because we both loved football. We loved to play and had nothing on our minds but playing. That didn't guarantee my making it in the NFL, though. One pivotal moment came in the first exhibition game we played in1956. That game, in Hershey, Pennsylvania, came very early after training camp opened, and I was a rookie struggling to make the team. I dropped a pass because I'm absolutely psychologically affected by the pressure of being on trial—that actually affected my physical coordination.

After the game, while sitting in my hotel room, some sad, dark thoughts crossed my mind. I was depressed. My whole world was football, and my world was getting ready to collapse and go away—and I had nothing else. When I went back to camp, I thought I was going to be cut, so it was going to be as if my life had ended. I lost my confidence. It was a horrible thing to go through, but I'm glad now that I did.

In retrospect, confidence wasn't something I was really aware of. When I lost it, that was when I began to realize what confidence is, and that without it you're a dead duck. That incident brought the importance of confidence clearly into focus.

Then, when I didn't get cut, I started to work my butt off in every way, shape, and form I knew how to. I didn't know anything else to do other than work, and I gradually began to regain my confidence. It helped that Weeb hadn't given up on me, and that was a key thing because I easily could have been cut, but during training camp Weeb made the decision to keep me over two number one draft picks.

When I reported to camp, that began six months of football, and I don't know that I gave anything else too much thought. If we lost a game, it was kind of like dropping a pass. I learned that you drop one, analyze it, figure out what you did, and what you can do to correct it, and then get to work on actually correcting the reason why you dropped it. But you cannot afford to let your mind dwell on it.

I have what you could call a mind trick, but I think it's based on sound thinking, too. It's exactly the approach I used in catching the football and the same approach I used later as a coach. You work your butt off in every way you can, you do everything you know how to do to prepare. You study your opponents and the situations that come up. You exhaust every way you can to prepare for a catch or a contest. Then, whenever you're not successful at it, you stop and look back and say, "Well, there wasn't anything else I could do. I did everything I could, but what can I learn from this?" That helped me keep my mind focused.

Like John, I didn't like losing. I didn't like dropping the ball, but I learned that I could not dwell on it and had to move on.

John had a strong arm; I had strong legs. When practices ended, John and I would continue working on pass routes for at least thirty minutes or so.

Because Weeb coached under Paul Brown, he was brought up in a system where the head coach called the plays for Cleveland, not the quarterback. Well, whenever Ewbank saw this free agent in training camp, and saw him throwing the ball and getting the feel for him as a competitor and a football player, things changed.

Remember, however, that at first George Shaw was our starting quarterback and Unitas was just a backup. He saw limited playing time in the first two games of the season, and saw some action in our fourth game on October 21, when Shaw sustained his terrible knee injury, a broken kneecap as a result of a wicked tackle. In that contest versus Chicago, Unitas threw his first touchdown pass, a 36-yarder to Jim Mutscheller, but we were blown out, 58–27. After that, Unitas took over, starting his first NFL game on October 28, 1956, against the Packers. We broke a tie in the fourth quarter and won, 28–21, when Moore broke off a 79-yard touchdown run. In that game Unitas and I connected for our first touchdown pass ever, a 43-yard strike.

Weeb immediately let Unitas call the plays, and he instinctively knew that this guy had what it took to do that. That was the key to it—Weeb understanding that Unitas was a natural play caller and a leader. Plus, in a system in which a quarterback calls his own plays another dynamic is set in motion: The quarterback will start studying the game, the strategy, and his opponents. And that's true for other offensive players on such teams, because they know the quarterback may ask them for their opinion. Of course over time a quarterback like Unitas learns who will prepare in this way and give him reliable tips on what will work.

In my relationship with Unitas, as I began to get more experience, I would tell him the route I thought would work, and then say nothing more. If he wanted to use it, he could. My job was to tell him. If I had nothing good, I would tell him that too. We didn't waste many plays. He once said he appreciated my ability to know what the defender "was doing to him, to come back and tell [me] the right thing." I was glad to be a part of a system where players were involved and had input for my entire career.

So, yes, Unitas called his own plays. But early on what Weeb delegated to him was a loaded six-shooter with only about four bullets in it. We hardly ever threw the ball deep, because Weeb did not like to do that. He had the misimpression that it was a low-percentage play. He wanted to throw short, so he discouraged us from working on the deep ball. But I discovered very early that Weeb was wrong about that, and I talked to him about it. I told him, "You can throw this ball short all you want to, and they're going to start reading your mail, and what you're doing is making it easy on these guys on defense. They know you're not going to go deep. You've got to let us go deep when it's there." He reluctantly agreed. We started hitting the long ball big time and showed him real quick.

From my early days on in football I was always looking for any edge I could get, from avoiding smoking and drinking to working hard with Unitas to studying my opponents. The philosophy I had was that you'd better believe you always look for an edge because the difference between winning and losing is only an edge. When you're in top competition, the difference can sometimes be an inch or one play. So it's a mental thing in which you start realizing the importance of the details. That is going to be the difference, and if you don't understand that, you're not prepared to compete at the highest levels, against the very best.

My guess is that of all the players in the NFL at that time, there weren't more than two of us who weren't working in the off-season. We didn't make much money as pro football players, but I never did take an off-season job. I spent my off-season studying football. I took two months off, and then I went back to work in March. I considered taking a job to make more money, but I thought, "I think I can make more money improving myself as a football player. I'll work at football, *then* I'll make more that way."

I usually stayed in Texas with my parents in the off-season, and we had good springs down there. My dad had a 6-acre practice field for his football operation with the high school. I had a great place to work out, even a field house where I could shower and dress. I'd run and work on pass routes, but there were times when I couldn't find anybody to throw the ball to me, so I had to just throw it up in the air, run under it, and catch it.

I used to simulate playing an entire game, keeping track of time and running patterns as I would under game conditions. Working out like this from March through June meant that once training camp began, I could play an entire real game with ease.

I spent a lot of time in the off-season, and during the season too, closely studying the guys I was going to come up against man-to-man. I did this by studying film—that's the only way you could do it. By the time we went into a game, I pretty well knew what I could do.

Preparing like this is a lot like how a baseball pitcher prepares. He studies batters and knows the ones he doesn't want to throw a curveball to. He throws those guys sliders and fastballs. And some of them he doesn't want to throw a fastball to, he throws a lot of junk at them. It's very similar to a receiver working man-to-man against a defensive back. I knew what I could beat him on.

As for linebackers, they were in my line of vision on plays where I had to block them. We had a lot of plays in our offense where I was not split out, where I was lined up like a tight end or a close side, weak side, end. There, I had to take on linebackers and defensive ends, one-on-one. So I also studied these linebackers very, very closely to see what worked against them—what weaknesses they might have, where they might be vulnerable, and what type of block I should use on them. Again, going into games I knew pretty well how I was going to go about trying to block them.

Weeb Ewbank was a brilliant coach, but he had a blind spot—no coach is totally perfect. His blind spot was that he was asking me, a 185-pound end, to block guys that weighed 30, 40, 50, 60 pounds more than me.

We played the Chicago Bears, and defensive end Doug Atkins used to weigh about 260 to 280 pounds. In our offense we had an off-tackle play where the formation had me lined up nose to nose with Atkins and I had to block him one-on-one. So I studied him to see how I could get the job done.

It never occurred to me that it was impossible, so I didn't approach it from that angle. I watched him get down in his stance. I lined up on the left side, in close, right next to our left tackle, Jim Parker. I had about a yard or yard-and-a-half split, probably. Atkins played the gap right between me and Parker, with his outside leg—his right leg—back. When the ball was snapped, that leg went into the air as Atkins started moving forward. Now, he's 6 foot, 8 inches, and that leg was in the air for a split-second or two, and that's what I decided his weak spot was. If I could pop him on his hip when he had that long leg up in the air, I could catch him off-balance. So that's what I did.

When I had to block a guy like Atkins, it was strictly on a formation we had where we positioned Lenny Moore wide to the right as a flanker, and there was a tight end and our halfback in the backfield set to the right. I was not split out as a split end, but in close, as a close side end. Then we'd run back to the left, toward me, and run right at Atkins on an off-tackle play where I'd have to block him by myself. On pass plays, though, I'd usually split out 4 or 6 yards, maybe even wider than that sometimes.

The hash marks are not in the same position on the field now as they were in my era. The football field is 160 feet wide, and, starting in 1933, hash marks were placed on both sides of the field 10 yards in from the sidelines. Depending on where the ball was spotted, the next play could begin with very little room between where a receiver lined up and the sidelines, especially compared to nowadays.

In 1972 the league moved the hash marks closer together so they were only about 20 feet apart, with both sets of hash marks 70 feet, 9 inches in from each sideline. Many people say that change helped offenses a great deal, including the running and the kicking games. I think it may have affected the passing game more than the running game.

I was always very aware of the hash marks, and my split. How wide I was split, or how close I was split would determine the route I was going to run or the fake I was going to use on a particular pass assignment. Learning how to split properly to give you the maximum advantage on a pass route is a huge part of being a smart receiver.

When I lined up, I took my measurements using the hash mark as a base. I would either be on the hash, a couple of yards outside the hash, or a yard inside it. I mixed it up so the defensive backs didn't get some kind of read on me about the route I was going to run. I didn't want to telegraph anything. I wanted every advantage I could get, and I didn't want the defense to ever gain an advantage.

I also considered the best way to start off the line of scrimmage. I could get a better jump when I used a three-point stance, but the upright stance let me see the defense better. So quite often I began upright, then I dropped to my three-point stance on the "set" signal. I'd use a quick jab step, putting my right foot back just a little to give me that extra drive.

I lived on my first step.

I gave a lot of consideration to avoiding serious injury: The most dangerous situations you get into as a receiver involve being hit downfield. But frankly, I never did take all that many hits. One reason was because I played defense when I was in high school and in my varsity years at SMU. I learned that you get lower than the lowest—whenever you have a collision with an opponent, you never let him get under you. Playing defense, I learned when you take on impact, you get underneath the guy you're having a collision with and you win. I learned how to take on blockers and people coming at me, how to deliver hits and to attack, how to take blows, and how to ward off blockers, dodging them and so on.

So when I became a receiver in professional football, I was in the zone catching passes around defensive players; I had an awareness of people around me, and it didn't interfere with my concentration on the ball—it was just an instinct. And when I was making the catch, I was conscious of protecting myself to the degree the situation called for.

One example of this is when I was surrounded by defenders: The number one thing is to stay airborne and not get hit with your knees and legs planted. If you're airborne and you get hit, all you do is fly through the air; you don't get a knee joint busted. Being aware of your foot position in heavy traffic becomes instinctive. So does your self-preservation, self-protection, and awareness of all your surroundings. For instance, when I caught a pass that took me to the sideline, and I was headed out of bounds, I knew I had to keep running hard so no upstart defender had time to take a cheap shot on me.

All of that is still important today, but we used to go over the middle more than today's receivers do—and that's a big difference. We did a lot of that, like on slants. I wasn't concerned whatsoever about getting hurt, or going over the middle against the likes of Chuck Bednarick and Ray Nitschke. They were good, don't get me wrong, but the way I looked at it, I was going to intimidate them, not the other way around.

When I was downfield, running pass patterns, and coming in over the middle, there'd be a time or two when the ball was thrown high and I saw the defender coming at me. So there were times when I'd focus on the defensive guy and forget the football, wanting to protect myself. I wasn't going to let anybody tee off on me when I was all spread out for a pass. If you get spread-eagled out there, and somebody is able to get a full body blow on you, that's not what you want. I never got myself into a situation like that.

My philosophy was that if I was in a dangerous situation where it was the ball, me, and a defensive back, and he was getting ready to bowl me over, I'd forget the ball. My motto was, "Live to fight another day, and don't get yourself in a position where somebody can really hurt you." That only happened a few times, but there wasn't any question in my mind what I was going to do in a situation like that.

Overall, I stayed pretty much injury free throughout my career. That's mainly because I was always aware of taking hits and delivering hits. It became instinctive with me.

I remember in one game a defensive back had me dead in his sights, and he was getting ready to lower the boom on me. I saw the situation playing out and lowered the boom on him—I delivered the blow, forgetting the ball. He was so surprised, he didn't know what to think.

Another edge I was always seeking—and it's another reason I was able to avoid injury—was top-level, superb conditioning. I got my body in shape to the degree that I avoided fatigue, one of the most common things that leads to injury. You start getting fatigued, you react a little bit slowly, and you get hurt. I did a whole lot of exercises like sit-ups, pull-ups, and pushups—strengthening stuff.

I ran backward and sideways a lot. I walked—taking long strides—in plowed fields where I had to do high knee lifts. I was building muscles in my legs. I was looking for every way to do this. I even used a device called an Exer-Genie, a long nylon rope wrapped around a metal cylinder that created a drag. You secured the device, put a harness around your waist, and ran against the resistance of the Exer-Genie. That created a pull, and it put your legs under a lot of stress. There wasn't any weight lifting in those days.

Gino Marchetti once said that I made it in the NFL for several reasons. "Raymond worked hard, he ran hard, he did calisthenics, he was in bed at 9:00. He did everything right—everything you should do as a professional athlete.

"He was phenomenal. You never saw him when he wasn't squeezing a rubber ball to make his fingers stronger or holding a football in his hands, securing it tightly. Walking to the gym, to the meeting room, he'd be squeezing the damn thing."

By the time I was a veteran, I had come up with a list of six drills for the short ball and six for the long ball. I wrote them on a piece of tape that I put on my wristbands. When practice was over, I'd stay out and get somebody to throw to me. I'd catch at least fifty balls a day in a variety of ways, including one-handed grabs, and in a variety of locations. I even practiced catching balls that were tipped by a defender, and, of course, I worked on my "tight rope toe dance" at the sidelines and end lines.

Eventually I got a Jugs pass-throwing machine that stood on a tripod—you could put a football into it and it would duplicate a forward pass. You could set it to pass at low, high, or medium levels. It had small tires that spun in such a way it could "throw" the ball at different speeds. I'd get about 25 yards in front of it and would work on, say, one hundred balls thrown 6 inches off the ground, something no human arm can do.

I'd go 40 or 50 yards downfield and work on passes over each shoulder, directly over the top, balls that fall a bit short that you have to stop and go back to get. I'd have a net to gather missed and overthrown passes. I found that drill and repetition are the ways to train your hands to react in games. Say you get a low pass in a game, you don't even think, you just react the way you've been trained. Often I'd work with the machine after practice when everybody else had gone in.

I even asked Unitas to throw bad passes to me so I could work on that part of my game, but I quickly realized that throwing bad passes could carry over into games. I told John, "We won't do this anymore. I'll get someone else to throw the low ones, the high ones, the ones behind me."

In addition to my strong work ethic, I was born with natural hands. I had real big hands. I strengthened them with Silly Putty, a silicone compound that our trainer—who was a physical therapist at a children's hospital who used to rehabilitate kids—gave to me. He told me to squeeze this putty, but I did more. I developed a sort of weight program for every finger. I would stick my finger in a thick wad of it and lift. Stick my finger in it and go downward, go to the right, go to the left. Up and down, out and in. I was working the finger joint in every direction. I'd do this a lot, at odd times—when we were in meetings, like when we were watching film, or when we were traveling somewhere, such as on airplanes or even when I was driving. I had it with me constantly. My fingers became extremely strong. It would take a real tough shot to hurt them.

I specifically worked more on my thumbs than on my fingers. To me, because the thumb is situated opposite the other fingers grouped together, it is 50 percent of the hand. As a pass receiver, if your thumb gets hurt, you've got a problem. If you take a blow that sprains a finger or puts it out of use for a while, it will recover real quick if you've been working to strengthen your fingers. You may even prevent injuries. When you block or the ball hits you wrong, it's an individual finger that gets hurt, not the hand. Luckily, I never injured my fingers by, for example, getting stepped on or hurt in a pile up.

Even if I had never worked on my hands, I would have been catching the ball in a superior way, because I was born with the ability to catch. I didn't learn to train my hands until I got into my second or third year of pro football. Then I took what I had to its highest level.

I was such a perfectionist. I'd search for just the right pair of football pants, and I'd take care of them myself, washing them and making sure the crease was just right. I even carried a bathroom scale around with me when I was on the road to keep track of my weight. I wore a strip torn from a towel around my wrist on hot days so the sweat couldn't run down onto my hands.

When I was in college, I wore glasses. After a year of not playing with glasses in the NFL, I went to Dr. Joshua Breschkin for contact lenses. He was one of the most instrumental men in my whole career, because he was on the cutting edge of contact lens technology and expertise. He happened to be right there in Baltimore, and I had access to him at a time when, if I didn't get some help correcting my vision, I was going to be in deep trouble.

I was able to play without contacts in high school and college, but my near-sightedness kept getting worse. By the time I was a rookie in the NFL, something happened. We played a night game, and with the sky providing a black background, boy, I couldn't pick up the ball at all. Things were fuzzy. I just couldn't judge passes accurately, and it was extremely difficult to overcome that. I knew I had to do something.

Dr. Breschkin fitted me with contact lenses that were designed to allow a person to play football with them on. They could handle all the extreme eye gyrations that a receiver goes through in a football game, plus they could withstand the taking of hits around the face and head. He made them larger than he normally made them for that reason. But he warned, "Because I'm making them larger, they're not going to be as comfortable." I said, "Comfort is not the issue. Stability and correction are." I wore them for twelve years, and they worked out perfectly. I wore glasses off the field.

The first time I had to deal with the glare of the sun was during my first NFL trip to the West Coast. For years we had to take that trip and play those games in December; that's just how the schedule was. The average fan wouldn't think about this, but the sun is in a different location in the sky as the months go by. When you get into December in Los Angeles, with the way the Memorial Coliseum was laid out, the sun became a huge factor in games when the receiver was going away from the sun. That happened in two quarters of each game.

When you were the receiver on the left side of the field, and you ran a route and turned inside or outside, the sun setting on the rim of the

Coliseum was blinding. It was a dangerous situation for a quarterback to throw to a receiver, because the ball may hit off his hands or helmet, bounce off, and result in an interception. I told John, "I can't see. Don't throw the ball to me during this time period."

Again, looking for an advantage, I told Dr. Breschkin about this problem. He got some goggles and dark glass and came up with a device I could wear on my helmet that totally shut out the glare; they were like a welder's visor.

The first time I unveiled the sunglasses was in 1958. After enduring devastating road losses to the Rams and 49ers to end the 1957 season, which cost us the division title, the time was right to fight the blinding West Coast sun. On December 6, in front of 100,200 spectators in the Los Angeles Memorial Coliseum, I scored the game's first touchdown against the Rams. We eventually lost 30–28, but the glasses were definitely helpful. In all, I caught eight passes, with four of them coming when the sun was shining in the direction of my eyes. Those four catches added 78 yards to our offense that day.

Another thing about playing on the West Coast: When we were scheduled to make the trip out West, the time zone adjustment I had to make in eating and sleeping was huge. After all, there is a big time difference between Baltimore and California. When we'd go out there, we'd play the Rams and 49ers in one trip, which meant staying there for about ten days. So I started to make an adjustment to West Coast time prior to leaving for that trip. For about a week ahead of time, I'd change my eating and sleeping habits to coincide with California time. I was always looking for an edge.

I enjoyed winning, and obviously I went to great lengths to avoid losing. I hated losing so much. That's why I did everything I could do to prevent it from happening. Then, *when it did happen*, at least I could look at myself and say, "Well, there wasn't anything else I could've done, so that's it." That's what was driving me. I never wanted to get into a situation where we lost a game and I would say, "If I had done this or that, we'd have won." Do it all ahead of time, and then you won't have to look back with regret.

So, yes, I tried to control and oversee as many factors as possible, but one thing I could not fully control or gain an edge over was that Raymond Berry hot temper. It manifested itself again in my first or second year with the Colts. I was driving in downtown Baltimore one day in this 1950 Chevrolet that my dad had helped me buy as a used car, and a guy in the traffic lane to my left was one of these guys who used his car as an intimidator. He did something like cut me off and then gave me the finger, and I took my car and just slammed into his from the side and drove off.

What I experienced at that point was my rage leaping into action. And one day in training camp in my second year, a veteran defensive back hit me late, flagrantly. He had been doing this kind of crap a lot, but I didn't realize what was brewing inside of me. He did it one time too many and, right there in front of everybody, I went after him in an absolute rage. I got him down and was on top of him. I ripped his helmet off and was hitting him with it. They had to pull me off of him. There was that time bomb ticking inside of me.

People who didn't know me deeply thought I was easy to get along with, thought I was a nice guy and all that stuff. They didn't realize the inferno that was inside of me. As a matter of fact, I didn't fully realize it myself.

The determination and drive that are part of my makeup are God-given gifts, assets I brought to my job that enabled me to exhaust every physical skill I had. They resulted in top-level performance, but that performance also was based on tremendous work, concentration, and focus.

I had several experiences a year when I might have gotten a ball in my hands, balls that I should have caught but that I dropped. I remember one game when I lit out a curse word that you could hear from Baltimore Stadium down to the Inner Harbor.

But that was just a part of my makeup; I was explosive. I grew up with a real bad temper. It was under control and out of sight most of the time, except in certain situations when it would be triggered. Then all of a sudden you'd see a different Raymond Berry that you didn't even know existed. Sometimes, if I dropped a ball that I knew I should have caught,

I would just explode out there on the field, and you could hear me even with sixty thousand people yelling in the stands.

From my rookie year of 1955 through 1957, the Colts were far from being the great team we would soon become—we would win just seventeen games while losing eighteen over that three-year span. Actually, in the two seasons before I became a Colt, their records were 3–9 and 3–9. In my rookie season we were a slightly below .500 team at 5–6–1.

As I mentioned, I was worried about my status on the team going into 1956, my second season. By late October of that season, I still hadn't caught a touchdown pass in the NFL. My first one came in Unitas's first NFL start on October 28 in our fifth game of the season, as I touched on earlier. It was a 43-yarder versus Green Bay, the team I'd wind up scoring against the most, eleven times. It was also, of course, the first ever Unitas-to-Berry touchdown pass and just his third NFL touchdown pass ever.

By the end of the somewhat uneventful 1956 season, I ranked ninth in the NFL for receptions and ninth for receiving yards with 601. Plus, my average of 50.1 yards on receptions per game placed me tenth in the league for that category, but I only scored two touchdowns.

In 1957 things got even better. Prior to that season, the Colts record during away games was a miserable 4–26, but that was all in the past. In a road win versus Washington on November 10, Unitas hit me on twelve passes for two touchdowns and a whopping 224 yards. This Colts team was talented enough to nearly match the much more famous team that would come the following season, except for one thing: We did not realize how good we were.

Weeb pretty much turned us loose to do what we wanted, and we started hitting the long ball big time. We had some spectacular plays. As a team, we reversed our 5–7 record from 1956. That marked the first winning season in the team's history. After ten games we were 7–3, coming off four straight wins, including home wins over the 49ers and Rams. We were even 3–1 on the road.

Then came the disastrous trip to play, once again, the 49ers and Rams. Since the Colts began their days in the NFL in Baltimore, they had won only one road game versus those two West Coast teams. Not quite ready to gel as a great team, we lost both games. Had we won those contests, our 9–5 record would have topped our division, as the Lions and 49ers wound up tied for the top spot at 8–4. Detroit won the division title game, then won it all against Cleveland. We'd have to wait another year before we would achieve what the Lions had done.

The memory of those two losses was one of the main reasons we went on to win two championships. We realized as a team that we had totally screwed up. We were good enough to win in 1957, but we took a cavalier approach to the West Coast trip. I think those losses so disgusted everybody that we were determined to never let it happen again.

By 1957 Unitas and I really began to click. He led the NFL in a handful of passing categories. And that year marked the first time in my career that I led the league in a statistical category, doing so with my 800 receiving yards. It was catching those long passes and getting comfortable in the first full season Unitas and I played together. My 67-yard touchdown that year was my longest ever to that point. In all, I caught forty-seven passes, second best in the NFL, just five receptions fewer than the league leader, Billy Wilson of San Francisco. My 66.7 yards per game average ranked second in the NFL, and my six touchdown receptions placed me third in the league.

In my rookie year I was just able to hang on and make the team. When I came back for my second year and ended up ranking ninth in the league for receptions, it was a total leap forward. By the 1957 season I began to realize that I could play with the big boys.

Yet my status as a top receiver was mostly done without much technique or route-running skills. A huge factor in my third season was watching the movie that was made about "Crazy Legs" Hirsch's life. I think I saw it around 1956. Earlier, he had one of the greatest seasons any NFL receiver had ever achieved. In a twelve-game schedule, he caught passes for 1,495 yards, almost exactly 125 yards per game. He was making these catches over the shoulder, directly over the head, with outstretched fingers, on the dead run. He'd catch it and run another 40 yards. He was spectacular.

Watching the movie was the first time I ever saw a great receiver at work. I could not have had a better example than Hirsch. He could catch that long ball 40, 50 yards downfield, with outstretched arms and never miss a stride. My mouth dropped open. It was the first concept I had of catching the long ball, and I started working on it after that.

I did that at Paris High School in the off-season. I got my dad's high school quarterback, Scott Odom, to throw to me when he was available. I told him, "I want to learn how to catch the ball over my head like Elroy Hirsch." He'd throw pass after pass, and I learned how to look at the ball all the way in and catch it in different locations until I got comfortable with it.

There was even a time when I'd have my wife throw passes to me in the off-season around May and June when I was getting in condition. My teammates, like Unitas, were spread all over the United States, so as I was on my own, preparing myself physically for training camp—you really didn't have anybody to work out with. As a pass receiver I knew I had to handle the ball before coming to camp. My wife Sally was a woman I met in 1960; I was so taken with her, I proposed and got married to her just a handful of months later. Even she was enlisted to help me. I had her throw to me, and she did a good job.

Another great influence in my career began in 1957. I was under one of the best receiver coaches in NFL history, Bob Shaw, an ex-pro receiver himself. In fact, he was the first NFL player ever to catch five touchdown passes in a single game. He did that in 1950 during his one season with the Chicago Cardinals, performing that feat against the old Baltimore Colts, in a 55–13 win. Since then only Kellen Winslow and Jerry Rice have ever matched that record.

Bob was more than just a bright guy. He was brilliant. He mainly played for the Los Angeles Rams, and he played with great quarterbacks like Bob Waterfield and Norm Van Brocklin and with great receivers, too. He knew what it was all about.

Hired by Weeb Ewbank, Shaw coached me in my third and fourth years with the Colts. He talked to me about concepts I had never grasped before. Once he left, during a season in which I was having trouble getting open, I started experimenting with what he had said, and I applied his lessons.

Shaw was probably responsible for the most critical development in my whole experience as a pass receiver. In just two years he changed my entire approach to pass offense and pass routes and my philosophy about working. Before Shaw, I didn't know any moves to get separation from defenders. He taught me inside approaches and outside approaches. He opened a whole new avenue of route running that, without him, I never would have understood at all.

When a defensive back lines up 4, 5, or 6 yards off of me—and most of them lined up head up on me—all I knew how to do before Shaw helped me was to come off the line in straight lines like it's drawn up in the playbook. Run 8 yards and break, and run 10 yards and break, whatever. Shaw taught me how to come off the line and maneuver to the inside and the outside to force the defensive back to start turning his hips and legs. I would get them in a position where I'd turn them inside and break outside, or the other way around.

And Shaw taught me to put more than one move on them. Usually they would let me do one fake, then they'd jump on me. So I developed double fakes, and they would invariably bite and I'd break wide open. I would get them neutralized, or I would get them turned in the wrong direction. They were reacting at the wrong time. If I wanted to break an outside route, I'd get the defensive back turned inside. Then I *had him*.

After I learned six different ways to run inside routes and six outside routes—and approaches such as using one fake, double fakes, even triple fakes, and some straight at the defender—I accomplished pretty much what I wanted to, because when I left the line of scrimmage, the defender didn't know where the devil I was going. For example, I could come off the line with an outside approach, and if the guy moved over there to cover it, I'd break inside on him. I studied the defenders to know what I felt their weaknesses were and I picked my move.

Legend claims I had eighty-eight different moves. The reason why the numbers got up to eighty-eight, although I never really counted them so I don't know the precise number, was that I had variations of each basic move. And I used so many fakes for a secondary reason that many people don't realize: It was a way to avoid being hit by defenders. I had a minimum of six different ways of running every route. I had outside approaches and inside approaches, and I mixed them up so that I had a lot of different looks.

I compare this to baseball Hall of Famer Juan Marichal, who had several basic pitches, but because he could throw each one from a variety of angles, it was as if he had an endless supply of looks with which to baffle batters. It was the same principle with me.

When Shaw came to Baltimore, he shaped my career in another way, one related to workload. He watched me, and he knew I was overworking. So he stayed on my butt about getting off the practice field in training camp when I wanted to stay after practice to work on routes. Now, doing some extra work is okay from time to time, but he knew it wasn't wise to do it too much.

During the season when we did stay out after practice, because Weeb understood how important this was for quarterback–receiver timing, Shaw would be there with us and then, when he knew I should get off the practice field, he would come out there and insist that I get off. He was trying to protect my legs.

I had two of the best years I ever had when Shaw was there. It was a classic case of the significance of one instructor who knows his business and how he can affect a developing talent.

Flash forward to November 9, 1958, for a funny anecdote. Shortly after we had lost a regular-season game to the Giants in Yankee Stadium, I appeared as a guest on the TV show *What's My Line*. The format of the program featured a four-person panel who tried to guess the occupation of contestants after asking them questions. One celebrity guest appeared per show, and the panel had to be blindfolded when the celebrity guest came on camera. Back then I was so unknown that I came on as a regular contestant, not a celebrity.

Panelist Bennett Cerf guessed my occupation quickly, and I only won $50. When we chatted on air, Cerf mentioned Unitas, but pronounced his name Uni-TASS. Amazingly, Cerf didn't know his name. OK, that was fine, but Cerf, and just about every other person in the United States, would certainly know his name in just a matter of weeks.

Chapter Four

The Greatest Game Ever Played

I AM PROUD TO HAVE PLAYED IN THE GAME STILL REFERRED TO AS THE Greatest Game Ever Played. But the rest of the 1958 season was great as well.

I led the NFL in two categories that year: I had the most catches (fifty-six) and most touchdown pass receptions (nine). I finished in the top five in several other categories. We were so impressive that season that we had the conference title wrapped up by the tenth game, right around Thanksgiving. We began the year at 6–0, but during the sixth game Unitas was badly hurt in a 56–0 rout of the Packers.

I'll never forget the play on which he was injured. Unitas was already on the ground when Johnny Symank, a defensive back, landed on his chest with both knees, breaking three of Unitas's ribs and puncturing a lung, causing him to be hospitalized.

Amazingly, Unitas missed just two games, and when he returned to face the Rams, he threw a 58-yard score to Moore on his first play from scrimmage. Colts radio announcer Chuck Thompson joked, "How rusty can a guy get?" Later Unitas threw Moore another touchdown pass, and he even ran one in from a yard out. We won easily, 34–7.

The next week Unitas engineered a great comeback against the 49ers. Down 27–7 at the half, we stormed back to win, 35–27. When we were up by just one point in the fourth quarter, Unitas threw to me for an insurance score. Without that pass his streak of consecutive games with at least one touchdown pass would have ended one shy of the all-time record, which was twenty-three.

We were guaranteed a playoff berth early enough that Ewbank rested a lot of players down the stretch, especially those nursing injuries. That's a big reason why we lost our last two games of the regular season. Prior to those defeats, our only loss was when Unitas was hospitalized. We lost our first game without him, 24–21, to the Giants in Yankee Stadium, the same team and at the same venue that would soon be historically linked with us. Actually, the loss to the Giants was the only one that year that came in a truly meaningful game.

Those last two games lacked the necessity factor. We just had no need to score more points than the other guys. We went to the West Coast with a record of 9–1, then lost to the Rams, by 2 points, and by twelve to the 49ers. They were two outstanding teams, no question about that, but our urgency was not there. We were already in the title game, and we knew it.

There's something many fans today don't know. Back then there were twelve teams in the NLF—six in the East and six in the West. Win your division and you go to the title game. What young readers may not understand now is the great concentration of talent we had back then: There were twelve teams, with thirty-five men on each team, packed with talent. Today there are thirty-two teams with expanded rosters. Today's players are talented, for sure, but the talent is really spread out. And that's why, when you look at the Baltimore Colts and the New York Giants from around 1958, you see a lot of Hall of Fame players. You can toss in a lot from the Green Bay Packers of those years, too.

The '58 season marked the first time I was selected for the Pro Bowl game and it was the first season I was a member of the first team on the All-Pro squad. These were totally separate honors. The Pro Bowl team was voted on by a different group than the various All-Pro teams, which were selected by United Press International, the Associated Press, and other publications like *The Sporting News.*

It was a thrill to be in the same Pro Bowl company as a slew of future Hall of Famers including Jim Brown, Jim Ringo, Yale Lary, Sam Huff, Ollie Matson, and Ernie Stautner. The list is an illustrious one and also included seven more Colts: four more future Hall of Famers in Unitas, Gino Marchetti, Jim Parker, and Lenny Moore, along with Gene "Big

Daddy" Lipscomb, Alan Ameche, and defensive end Don Joyce. The winners' share was something like $800, and the losers earned around $600. By the way, this was the first Pro Bowl game to be televised nationally.

But of course the big television event of the year was the title game. Our opponents, the Giants, had given up the lowest point total in the NFL, 183, but our defense was ranked second best, surrendering just 203 points. In addition, we stood number one with the top NFL offense. We had scored 381 points, good for an average of almost 32 points per game, while the Giants had scored just 246 points, or 20.5 points a game.

The Giants had won the championship just two years earlier, while the Colts were only in their sixth year of existence. Weeb went into the title games in both 1958 and 1959 with a simple plan. We had somewhere in the range of just ten runs and twelve passes that we'd been running since training camp. Each receiver had about four routes he'd run, and the timing with the quarterback by then was automatic.

Weeb felt there was no way you could master and execute an offense at a high level when you had a game plan that was inflated with too many plays. He believed execution would fall off, and that even players' physical abilities wouldn't operate at full speed, because there would be hesitation, doubt, and indecision with so many scarcely rehearsed plays. You can call plays in a game that you may not have worked on for three weeks under a complicated system, and that goes along with having a massive game plan. The quarterback would have to carry a huge load that way, and that's not good.

As always, I was looking to gain any edge I could gain. So before the game began, I went onto the field alone to examine it. This was a pregame routine that had begun early in my career after I had slipped a few times. I always wanted to know if there were any spots on the field that were wet, muddy, or frozen over. I also did this to decide which pair of cleats I'd wear that day.

Usually if there were muddy or soggy conditions, I'd wear my mud cleats, which had two extra spikes around an eighth of an inch long or so under the balls of my feet. They helped me to pivot better. With those, when I planted and pivoted in mud, I would go deeper into the surface, and that gave me footing where I might otherwise slip and fall on my butt. On most fields, my regular cleats were better; they didn't hurt my feet or slow me down like the mud cleats did. Ninety-eight percent of the field called for my regular cleats, but the remaining *2 percent* were comprised of an icy spot near one of the goal lines and another slippery spot I saw, one that would be on my side of the field at times, near the Giants' bench. I knew that if in a critical stage of the game I had to make cuts in that place, the regular cleats wouldn't get the job done. That's why I went with the mud cleats—the important attention to details.

In the locker room before the game, Weeb gave a pep talk. He named every player on the team and said how each of us had some shortcoming or how many of us, like Unitas, were castoffs. His comments about me were about how I came out of SMU as a twentieth-round draft pick. "Nobody wanted you but the Colts," was how he led off, and he was totally accurate about that. His talk inspired a lot of us, but I actually wasn't paying attention. I was focused on the Giants. So, to be honest, Weeb's speech didn't have any effect on me.

People remember our drives to tie and win the championship, but we also scored an important touchdown on our last possession of the first half as time was running out. That drive went 86 yards and lasted fifteen plays. During that stretch Unitas hit me on a 5-yard completion, a 9-yard pass for which I was ruled out of bounds as I made the catch, a look-in pass for 13 yards, and the touchdown with 1:20 showing on the clock.

On that play we were in a situation where we had just picked up a first down and were 15 yards out, trying to add to our 7–3 lead. The situation may have called for an off-tackle play, but when Unitas got in a spot like that, he would invariably do something different.

So we went into a formation in which Lenny Moore or L. G. Dupre flanked to the far right and I was the split end on the left, but in this formation I didn't really split. Instead, I came in and lined up close. That gave the impression that we were going to run the ball toward me or to the other side of the field. So the Giants defense was expecting a run. What Unitas called was a fake. He took the snap, spun, and ran behind where I was lined up, acting like he was going to hand off to Ameche. Ameche started in to the left tackle area, while I acted like I was blocking. Then Unitas put the ball in Ameche's belly and pulled it out. In the meantime, after I had faked the block, I slipped between the linebacker and the defensive back. I was standing in the end zone, wide open, and Unitas hit me for a touchdown.

The Giants ran just three plays after the ensuing kickoff, and we went into the locker room with a 14–3 lead. Early in the second half, an odd event took place. I caught a pass in front of the Colts' bench, and Sam Huff hit me late; he hit me dirty. He didn't hurt me, because I was well padded up, but it happened right in front of Weeb. Now, you had to know Weeb. He was a short, dumpy kind of little guy, but he was a competitor with a capital C, and he got upset at Huff. He went after him. Huff was sort of humoring him. He outweighed Weeb by a hundred pounds, but Weeb got real hostile—I think he tried to throw a punch—but there's Huff, he's got his helmet on with his mask. All Weeb could do was hurt his own fist.

The lead melted away when the Giants scored a touchdown late in the third quarter and another early in the fourth quarter to take a 17–14 advantage.

Then came the historic 86-yard drive to send us into overtime. The prologue covered this drive already, but I have to say here that Unitas and I sure were in sync. Among the seven plays, not counting the game-tying field goal, we connected on three passes, all in a row, for 62 of the 73 yards we advanced before Steve Myhra's kick tied things up.

At the end of regulation, the Giants won the coin toss to start overtime play, but they quickly faltered, going three and out. Our defense forced them into a fourth-and-1 situation from their own 29. They punted and we took over on our own 20. It seemed like we had the length of the field to go. We had a *long* way to go.

One big thing in overtime was that there were no time constraints. We didn't have a clock to work against. We could do what we wanted to, and take the time we wanted to use, and run whatever we wanted to. Of course we did have to keep making first downs against a tough defense.

So Unitas started hammering the ball on the ground while also throwing the ball to mix it up like he usually did. Here's the breakdown on the plays we carried out: run, long pass, run, short pass, run, pass (but Unitas was sacked), 21-yard pass to me, run, another run, 12-yard pass to me, run, short pass, and then the dive into the end zone by Ameche for the game-winning touchdown. Now that's mixing things up.

Unitas's whole approach to things was that whatever they thought he was going to do, he'd do the opposite. He liked to keep them guessing, but he also was dealing with a full deck of cards. He had Moore flanked, and Moore could also run the ball. He had Ameche in the backfield with Dupre, who was no slouch. And he had me on another flank and tight end Mutscheller, who was a great blocker and catcher. Unitas had weapons everywhere, the entire arsenal. He had great players to call on, no matter who he gave the ball to.

We had a totally balanced attack, and this was a huge part of the Baltimore Colt story. It is what you need to win a championship. A totally balanced attack makes the defense play honest. That was one of the big problems the Giants had—they had to defend the entire field, and that was not an easy assignment at all. They couldn't gang up in one place or another, because they didn't know what the heck we were going to do; and Unitas played this to the hilt. He was totally unpredictable. It was one of the things that made him so difficult to defend—you could never tell what the guy was going to do, what he was going to call.

Weeb understood balance, and he had the personnel to attain it. We could run the ball and we could throw it. And we could run the ball wide, up the middle, or off tackle. And we could throw it short, medium, and deep.

So, on that historic drive, Unitas just started doing his thing, mixing things up beautifully. After an 11-yard run by Dupre to open the drive, Unitas unleashed a deep one to Moore. Although it was incomplete, it reminded the Giants that they'd better defend that guy deep.

Six plays into the drive, we were faced with a third-and-14 situation. John's pass to me deep on the sideline was good for 21 yards to keep things going. That placed the ball at the Giants 42-yard line. I was the third receiver Unitas looked for as I ran a "come open late" route. I ran through a slippery spot on the field, a spot I had noticed before the game, and Karilivacz slipped and fell on that area. Wearing my mud cleats had paid off.

Under Weeb's system, on pass plays Unitas was instructed to have a first-choice receiver, a second, and, if neither one of them was open, a third choice. Very seldom did Unitas go to the third option—it only happened one time in my entire career. Moore was the first choice on a 10-yard out, and Mutscheller did a 12-yard hook. I was on an 18-yard sideline pattern. Unitas had never come to me on that play, but in this particular situation I ran the route, turned around, and the ball was coming because Moore and Mutscheller were both covered. For as long as we had that pass pattern, that was the only time he threw to me.

On the very next play, Ameche got sprung for 22 yards up the middle on a trap play, bringing us to the Giants' 20-yard line. In a little while I'll relate what happened on the play that prevented Ameche from ending the game right then and there.

Two plays later John hit me on what was my last catch of the day, a 12-yard pick up to the 8-yard line. He hit me on a slant pass. One interesting event took place then. NBC, which was broadcasting the game, lost its signal, and millions of fans sat frustrated in front of their TV sets. Shortly after that, a fan, who observers thought to be drunk, stumbled onto the field and, in the time it took to subdue him, NBC was able to restore their feed. Later it was revealed that the fan was actually NBC employee Stan Rotkiewicz, who was at the game to serve as a statistician. His drunken act bought time for the repairs to be made, but it broke up the flow of the game, and it stopped the clock. Nevertheless, I don't think it was a big deal or that it had any effect on the outcome of the game.

Then, on first down Ameche picked up just 1 yard up the middle before Unitas threw to Mutscheller on the right sideline for a gain of 6. Mutscheller went out of bounds, slipping at the 1-yard line on one of the frozen places on the field. Weeb had told Unitas to keep the ball on the ground. If that didn't produce a touchdown, we could always kick on fourth down. But Unitas, having seen how the Giants defended Ameche on the previous play, threw, crossing up the Giants.

The play, despite what some people may think, was not one Unitas conceived on the spot, even though it was not the play Weeb wanted us to run. We had the pass play in which Mutscheller ran that route in our repertoire, but Unitas may have had added some special instructions to Mutscheller in the huddle, because he *would* do that. He would call a play and then say something like, "Jim, I'd like for you to do this and that on the route." That's probably what happened, a variation on one of our plays.

Unitas was later asked why he threw a risky pass with the Colts so close to the goal line. He replied, "You don't risk anything when you know where you're passing." Knowing he always had the safe option of throwing the ball out of bounds, he also commented, "When you know what you're doing, they're not intercepted."

When Mutscheller returned to the huddle, Unitas didn't criticize him for not scoring. I've heard it said that he joked, "Jim, I tried to make you a hero." Now, I don't really remember that, but it sounds *exactly* like Unitas. He especially liked to laugh and joke off the field.

It was third down now, and we could smell the end zone. In that huddle, we didn't even consider kicking a field goal. Myhra was an erratic kicker. He had made just four field goals on ten tries during the season, so we weren't totally confident about him. And earlier in the game, he had missed two field goals.

Later, when Unitas was asked why we didn't just go for a short field goal to win it, he said, "No offense, but I couldn't trust Myhra. We *had* to score." I agreed with him. And like the rest of the team, I had faith in his ability to take us into the end zone—and he did.

Unitas handed off to Ameche, and after he capped the incredible drive with his famous 1-yard plunge over right tackle to make it 23–17, we were the world champions.

We had run thirteen plays, methodically marching 80 yards. We were finally able to exhale, bringing the city of Baltimore its first NFL title in the history of the Colts.

Interestingly, the rule about playing sudden death in overtime had never come into play during a regular NFL game, so a lot of us were confused after we tied the Giants in regulation. It remains the only sudden-death NFL championship game played, including Super Bowl contests.

One of our defensive backs, Andy Nelson, later said he didn't know that this game would go beyond the regulation four quarters. Some of us thought the game was over, and we ended up in a tie because that's the way things always had been. Players were looking at each other, asking, "What's happening here?" The overtime dimension to the game was new. I didn't even know what overtime or sudden death was. I think we all learned it at the same time. I remember standing on the sidelines with the officials and the captains out on the field and there was another coin toss. I can't recall who told us what was going on, but I think the referee explained it.

After the field goal to tie the game, though, I just felt we were going to go on and win it. It was a psychological experience that I don't think we were even aware of at the time. But over the years and having been involved in a whole lot of competitive contests at various levels, you realize that there is an inner sense of confidence that comes in certain situations that's really hard to explain. That overtime experience going against the Giants was one of those situations. It was like we knew we were going to win that ball game.

Looking back now on my condition, I did start feeling some fatigue in that overtime period. I had been tracking my weight that entire season, starting in training camp. I had scales and I'd weigh myself practically every day—before and after practice, before and after games—and I kept records on it. And what was interesting was that as the season went on, I went down from 184 pounds in camp to about 178 going into that game against the Giants. After that game, I found I had lost 7 or 8 pounds that day alone. It was not hot, but running all those pass patterns and playing almost five quarters took its toll. I was as lean as a snake going into the game, but I lost a lot of water weight.

Many of the Giants would later say that by the end of the game they were drained. I was worn out. I had been running pass routes all afternoon, so I had a good reason to be worn out. We threw the ball forty times that day. I don't really remember fatigue being a factor in overtime, though. I'm not sure I was even conscious of fatigue at that point.

I think maybe when we went into overtime I got a surge of energy. You hear people talk about "Getting in the zone." Well, I think I was totally in a zone, and John was too. We were just so focused on winning. I think the apocalypse could have come and it wouldn't have caught our attention. We were focused on doing what it took to move that football down there and win that game.

I don't remember any mental fatigue, either. Adrenaline was pumping and, again, I'm not sure I was conscious of physical fatigue. But I do remember when Ameche broke up the field on the trap play in overtime, the one where he gained 22 yards. Then there was a tip off to my fatigue. And here's what I alluded to earlier in this chapter: He would have scored if I had done what I was supposed to do downfield, which was to leave the line of scrimmage from my split end spot and get that safety out of the way. But I was really tired at that point.

Normally, whenever you hand the ball to the fullback up the middle, you make 3, 4, maybe 5 yards, but you're not going to break a long one—never happens. Darned if it didn't happen on this one. I gambled because I was tired, and I was loafing, and I couldn't get in position to block the safety, Jimmy Patton, because I was too late. Wouldn't you know it, Ameche breaks through there clean as a whistle and he's in the secondary, and the only guy who stops him is Patton. And I'm sitting there watching this, knowing that if I had done my job, he would have scored.

I heard Unitas talking later, and what he said gives an interesting insight into his on-the-field observation skills. He said that the reason why he called that trap play was that he had been watching Huff. From his middle linebacker position, Huff had been starting to cheat back and toward me because I was catching so many passes. Huff confirmed this later on when he said, "I was trying to help Karilivacz out with Berry, and I got too far out of position."

Now, you're talking about just a couple of yards, but that was enough. It put Huff in a position where our right tackle, George Preas, who had to execute a crossover block to get the middle linebacker on our trap play, could get to Huff. That's when Ameche blew up the middle. But if Huff had been playing the defense like it was designed, it would have only gone for a gain of a few yards at most. Unitas saw Huff cheating, so he went to that trap play. Little things can change a lot in sports.

I once told author Dave Klein about how Unitas acted when he was under fire. I said, "Old John never did get excited. He never did show any emotion. You'd think we were playing an intrasquad game back in Baltimore during summer camp. He was just a businessman, a professional, and it was time to go to work. He called all the plays." And he was shrewd doing so.

We were on the far end of the field when Ameche went in the end zone to win it. I can remember the last moments like it was yesterday. Our locker room was on the other end of the stadium—you had to go all the way over there to reach a ramp under the stadium, then go on up and into our locker room. So we had to go the entire length of the field to get there.

Now, my job on the play, since I was on the left side of the field and Ameche ran off tackle to the right, was just to do a cutoff block. I wasn't at the point of attack, but I did have a block to execute on the line. I did that, and then I saw him score. As soon as I saw that, I turned and started running, full speed, toward our locker room. And the reason for that was I remembered our final game in Memorial Stadium that season.

After we beat San Francisco and had clinched the title, the fans started pouring onto the middle of the field. The noise level was such that you could scream and shout and not even hear your own voice. Some players got knocked down, but some were safe because the crowd lifted us up. Some fans got trampled, though.

Visualize being up in the press box looking down at this mob with the focal point being the center of the field. You've got this massive group of people all pushing toward the middle. People there started falling, getting crushed. The overwhelming pressure of the mob on the field was one of the most frightening things I had ever experienced. I didn't want to go through that again.

So we had that memory lingering in our minds, and a bunch of our offensive players took off running. We weren't thinking that such a reaction wasn't going to happen in Yankee Stadium—that there wasn't quite the frenzy like the Baltimore fans had after that win against San Francisco—but we still hurried off the field. I've since heard that fifteen thousand fans from Baltimore did make the trip to Yankee Stadium, so there certainly could have been another swarm of supporters on the field who might have been overzealous in their celebration.

All the time I was running for the locker room, this was the refrain going on in my head: "God just did that." I really felt in my heart that God was responsible for that. One of the unusual things about it was that

I never really gave God any thought like that before. It was a first-time experience, totally alien to anything that had ever gone through my head before. It was so strong that when I ran all the way to our locker room, it stayed on my mind.

I went into the locker room and then went back into a toilet stall and sat down where nobody was around me. I thought about it many times, and the best way I can come up to express it is that I was immersed in this awareness of God. It was so strange, but that's what happened. I guess you might say it was my first experience with God revealing Himself to me, because that was what was happening.

You study Scripture and you'll see this surface periodically—God revealing Himself to someone. It is not an isolated experience. It's there. All I know is it happened to me right then and there, and I haven't been the same since.

In the meantime, Unitas's reaction to the game was quite different. Nelson said, "John Unitas was a cool customer. Nothing excited him. He walked off the field after that game and he wasn't turning back flips or jumping up and down. His eyes were focused straight ahead. Like it was just another game. I thought, 'This man just played the greatest game of his life and it's like another game to him.' He just casually walked off. He took it all in stride.

"When we got to the airport there were 30,000 people waiting for us. Some of them climbed on top of the team bus. I rode home with him that night, and he never said two words. I got out of the car and he said, 'I'll see you tomorrow,' and that was it. It was as if he were saying so long to a buddy, leaving a factory after putting in an eight-hour shift." That was Unitas for you.

Later on the game would be dissected time and again. Nelson said the key was, "The two-minute drill. We worked on it in practice every day. Between Raymond Berry and Johnny Unitas—that's what made the game so famous. They knew what they wanted to do—they had worked on the pass routes they wanted to run. That just didn't happen, it was planned for many, many days ahead. We were ready for it, and we used it quite a bit."

I think Weeb learned the drill under Paul Brown, but the way we ran it that day was something special. As I said, you found yourself shaking your head, saying, "Good grief, I've never seen anything like that before."

On the day, my twelve catches and 178 yards in receptions set records for an NFL title game. The old records were eleven receptions in the 1950 championship game by Cleveland's Dante Lavelli and 160 yards on catches by Washington's Wayne Millner in 1937.

Of Unitas's twenty-six competitions of forty passes, almost half went to me, and more than half of his 349 yards came when we hooked up on completions. The record twelve catches in a championship contest wasn't broken until 2014 (by Demaryius Thomas in the Denver–Seattle Super Bowl) and, even today, through 2015, my twelve receptions rank number two for a title game; and they're tied for the eighth-best total ever for any round of playoff games. Plus, I believe the 178 yards stands third best in title games, and nineteenth best for all postseason play (again, through 2015).

Other records set that day were our seventeen first downs on passes and our total of twenty-seven first downs. New York's six fumbles were also a new high for a title game. Finally, Unitas's 349 yards through the air broke Sammy Baugh's record of 335 set in 1937 for Washington.

The classic 1958 game still lingers in football lore (despite eight total fumbles and eight sacks). It gained instant fame largely because of our two dramatic drives and because it was the first championship of any major sport to go into, and be decided by, sudden-death overtime. Furthermore, it was televised nationally back in a time when watching pro football games on TV wasn't a prevalent practice. An estimated forty-five million watched the game, making it the most widely watched football broadcast to date. All of these factors combined to make this contest what many still call The Greatest Game Ever Played.

The pro football Hall of Fame website goes as far as to say, "Professional football was on the rise in the 1950s and reached a crescendo during the latter part of the decade. Much of the popularity can be traced to a single game—the 1958 NFL Championship Game between the Baltimore Colts and New York Giants." In all, fifteen future Hall of Famers, including twelve players, took part in the contest, seventeen if you count the owner and the vice president/secretary of the Giants.

Winning the game also led to a nice honor: In January my hometown celebrated with a Raymond Berry Day and a testimonial luncheon. Winning the championship also had to be a factor when the Texas Press Association named me the Texan of the Year in 1968.

The 1958 championship game remains the highlight of my career, and it came against the number one defense in the NFL. It was my biggest professional achievement, alongside being inducted into the Pro Football Hall of Fame on the first ballot. Of course back in the 1950s, becoming a Hall of Famer wasn't even a remote thought in my head. I still had a lot of work and a lot of playing days ahead of me—and another championship, too.

Chapter Five

"Unitas to Berry"

The words "Unitas to Berry" mean more to me than the refrain of many PA announcers making a touchdown call for the audience, much more than simply a recitation of the many passes we hooked up on. Our names linked together represent our diligence, our productivity, and our friendship.

Unitas and I were of one mind from the very first time we ever met. Outside of family, he was 100 percent football, and so was I. It was our focus and our interest—we had nothing else that we were concerned with. He had three interests: one was football, the second was football, and the third was football. He was single-minded in his approach to the game. We weren't interested in any half-ass operation, so we were on at the word, "go," all the time.

I can never get away from the fact, though, that perhaps the single most important thing that happened to both of us was being hired to play for the Colts under team owner Carroll Rosenbloom and head coach Weeb Ewbank, who had been an offensive line coach under Paul Brown at Cleveland. They defined leadership. But at the time, we had no clue that we were in the ideal environment to let our physical abilities flow. We clicked. By the time I retired, all but five of my sixty-eight touchdown catches came from Unitas. For some time the sixty-three Unitas-to-Berry scores were a record for one quarterback throwing to one receiver. The first two men to break that record were Dan Marino and Mark Clayton.

There was a great marriage between Weeb and Unitas. Weeb had an instinct about Unitas's ability and saw him as a field general, a strategist at calling plays. If it hadn't been for Weeb, John Unitas would have never had a pro career. Now, combine John Unitas with Weeb Ewbank, and you've got yourself two world titles and a whole bunch of victories.

Mike Ditka said the Colts changed the game of pro football significantly when Unitas started putting the ball in the air quite a bit. Ditka told a sportswriter, "John was a terrific player and he was put into the right system—he had a great tight end in John Mackey, he had great receivers in Jim Mutscheller and Raymond Berry. John Unitas was a special guy . . . The advent of the forward pass being *really* a weapon was with Johnny Unitas more than anybody."

If he'd have been under any other head coach in any other system, Unitas would not have been what he was. Weeb's system was utter simplicity and utter soundness, and that is one of the most difficult things for any coach in the business to accomplish.

Unitas was a man of few words, and he was a man who sought out the simplest way to get it done.

And that fit well with the Colts when he first arrived there. I don't think people have ever made enough of this point, so I'll say it again: Weeb Ewbank's offensive philosophy and his offensive system were utter simplicity. He and his offense were a whole lot like Unitas was with his quotes. He didn't have much to say, but his messages were powerful. And with a simple offense, Unitas wasn't overburdened with too many playbook pages. He knew how to select and use his personnel. So he'd call the plays on the field as he instinctively felt like.

I just happened to have some perspective on this offensive system that helped me to understand it. My dad was a Texas high school football coach for thirty-five years. I grew up watching him, hearing him, being around him on the sidelines, and I played for him. My dad had a wry sense of humor. I often heard him repeat one of his sayings, which he learned in the coaching business. He would chuckle and say, "Any fool can make it complicated."

I didn't even understand it at the time, not being old enough to grasp what was happening. But I understood it after I had a lot of experience in the assisting coaching business and being on a lot of coaching staffs under a lot of different systems. The two things that really began to get clearer and clearer to me were the sheer simplicity and soundness of my dad's offense and Ewbank's thinking, and their approach to football. It was, "Don't do very many things, but do them well, and your players just instinctively know what to do. And they'll adjust to anything the defense does. You don't have a whole bunch of adjustments for a whole bunch of plays, you've just got one play and you know how to make it work, no matter what they do."

We certainly did adjust to what defenses did. Unitas and I even had our own audibles that we worked on. We could put them into play depending on the tendencies of the guys who covered me on defense.

Playbooks for teams like the Colts didn't bulge—you could easily print them out—but a game plan could also be easily constructed. Not unlike the Green Bay Packers of Vince Lombardi, the Colts ran their plays, and even if the opposing defenses had a good guess about what was coming—such as the Packers' famed sweep—it was a case of, "Just try and stop it."

Lombardi and Ewbank were two peas in a pod. Forrest Gregg played for Lombardi, and he is one of my closest friends. We played at SMU together, and we played in the trenches side-by-side for two years on varsity. We talked about Lombardi. He agreed that Ewbank and Lombardi had exactly the same approach. They had good football players, and, by the way, both knew how to spot talent in unknown players.

I've been places where the systems were so complex, so complicated, that the players didn't know their butt from first base about what they were doing out there on game day. And the execution on the field showed it. So did their win–loss records.

What it amounts to is that Ewbank knew exactly what he wanted his team to do and how to get them to do it well. Being under Weeb's system was the number one reason why Unitas and I had the careers we had. Later, Weeb and his system would help Joe Namath do what he did.

The other thing that Weeb had going for him was that he had come into the league as an assistant coach under Paul Brown. A very small man physically, Brown always wore a suit, tie, and hat the day of the game, and he was cerebral. He exemplified something that I learned from studying him and Ewbank: It takes a genius to keep things simple. Weeb experienced up close one of Brown's tremendous strengths—Brown had very, very few plays. He was one of the most brilliant coaches who's ever been in the football business, and he used only about six to eight running plays, and, I don't know, eight to ten pass plays—simplicity and soundness. Weeb either had that same philosophy himself when he first coached there, or he learned it from Brown, and he never varied from it.

The significance of it all is that when a player is absolutely, undoubtedly sure of what he's doing when the ball is snapped, his physical and mental abilities flow at full speed. When the opposite is true, the player leaves the line of scrimmage and pads around here and there because he's not really sure what he's doing.

So, the Colts under Ewbank knew how to run our stuff—we knew how to shoot our weapons. It didn't make a difference what the enemy was doing.

And I don't think people comprehend the significance, the importance, of the owner. The Baltimore Colts never would have been *the* Baltimore Colts without Carroll Rosenbloom. He was a very generous owner and a people person. He was *the* key man, a leader who had sense enough to look around the league and select Weeb to be the head coach. Anybody could have hired him; he had never been a head coach. What did Rosenbloom know and see in this guy? Rosenbloom was a brilliant man, and that was a brilliant hire. He certainly knew something that other people didn't know. That step he made to hire Weeb set the whole tone for the championship Colts.

To end up in Baltimore with Rosenbloom as the owner, Ewbank as the head coach, and Unitas as the quarterback was a scenario you couldn't re-create in a thousand years. I've seen great players from all around the NFL over a lot of years, and I'd see a great player with some half-ass team that had bad ownership and coaching. If you put him in the Baltimore Colts environment, he'd be a totally different guy.

And talk about leadership: Unitas was the ultimate leader. Lenny Moore once said, "Johnny ran the huddle. If they sent something in from the bench, and he didn't like it, he wouldn't call it. Usually if something came in from the bench, that's something you're supposed to immediately call. If Johnny didn't like it, he'd say, 'Hell, that damn thing won't work,' and he would go on and call whatever he wanted to call. And when he came off the field, the coach might say, 'John, why didn't you call my play?' He'd say, 'Hey, I'm here—I can see what's happening.' No, Johnny was completely in charge. He took care of business at quarterback."

I agree. I remember a situation when Ewbank sent in a play and Unitas didn't run it. Later, Weeb questioned me as to why he didn't call the play, and I simply told him, "John didn't think the play would work," and Weeb just said, "Oh. That's OK."

In 2002 I wrote an article about Unitas for *The Sporting News*. In it I spoke of his many attributes, such as the way he "was absolutely locked in on moving the ball any way he could move it, getting it into the end zone and winning. And he couldn't have cared less about hype, publicity or who got the credit. All those things were garbage to him, and everybody on our team knew it. When you have that type of attitude in your leader, it's going to cause the ones behind him to fall into the same pattern. What we had in Baltimore was a totally unified team that didn't think about individuals at all. It was a great place to play because of that, and John set the tone."

Unitas truly was a field general. He had this rare ability to make the game conform to his will. He controlled the tempo, decided the tactics. He was a chess master who played the game several moves ahead of everyone else.

Legend would have it that Unitas would draw up an impromptu play on the spot in the huddle, using his finger to draw up the play in the dirt during games. That's all bull, but he did direct things.

Tom Matte, a Colt running back, learned firsthand about Unitas's being a field general. He said, "The thing that Unitas made me understand—and this is where John was so important to me—is he'd say, 'Tom, what you've got to do is not only understand what you're doing during this play, but you have to understand everybody else's position. So what I want you to do is I want you to learn the centers, guards, tackles, outside receivers, and I want you to understand what the patterns are doing. For instance, if you're running a closed flare on the weak side, you're clearing it out because Raymond Berry is going to come in right behind you. You're in a clear out mode, so you got to get moving—just don't think, 'I'll go out there and I have to get open.' That doesn't mean shit. What you've got to do is clear the area out for Raymond to come underneath and I'll hit him.' So he made me learn every position, just like John himself had done, so I could understand what a complete football play was, and that was really important."

Mike Lucci, a linebacker for nine NFL seasons, recognized another talent Unitas had: "Unitas had a great feel of the game, of the field, and he did look you off a lot. I mean, he'd go and come back to a receiver, or he'd look one way and then come back to where he intended to go all along. He had a great ability to do that."

One time when Unitas got hurt in a game, Weeb told him he was taking him out. Weeb said that Unitas "looked at him straight in the eye and said something like, 'Listen, you are not taking me out. If you do, I'll kill you.'" I didn't hear that firsthand, but I sure don't doubt the accuracy of it.

Unitas was tough, no question about it. He had a total disregard for his own safety.

We played the Chicago Bears twice a year in our division. They were "The Monsters of the Midway," but it didn't make any difference what kind of monsters they were, Unitas was not able to be intimidated. In 1960 against the Bears in Wrigley Field I saw a classic case of his toughness. There was less than a minute to play, and the Bears were up by 3 points. Now, the Bears were a dirty team to begin with, and Doug Atkins, a huge defensive lineman, came in there and blasted Unitas in the face, busting his nose. Gushing blood, Unitas didn't call a time out. He just reached down on the field, got some dirt, and stuffed it up his nose. With the flow of blood stopped, he stepped back in the huddle. Then he threw Moore a 39-yard touchdown pass to win the game. That was Unitas. You hit him in the mouth and he'd just spit out his teeth and go back and beat you. With that temperament, if he had been big enough he could have been a Hall of Fame linebacker, a great middle linebacker.

Another characteristic of his that comes to my mind is his fierce competitive spirit—he was beyond intimidation. He had an icy composure, even when he was under fire. Put that competitive spirit with his instinct for the game, and he was unstoppable! You could not intimidate him. He was a tremendous competitor, and he instinctively knew what to do with that football in all kinds of situations.

But he couldn't have been Unitas without the physical attributes, of course—he had the fastball, and when he needed to, he could throw with a soft touch. He could throw every pass—short, medium, long. He could rifle it or arc it, depending on the defensive situation, and he had tremendous accuracy.

Here's something else I wrote in *The Sporting News* article: "I think John's best pass was whatever was called for. He didn't have any limitations. He had all the pitches. He could touch-throw it, he could throw it long, short, medium, inside, outside, deep, wherever. But when he really had to put the power behind it, I don't think anyone in the league was better. He could rifle that ball to the outside as fast as anybody."

Another thing Unitas had going for him was great footwork—he'd been well trained by his college coach at Louisville on drop-back fundamentals. He was an expert at getting to the pocket with three-step drops, five-step drops, and seven-step drops, and he knew how to get those feet in position to deliver accurate passes. He was a master of fundamentals in that respect. So he had the physical talent *and* the training to be sound in everything he did.

I have been asked what our favorite play was, and it was probably what we called the "Q" pattern. I once told a writer: "The 'Q' pattern was based on our 10-yard square pattern. I'd go down about 10 yards and make my break, like I was squaring inside. Then, when the defensive back made his move and tried to go inside with me, I'd plant my inside foot and head to the corner. The defensive back would overrun me, and I'd have clear sailing to the outside. For a couple of years there, it was like a lethal weapon."

Weeb saw us working together and he encouraged me. "Keep working with Unitas," he said. At first, I didn't grasp the significance of what he was saying, but years later I realized that Weeb saw in Unitas something that very few other people did. So it was like he was saying, "Work with Unitas. This guy has got what it takes, and he's going to be around for a while." He was a wise enough coach to know that Unitas and I were diamonds in the rough, and that we'd both benefit from our private sessions.

One of the keys to this relationship and the timing we had together was that the work level and the work ethic of the two of us were exactly the same. He wanted to work after practice, and he had an arm that never wore out, never got tired. Practicing extra was a rarity in the NFL at that point, but after practices ended, Weeb had sense enough to leave us alone. He didn't have all the weight training and film study and all the stuff that goes on with today's so-called high-powered operations.

If you let a quarterback and receiver stay out there and work on timing, you can develop a pass offense that will go to levels you can't believe. That was a part of the Baltimore Colts system when Weeb was there. He had seen it work in Cleveland with Otto Graham and all his great receivers. When Weeb structured his two-a-days, or during the season our one-a-days, we'd stay out there and work on timing.

Unitas would take either a three-step drop, a five-step drop, or a seven-step drop and that was it. His drop coincided with what route I was running and how long it took me to get into the break. For example, when I ran a 6-yard out, he took a three-step drop and fired it.

We worked on conditions that could come up in a game. You might be looking over your right shoulder, but Unitas gets under a heavy pass rush and launches one that comes over your left shoulder. So while you're racing downfield, you've got to make a total turn, just like a center fielder that takes off after a fly ball and then has to make a turn to get under it. It's called the wrong-shoulder drill.

Sometimes he'd launch a long ball, but it would get deflected. The ball's short, so you'd have to stop downfield and fight for it. We had six different situations for the long ball and twelve for the short pass. The whole routine was just drill, repetition, drill, repetition, because you don't know when these things are going to happen in a game. You prepare for any eventuality, and then in games, the body reacts the way it's been trained—you react and you catch, so your success level is off the board.

Lucci was well aware that our hard work paid off. He said that the combo of me and Unitas was more precise in our execution than other combo he could think of. "They had great timing even though back when Berry and Unitas were playing, you could not only grab receivers, you could hit them again at 8 yards or 10 yards as long as the ball wasn't in the air. It was more disruptive. The whole game has changed tremendously from that standpoint." He's right, but we still got the job done even under the liberal defensive rules of the day. It got to be where I had my moves and fakes down like dance steps. I could run them in my sleep.

You talk about multiple moves. Unitas and I watched the Green Bay Packers' Bart Starr and Max McGee run the quick post pattern. McGee would go down about 8 or 9 yards and just break in and, boom, the ball's in the air from Starr. McGee would catch the ball anywhere from 15 to 18 yards, and they'd pick up 20, 25, whatever, total yards.

So Unitas and I started working on that route. I'd be split out to the left, and the breaking point was around 8 or 9 yards from the line of scrimmage—with me it was a six-step move. I got my right foot back, my left foot up, and my right hand on the ground when I got down in my stance. So when I came off the line, it was right foot, left foot, right, left, right, left, and on the sixth step I was breaking on the quick post pattern—a very simple little route. Unitas took a quick five-step drop, turned, and fired the football to a spot. He only knew I was breaking at a forty-five-degree angle, but he knew when I'm going to get there.

Well, he didn't have to know that I was going to mix up those six steps. I had five or six different ways of running a six-step quick post, all of them with multiple fakes designed with outside approach, inside approach, one fake, double fake, triple fake before I broke. He just had to know one thing about what I was doing—the other stuff didn't make any difference, because the timing was still there. At six steps, I was going to break.

That was how we began to work on faking, finesse, and how to beat man-to-man coverage, which is what we were faced with—skilled man-to-man coverage; every team had it. You had to be able to get open against man-to-man, or you couldn't play in the NFL.

Incidentally, Unitas did approach some things differently than I did. He very seldom studied film, but I studied film all year long, in season or off. I was always trying to spot something that could help us. I'd feed him information as a result of my studies, and he knew he could count on it being reliable.

So, by the time John and I had worked together for two years, I pretty well was telling him what I could get open on and what wouldn't work for us. Consequently we didn't waste any plays. Another way of putting it is, when he called me on a route, we hit it because it was there, and I knew it was, so that's why we called it. I had an understanding with him. I'd say, "Let me bring you what I can get open on, and if I don't bring anything, it means I ain't got anything and there's no sense wasting plays. Run something else, throw to somebody else."

Moore recently told a writer:

> *Thank goodness we had a guy like Raymond Berry who always tuned John in as to what could happen from our offense versus the defense. Raymond studied films along with Unitas, and they used to see what they could do and what they couldn't do.*
>
> *In fact, how I ended up getting involved in a lot of the play calling was because Raymond came to me and told me, verbatim, "Lenny, I've been watching these films of these teams, and I just came to the conclusion we need more of you in our offense with your speed and your talent. You can do this, and that will give us an extra addition to what John already has." I'm thinking to myself, "What the hell is he talking about, because Weeb Ewbank writes up the game plan and then John executes whatever the game plan is . . ." I just went along with what Weeb and the other coaches worked out on the board—these are our plays that we're going to run, what we think we can do, but that's as far as it went. Raymond took it a step further, feeding information to John.*
>
> *Raymond said to me, "But here's the situation—you've got to go to John you've got to work with John." What he was telling me was that Johnny's not going to go to me unless he's sure that I fully understand what is going on out there.*

Let's say Moore was out on the flank position where he could recognize what he could do against a defensive back because he would know how he was playing him. The key was to take that information back to the huddle, to tell John he could succeed on, say, a slant in or a slant in, take off.

Unitas would work hard with a teammate, but he wouldn't approach that player initially, especially if he didn't have confidence in him or felt the player wasn't interested in improving himself through extra work. If a player worked with Unitas, the two could nail down their timing and perfect plays, which could then be unleashed on opponents. Then, and only then, would Unitas have full confidence in the player. As Moore said, "He'll know he can go to you any time you bring something back to him because you two have worked on it after practice."

Former Colt Rick Volk noticed that Unitas and I put a lot into our practices. He remembered me working on that out pattern, going down, making an out move, and then working that sideline. Volk said, "John would throw it out to where only Raymond could catch it and go out of bounds so the clock stops—and they could work it down the field that way and not take a lot of time off the clock. Then we could set up and go again.

"If you saw the 1958 championship game, with Berry running those patterns, and then I look at the quarterbacks today . . . they're doing basically what John and Raymond were doing in those days."

I think Unitas pioneered other things quarterbacks do today, too, such as the play calling at the line of scrimmage by, say, Peyton Manning—no question about it.

Moore was nice enough to say that I was the kind of player who wanted "everybody to work to the limit of their talent," and that I was the one who turned all of us around. He said when the Colts were able to gel and work to our full potential, we became a major force in the NFL. Quite a compliment, but Unitas and a lot of other players such as Moore were essential to our success in their own right.

There was another thing Unitas and I worked on during the last six or seven years I played. I had a young man with a stopwatch and a clipboard, and he clocked every pass play that we had for those years. He watched when the ball was snapped to Unitas and started his clock. When that ball left Unitas's hand, he stopped his clock. From snap to release, he clocked it, and I began to realize the amount of time our quarterback had back in that pocket to get the ball out of there. I told Unitas about all of this because we had these great pass-rush teams we were up against and our offensive line couldn't hold—they had to pass protect the best they could under the rules. I began to realize we had to get that ball out of there, and 2.4 seconds was pushing the envelope.

So we structured our pass patterns to fit the time we had to do it in. That way he very seldom got hit or sacked. If we got in there and threw it in 1.9, 2.0, to 2.4 seconds, it worked. Every once in a while we might push it to 2.6 seconds, but that was gambling.

In early 2013 I read an article, and it was the first time I had ever seen something like this mentioned in all my reading about the NFL over fifty-some years. The piece was about Peyton Manning, I believe, and the fact that he doesn't get sacked very often. They specifically mentioned 2.4 seconds, and I said to myself, "These people have discovered the secret. He knows that you've only got so much time to get the ball out of there before all the monsters get there."

It's also vital for a quarterback to come into the league and learn that a key to success is to not make, or force, foolish passes. Unitas played college ball at the University of Louisville back when running offenses were dominant. He was different from a lot of young quarterbacks, because he threw a whole lot of passes. I think when he came to the Colts, he had already acquired all types of skills and a philosophy and good judgment about delivering the forward pass. Then he worked under Weeb, one of the greatest coaches of quarterbacks that ever came along. So he had the best of both worlds: He learned a lot in college and then he came into pro football under a master.

My hands were my best asset. I was born with good hands, and I learned how to train them. I worked on strengthening my hands year-round, plus I just had big, big mitts.

I became used to handling Unitas's fastballs. There was a big difference between the speed of a Unitas pass and that of some of the other quarterbacks I worked with, no question about that.

I look at one year when my quarterback was George Shaw, and he was an extremely accurate passer and a very good one. His ball came in, with a slight nose up and very catchable velocity, a totally different speed than a Unitas bullet. I'm sure that over the years there have been others who threw as fast as Unitas, but not too many.

Another unique characteristic of the era that I played in—especially in my first eight years when we only had twelve teams in the NFL—is that practically every team, maybe ten out of the twelve, had a great quarterback. We played against guys like Norm Van Brocklin, Bart Starr, and Bobby Layne—Hall of Fame level players. The concentration of talent was just extremely high. I know that Van Brocklin had a real good fastball, for example, but Unitas was the top bullet thrower then.

I was unique. I was a pass catcher who, from the very earliest days of playing football—even going back to elementary school—had a natural technique and method of catching that was not normal. It wasn't standard operating procedure, at all. And that technique involved leaping and catching the ball against my body. I did that the entire time I played. I never tried to break that habit, because it was a tremendous advantage to go up for a ball. And when you're contesting a defensive back for a football, getting your whole body in there is a plus—it totally limits his ability to strip you of the football.

So I was a leaper, a jumper, and a body catcher. I could make great catches with my hands, but I had this other style that also worked to my advantage. I even left my feet when it wasn't totally necessary, and I didn't hold my hands in the traditional method receivers are taught. My favorite way to catch was to secure the football by my chest and then crouch down so I was in position to go in any direction. Now, when I went up for a ball on my chest and caught it against my body, I had my thumbs outward. I attacked the football, leaping at it and having it hit my body, then enveloping it with my hands in an instant. It worked for me, and it's something I don't think is really teachable—it's something I was born with. I don't even remember how it started—it was natural; I just did it.

I didn't even mind getting walloped by a defender as long as I was floating. When I didn't want to get drilled was when my legs and feet were planted. So, I would leap for the football and be high in the air and take all kinds of licks, but all I did was float around—it didn't really bother me.

My old Colt teammate Gino Marchetti recently shared a story from my final season in the NFL. He said, "Raymond would always catch the ball. I saw him drop a pass one time in Baltimore against Green Bay during the season after I retired. And you know what, you could hear a pin drop in that stadium. You could hear the fans saying, 'Oooooo,' when Raymond Berry dropped a pass, because it just never happened. The fans were in shock."

He's right. I hardly ever dropped a pass. One newspaper account written after I retired said I dropped twelve passes over my thirteen NFL seasons. Poet Ogden Nash once compared my fingers to flypaper. Fans would be surprised to see me drop one, especially if we were playing at home with people who had followed my career year after year after year. They understood what they were looking at, knowledgeable of the fact that what they just saw didn't happen often. They'd look at each other and say, "What in the world happened there?" Of course, I was out there on the field asking the same thing.

There was an incident involving Unitas that I'll never forget, when the ticking time bomb inside me was triggered. It happened in a game in my third or fourth year. A defensive player I had been watching on film for a couple years was just a dirty football player. He'd pile in on guys late and hit them illegally. I was aware of this during a game we were playing against him when Unitas went back to throw. He couldn't find anybody open, and he scrambled up the middle for 8 or 10 yards and went down. I was downfield watching it all. I came up on the play as Unitas was down with his back exposed, and this guy came in and laid his knee with everything he could right into Unitas's back.

When he did that, I exploded on him—that's how quick my temper was triggered. I went after this guy. I got him down, and I ripped his helmet off. I went after him with everything I had. He's lucky he got out of there alive is what it amounts to. If I had got ahold of his throat, he probably wouldn't have. I think if I'd had a weapon . . . In any event, back then they didn't even kick me out of the game.

All of the Colts loved Unitas, but he and I were very close. I never had a brother, but he was the closest thing to it. For the first five or six seasons I played, as soon as the season ended, I went back to Texas. So

I wouldn't see him again until we got back in training camp, and that's when we smoothly took it up again. We were of one mind about so many things, and our focus on football was an obvious common interest that brought us together.

Unitas's son, John C. Unitas Jr., wrote a biography of his father. In it he stated that he believes only three people truly understood his father, and I was one of them. I certainly wouldn't question his observation about that. The fact is Unitas and I have a lot of background together, and we spent a lot of years very close, so that's a pretty accurate statement.

Some years Unitas and I did socialize in the off-season. He started a family much earlier than I did, and I got to know his first two children, Janice and John Jr., very quickly, before I even got married. I was very close with Dorothy, his first wife. She kind of treated me like an older son. We had a great relationship.

Many times when we got together it was at their home. When I'd stay in Baltimore in the off-season, Dorothy would invite me over to eat with them. So I did spend a lot of time with the Unitas family, and I got to know their children, which was a pleasure.

After I got married, Dorothy was a great friend to Sally, who was young, just out of college. Sally was in need of someone to show her the NFL spouse ropes, and that's exactly what Dorothy did. She reached out to Sally at a time when Sally came into the world of professional football, not knowing anybody. To have one of the wives reach out was a huge help.

After I retired as a player, I immediately moved away from Baltimore because I got into coaching, so my days back there were few and far between. I didn't get to see any of my teammates very much for a while. In the last fifteen years or so, I've gone to functions in Baltimore for card signings or speaking engagements, so I've been there more often lately. I used to get to see John periodically, and we stayed in pretty good touch, and we'd make appearances together. A lot of times promoters wanted to have both of us together.

In 1978, to commemorate the twentieth anniversary of the 1958 title game, CBS televised a two-hand-touch football game between the Giants and us. Unitas hit me for the second and third touchdowns of the game, giving us a 21–0 halftime lead. Sonny Jurgensen, who served as a referee, approached some of the Giants and teased, "Twenty years have gone by, and you still can't cover Berry." We won this one, 28–14.

If you want me to pick an elite group of the greatest quarterbacks ever, I can give you twenty names pretty quickly. I've seen so many that the list goes on and on. However, if I had to pick my top all-time quarterback, it's still Unitas, no question about that. He just had that combination of qualities, traits, and talents that made him the whole package, yet more than that. He was not just a tremendous passer, he was a leader and a very astute play caller.

John died in 2002, exactly a year after the tragedy of 9-11. I had no clue. It was a shock to everyone. It happened so fast. We were living in Colorado at the time, and I was temporarily out of coaching. When the call came about his death, we were free and able to fly back to Baltimore for the funeral.

His entire group of children felt very close to Sally and me, having spent so much time with us. They were comfortable with us, so our being there was sort of like members of the family being there.

In my eulogy I called John a "once-in-a-lifetime quarterback" who elevated the Colts and our fans "to unreachable levels . . ." I said he "made the impossible possible. You filled our memory bank full." I added that, "The Colts were a team, and your example and leadership set the tone."

I pointed out that I felt his toughness was his biggest asset. I commented, "You were more than a teammate to me. You were a special friend. And I came to love you like a brother." I concluded by saying, "So, as we come here to celebrate your life, we don't question His timing, but we are going to miss you, Johnny U."

The relationship we had was so close that as I've gotten older I've gotten more sentimental about these things. There's no question that we were very, very close and we did so many things together that memories of him bring nostalgic reactions.

After John's death, two of his children, Janice and John Jr. sort of adopted me as a dad. His kids are still important to me.

Losing such an old, great friend was a terrible loss. Of all the Colts, I was John's dearest friend, and I felt the same about him.

Chapter Six

1959–1967, Sometimes You Win . . .

The six or so seasons following 1958 were among my best years, the peak time when my pass-route running was very precise and multiple.

The 1959 season turned out to be one of my most rewarding, especially because we won the championship again, and it is extremely difficult to repeat as a champ in any sport. On a personal level, the statistics I put up made this one of my two best seasons ever. I led the NFL with my fourteen receiving touchdowns, a new franchise mark. Only two players scored more points than my 84 that season. I also topped the league with sixty-six catches, 959 receiving yards, and my average of 79.9 yards per game on catches. I became just the fourth man ever to win the Triple Crown for receivers, leading the league in receptions, total receiving yards, and touchdown receptions in the same season.

We were screwing around there in the early part of the season, though. We won our opener against the Lions easily, but lost to the Bears in the next game, 26–21. Then we ran off three wins in a row, on the road versus the Lions and the Bears, then at home against the Packers. But that stretch was followed by a short losing streak, falling to the Browns and the Redskins. At that point our record was nothing to brag about. We were talented, coming off winning it all, but we were just bumping around.

I don't think we were approaching the early games any differently at all. But somehow we were struggling. After the seventh game, our record stood at 4–3 due to a humiliating loss to the Redskins, who would end the season with a 5–6–1 record.

Then we got hot. We never lost again. Unitas, who would go on to win MVP, started cranking it up. He threw for nearly 3,000 yards and thirty-two touchdown passes, a career high as well as a new record for a twelve-game season. In fact, he is the only quarterback in the era of a twelve-game schedule to hit the thirty touchdown plateau. I was proud to be on the receiving end of fourteen of those passes, the highest total for any of my seasons and the sixth best total by a receiver ever at that time.

We defeated the Packers in a tight one, 28–24; crushed the 49ers at home by 31 points; then handled the Rams easily, 35–21. Next, we made our usual trip to the West Coast for our final two games of the season and, because Chicago was on a tear, winning their final seven games in a row to go 8–4 on the year, we needed to win both of our California games to win the division outright. We did. We beat San Francisco by 20 and Los Angeles by 19, scoring 21 unanswered fourth-quarter points to pull away and put that game on ice. Prior to those two wins, the Colts all-time road record against those two teams was an abysmal 1–11.

The Colts were a great team to watch, what with all of our tools and how we executed plays. We had a true team spirit, too. We were an unselfish group of men who wanted to win. You couldn't have been in a better environment or atmosphere.

The Colts of this era were simply stacked with talent. When the NFL produced a book to commemorate the league's first fifty years, they picked an elite All-Star team. The top sixteen players, based on positions played, were named, with another group of greats listed as the best runners-up ever. Unitas, Marchetti, and Mackey made the top sixteen. Four more Colts were in the next group: Moore, Parker, Art Donovan, and myself. Seven of the greatest players ever to suit up were Colts, and all of us were contemporaries.

As a team we led the NFL with our total of 374 points scored, an average of just a bit more than 31 points per game. That was 84 points more than the second-best offensive team in the league, and we held our opponents to just 251 points. While that was only the seventh lowest total in the NFL, the point differential of 123 was the highest in the league.

As for the title game, again versus the Giants, I remember one thing: I think their defense was bound and determined to stop me. What they forgot was Lenny Moore. And you don't forget Lenny Moore. He caught some big ones on them. Unitas hit him three times for 126 yards, including a 60-yard bomb to open the scoring.

Actually the Giants didn't exactly forget Moore—Tom Landry later said that his plan was to stop our running game and double team Mutscheller and me, knowing we had too many weapons to shut down. His hope was that the Giants could overcome whatever damage Moore might do.

Another thing I still remember about this game was that it rocked along there for quite a while, very, very close. The Moore touchdown was our only score through the first three quarters, and New York only had three field goals at that point.

What the Giants were doing was overloading the defense on me. Moore was sitting over there, one-on-one, and John went to work with him. When they overloaded on me, Unitas had sense enough to go to Moore and Mutscheller, which he did a lot. He hit Mutscheller and me five times each, with my catches totaling 68 yards. And we had Ameche giving us a real sound, solid running game; and the defense did their normal thing.

Our offense did sputter for some time, though. Then all of a sudden, Unitas got it together. He scampered in from 4 yards out, then hit Jerry Richardson for a score. Later Johnny Sample returned an interception for a 42-yard touchdown, and Myhra added a 25-yard field goal. The Giants' 9–7 lead vanished as we rattled off 24 consecutive points in the final quarter. A late Giants touchdown pass from Charlie Conerly to Bob Schnelker made the final score 31–16.

We had held the Giants to just the field goals and one other meaningless score. I'm glad when people bring up our defense. If you talk to any Colts offensive player who's got half a brain, what you understand about the championship Colts teams is that *the* most important part of those teams was our defense. Our defense was dominant.

And what it meant was—and I remember this happening many times—we could go out there offensively and mess around, but our defense kept getting us the ball back. Now, eventually you have to deal with Unitas, and it's going to be over with. Without a great defense, things are different all of a sudden. Without them, we weren't the same; we might not have even been heard of as champions.

You can go back and look at the scores. It took us a while to get untracked and go, but our defense kept stopping them, getting the ball, and seemingly we were never behind.

So, if you had to list the factors that brought about our championship teams in Baltimore it would look like this: First, we had Carroll Rosenbloom who, as mentioned, had enough sense to hire Weeb; second we had Weeb as the head coach; third we had our defense; and finally, we had Unitas and the offense.

By the way, when we won our title in 1958, the winners' share was $4,718.77 per man, and it was about the same the following season. Yes, that's not too bad considering I was earning only about $12,000 a year or so. But our check for winning it all was a far cry from what today's Super Bowl winners get, a reported $165,000 for the game played in 2015. I had come into the league making $10,000 because Doak Walker and Fred Benners of SMU had played pro football and advised me to get that kind of a salary based on my college credentials. The Colts general manager went along with the amount, but said, "OK, we'll give you $8,500 salary and a $1,500 bonus." That made me one of the better paid rookies in the league.

I didn't think that much about it at the time, but when I came back to sign for my second year, he wanted to give me the same *salary*, $8,500. Of course he had laid that trap from the very beginning, but I didn't have enough sense to realize it. I told him I wasn't going to go for that. I said, "Ten thousand dollars was what we agreed on—you're the one who suggested breaking it up." We hassled around, going back and forth. He finally said, "Well, if you have a good year, I'll give you the extra $1,500." I agreed, and when I ended up in the top ten for receptions, I got the full $10,000. Bottom line: The salaries weren't exactly sky-high in my era.

Back then in order to get any playoff money, you had to make it to the championship game. When I first came into the league, you either won your division or there was no postseason. There was only a championship game, no other playoffs.

There's no question that the 1959 title gets lost in the shuffle, overshadowed by the classic 1958 championship game. It was a totally different game; the 1959 contest rocked back and forth there for a while, then we blew the Giants off the field before it was over with. So there wasn't any particular suspense about the outcome of the game after a certain point. We were a dominant team and we exerted it, so it became clear.

Still, I think the 1959 Giants were a better team than their 1958 team. They had Dick Lynch as a defensive back, and he covered me that season. He was an extremely skilled man-to-man cover guy and a big improvement over the coverage of me in the 1958 game.

In any case, the 1958 title game was like two fighters in the ring knocking each other down, getting up, and going fifteen grueling rounds. And it going into overtime made it special, an unprecedented experience for the NFL, the viewing public, and the players and coaches involved. The fans didn't have a clue about overtime, and all of a sudden we've got a whole different way of playing a football game.

On a personal level, one great thing about both titles was that my parents got to see the deciding games in person. My dad was coaching high school football in all of the years I played, so he was totally occupied on Friday nights, and Texas was a long way off from NFL cities, so they rarely got to see me play except for those big games.

After our success in 1958 and 1959, some very disappointing seasons followed. It's not like we expected to win titles every season. We approached each season with a "one game at a time" philosophy. But I do know that when we came back in 1959 after winning the championship, we did feel like we could win every game. We were very confident, and we had the right to be. We were expecting to win, and we did, but just not often enough to excel as we had. We had a defense that could get the job done, and we had Unitas.

But from 1960 through 1963 the Colts were basically a .500 team, going 6–6, 8–6, 7–7, and 8–6, yet we still had some great players. Losing was very frustrating.

The Colts were in the West Division, and we didn't play in the South in my early days, except maybe for a preseason game or two. But when the Cowboys were given a franchise in 1960, we went to Dallas to play them. This is where it hit the fan with the Colts and racial problems. Our black players found out they weren't going to stay in the same hotel as the white players. All of us were blindsided by this.

We played a preseason game at the Cotton Bowl in August one year. We landed and then saw that they were taking the black players to one location and the white players to another. We didn't see them again until we got to the stadium the next day and went into the locker room. The first thing I did was walk over to them and apologize for what had happened. I said, "This was something that none of us knew was going to happen."

We went ahead and played the game, but it was a wake-up call for all of us; we had never traveled into an area that had such attitudes. It was a shock. But I guess in some ways the whole United States was waking up to this situation—a new era. When I was growing up in Texas, things were just the way they were, and you didn't think anything about it. The races did not intermingle whatsoever. So my awareness of the problem wasn't high to start with.

By the time we played that game in Dallas, the integration of the South was in progress, but it was far from complete. Changes were a long time coming. At one point the team that was in the southernmost city was probably Washington, so the NFL wasn't prepared to cope with the issue.

Injuries hurt us a lot in 1960. We lost Ameche, and I think that was the story of that season. This was his final year, and he started ten games but carried the ball just eighty times, down from close to two hundred carries the year before. He ran for a mere 263 yards and averaged only 3.3 yards per run with just three touchdowns to his credit. Moore led the team for total yards rushing with just 374. We lost our running game, and we lost four games in a row at the end of the season.

With no ground game to speak of, Unitas and I did hook up quite a bit. I set an NFL record that season with six consecutive games in which I had 100-plus yards in receptions, one more than Hirsch and a few others, and still a record for the Colts franchise. In the second game of the 1960 season, I caught a touchdown pass in my seventh straight game dating back to the eighth game of the 1959 season. That set a new team record that still stands today. For the entire 1960 season I had seven 100-yard games, also a Colts record.

When we played the Cowboys in the Cotton Bowl on the day before Halloween that year, I was back in my home state, appearing in the same venue where I had played many games for SMU. My dad and some members of his Paris High School football squad were on hand, and they got to see me and Unitas connect on four completions, with three going for scores and all of them in the first half. We led 31–7 at the half and cruised to a 45–7 victory. My scores covered 68, 52, and 70 yards, good for the longest reception of my NFL career. Plus, the 68-yard catch stood up as my second-longest pass reception of my career. Overall that day Unitas and I piled up 195 yards on four receptions. Incidentally, that was the only time I played against the Cowboys in Texas.

That win boosted our record to 4–2, and two more wins in our next games versus Green Bay and Chicago gave our fans false hope. When we dropped the next four games, we ended up with a very disappointing 6–6 record, quite a let down for us.

What's more, during the eleventh game, in Los Angeles, John's streak of having thrown at least one touchdown in forty-seven straight games came to an end. His record streak towered over the previous best, which stood at only twenty-three games in a row. The last time John had played in a game and did not throw a touchdown pass was in his rookie season. The streak began on December 9, 1956, in a game versus the Rams, and it lasted until our game of December 11, 1960, just over four years. During the streak, the Colts went 31–16, and he threw 697 completions (on 1,298 passes) for 10,645 yards and 102 scores, an average of better than two touchdowns per game. He hit seven different Colts for touchdowns, including thirty-eight to me and twenty-seven to Moore. This incredible record stood for almost half a century. But in a way, I didn't think about the streak that much when it was going on—I guess you just expected Unitas to do what he was doing because that *was* what he did.

On the year, he threw for a staggering NLF-record 3,099 yards and a league-leading twenty-five touchdowns while topping the league in three more major quarterback categories including completions with 190. He became the first and only man to throw for more than 3,000 yards over a twelve-game schedule. I was happy to help account for more than 40 percent of those yards.

Statistically speaking, 1959 and 1960 were my finest seasons. In 1960 I led the NFL in receptions for the third year in a row with seventy-four, the fourth-highest total in NFL history to date, and I led for yards gained on receptions for the second straight season, with my career high of 1,298 yards. In fact that total was a new team high and the third best ever in pro ball, and it was achieved in just twelve games. Even counting running backs, the total was the fourth-most yardage from scrimmage on the year. Ahead of me were John David Crow, Jim Brown, and our flanker Moore. I even led the league for the second consecutive year with my average of 108.2 yards per game on catches. My ten touchdown catches would stand as my second-highest season total ever, four fewer than my personal high from 1959.

Still, coming off back-to-back NFL championships, something only four other teams had ever done through the end of the 1950s, the 1960 season left us unfulfilled. In fact it was a year that had high points and then one of the lowest points of my entire life. I had a great year in 1958, a tremendous one in 1959, and came back in 1960 so fired up to work with Unitas during and after practice, and we were hitting the long ball. What I didn't realize was I was overworking. I had this mentality that was the perfect seedbed for stupidity.

I didn't understand that the body has to rest. You cannot keep pushing it, and you especially cannot keep sprinting full speed. Legs are not able to keep doing it as much as I was doing it. I was so carried away with enthusiasm, I'd catch a pass in practice and run 50 yards with the ball, full speed, dodging, doing all this faking and all.

Before my injury that season, I caught three touchdown passes in back-to-back games, the only two games in my career in which I caught three touchdown passes. I accomplished this feat in the season's sixth and seventh games versus Dallas and Green Bay. I had those four receptions I mentioned earlier against Dallas that went for 195 yards, and against the Packers I caught ten passes for 137 yards. I put up big numbers in the early games of our schedule, especially when you toss in eleven catches for 186 yards against Detroit in the fifth game of the year.

However, doing all this and running myself to death in practice week after week caught up with me. It happened near the end of the season. In practice that week I noticed my hamstring on my right side began to twitch. When that happens, it's the body's way of telling you, "Pull into port, my friend." But I kept sprinting like crazy.

One day I took off deep, and boom. The hamstring went. Had I used any sense at all and rested properly, there's no telling what kind of statistics I could have had. Without the injury I think I could have broken every record there was for things like yardage. I ended up 197 yards shy of the record that existed then. As for most receptions in a single season, I was ten short of the record.

I guess there was a chance I also could have approached the season record for receiving yards per game, which was held by Crazy Legs Hirsch (124.6). My average of 108.2 was the fourth highest ever, and it still ranks thirteenth on the all-time list. Overworking was the biggest mistake I ever made as an athlete.

Sure, the numbers I did put up were impressive, but in the final two games I only caught three passes for 34 yards. I think I limped through the last several games of the season. I was playing with a hamstring pull, and I couldn't go deep, but I had such a reputation that the Colts just kept playing me anyway. They figured the defense couldn't figure it out in that short of time. I was drawing double coverage, so they wanted to continue doing that.

Luckily, the defensive backs didn't know I was hurt. They were going by my reputation, so they kept giving me ground in front of them to defend against the deep ball. So we were able to hit on a few passes toward the end of the season.

Not too long after I first started giving speeches in the off-season, around 1961, I went to South Carolina and spoke to a Christian organization. I met Bobby Richardson, the Yankees second baseman during those years. He had become a Christian, and he was just a great guy. We stayed friends for many years.

Richardson had unbelievable quickness. He was like a cat out there, and the plays he could make! He was a solid hitter, too. He still owns the record for the most runs batted in during a World Series, twelve in 1960, and he shares the record for the most RBI in a World Series game with six, also set during the 1960 Series.

Back then the Yankees always came to Baltimore in April to play the Orioles in a four-game series. Bobby would call me when the Yankees were getting ready to come to town. I could walk to Memorial Stadium from where Sally and I lived at that time, so I'd go there to watch those games, and I got to go in the locker room and meet the great players of that era—Mickey Mantle, Roger Maris, Tony Kubek, Whitey Ford, Elston Howard, Moose Skowron, and Yogi Berra. Getting to know the Yankee players was quite an experience, one of the real high points of the early 1960s. It was just a classic championship team. What a lineup!

Meanwhile, I think the hamstring pull I had suffered was a contributing factor to my tearing cartilage in my knee around this same time. So I had a hamstring in one leg and torn cartilage in the other at the end of 1960. In the off-season they tried to put things off, hoping I would get well, but finally I had to have surgery very early in training camp because it collapsed on me. I ran a fake and just crumpled, hit with a sharp pain. I had gambled the wrong way. I should have had the operation in the off-season. They had to take the cartilage out, and I was out for eight weeks, missing our first two 1961 regular-season games.

When I resumed playing, I was limping around before I finally recovered for the next season. But really I was never the same after the operation. During the 1961 season I caught seventy-five passes, my career high actually. It was also the most ever in team history and the seventh-highest total ever in NFL play to that point. However, my totals over the next three seasons dropped off to fifty-one, forty-four, and forty-three. My knee started to swell a lot, and I had to get it drained every week. It limited what I could do in practice. It was a pain in the butt all year long in 1961.

None of my seventy-five catches in 1961, which did rank second in the NFL, resulted in a touchdown. What we ended up doing was throwing a lot of garbage stuff—little short and quick stuff. I was coming off a year in which I had led the NFL in a lot of major categories. The defensive backs played me cautiously, having no idea that I was playing on a gimpy knee. They didn't really press me because they were remembering my reputation. They didn't understand I had lost one gear.

Even though I missed two games due to injury, I almost led the league for the fourth straight time in receptions. I went into the final game of the 1961 season six catches ahead of the number two man for receptions, Red Phillips of the Rams. In the finale I caught four, but Phillips hauled in thirteen to overtake me, seventy-eight to seventy-five. He averaged only 7.7 yards per catch, causing some reporters to ask Rams coach Bob Waterfield if he had intentionally instructed his team to throw a slew of short passes to Phillips to help him overtake my lead. Waterfield said no, insisting his game plan was to use short stuff to set up the long pass.

My average of 11.6 yards per catch was the lowest of my entire career, but I managed to finish in the top ten in two other departments. However, on the year we went 8–6, good enough to finish only third in our division.

The 1962 season was the first season in which the NFL played a fourteen-game schedule. This was once more a year of utter disappointment, as we finished at .500 with a 7–7 record, meaning we finished in fourth place in the seven-team West Division.

I missed out on making the Pro Bowl for the first time since 1957 (although I would make that team two more times in 1963 and 1964). I had twenty-four fewer receptions than I had in 1961 despite playing in all fourteen games.

Our mediocre seasons during this time led the Colts to fire Weeb Ewbank, despite his knowledge of the game and what he had brought to the city of Baltimore and our team. Team owner Carroll Rosenbloom and general manager Don Kellett brought in former Colts player Don Shula to run the team in 1963. Shula was thirty-three years old when he took over, just three years older than me. While he would go on to become the winningest coach in NFL history, he could only manage a third-place finish that season, with our record standing at 8–6.

Shula had been a veteran player when I reported to the Colts, and he really took me under his wing and helped me a lot. Few people remember this, but once in an exhibition game, he had to serve as our emergency quarterback, even though he was normally a defensive back. He got in for one play, the only time he ever played that position in the NFL—and he got sacked.

In 1957 Shula played for Washington. That was Shula's last season before he went into coaching. In one game he was assigned to cover me man-to-man. That was the game of November 10 in which I caught a dozen passes, a Colts team record and a total that remained my personal best for my entire career—I also caught that many in the 1958 championship game. Two of the passes versus Washington and Shula went for touchdowns. The catches were good for 224 yards, my highest total for yardage ever and a new franchise high. He once paid me a nice compliment, saying no defensive back could, on a consistent basis, cover me man-to-man.

Shula had a laundry list of strengths. He's one of the greatest competitors you'd ever want to be around, and his teams played that way. And, he was tough and smart. He knew football, and he played defense. It's been my experience that a football player who played on defense who later goes into coaching has got a tremendous advantage over others.

Tom Landry was that way; he specialized in defense and then became one of the greatest offensive coaches of all time because he understood what screwed up his defense. The offense he put in at Dallas was what he knew bothered him, what was difficult to defend against, and that's what he was going to use against opponents.

Don Shula knew defense, and he had great quarterbacks over his career, especially Unitas and Dan Marino.

In 1963 Unitas, at the age of thirty, exploded for 3,481 yards in fourteen contests to lead the NFL. His total represented a career high. I wasn't too big of a part in his success, playing in just nine games and catching forty-four passes for 703 yards and only three touchdowns. I was out with an injury from our third game to our eighth game, but I still ranked fourth in the league with my average of 78.1 receiving yards per game. It was good for 16 yards per catch, one of my better averages in that department.

They say that close only counts in horseshoes and hand grenades. Well, in 1964 we came tantalizingly close to winning another NFL title—until we ran into a tough but underrated Cleveland Browns team. They were certainly underrated compared to our team, that is.

The season began on September 13 with us losing to the Vikings 34–24. We then rattled off ten wins in a row, not losing another game until December 6. After that loss, our regular season ended with us bouncing back with a 45–17 destruction of the Redskins.

Statistically, I did about the same as I had done the year before. A bit healthier perhaps, I played in twelve contests, caught forty-three passes for 663 yards, almost exactly 15.5 yards per catch, and six touchdowns. This was the season when I broke Billy Howton's record for career receptions, ending the year with 506, three more than Howton. The record-breaking catch came in our season finale against Washington on December 13, in that 45–17 win.

In that same game, Moore scored his twentieth touchdown of the season, a new league record. That touchdown also meant that he led the NFL for the year in two categories: most touchdowns and most total points scored, 120. He scored sixteen times on runs (tops in the league) and three times on catches, and even recovered a fumble for a touchdown.

This was my last season making the Pro Bowl. The thing I remember most about the Pro Bowl games was getting to meet the players you had played against, but didn't really know. After spending the week with them for the Pro Bowl game, you felt like you really got to know them. It was a great experience to be selected and play in those games if for no other reason than it gave you the chance to interact with those guys.

Entering postseason play with a 12–2 record, we were primed and heavily favored to win it all. We ended the season ranked number one in points scored with 428, and our defense was the stingiest in the league, surrendering just 225 points. That means our average score per game was 30.6 to 16.1. We had six future Hall of Famers on our team, the NFL's MVP in Unitas, and Coach of the Year Shula.

Meanwhile the Browns, winners of the East Division with a 10–3–1 record, had the league's second-best offense, but just the fifth-best defense, based on points for and against. Not that it meant much, but their average score per game was 29.6 points to 20.9. One source had the Browns total defense ranking last in the NFL and contended that the contrast in our defenses gave us the edge going into the game.

The game was scoreless at the half, with a very brisk wind of about 15 to 20 miles per hour coming off Lake Erie right there by Cleveland Municipal Stadium. That was definitely a factor in keeping the offense down. The wind chill factor plunged the temperature down to 23 degrees. It was the pits. We not only lost the game, we didn't really play all that well. It was just a real down experience. We didn't just lose it, we lost it bad. I was held to three catches for 38 yards. About the best thing I can say about losing like we did is it really made us appreciate winning a championship game.

Blanton Collier was the Browns head coach, and he was quoted as saying that going into the game he wanted to force Unitas to have to go to his second receiver. Knowing I was Unitas's favorite receiver, Collier set up double coverage on me. He later said, "I told Walter Beach, our right corner man, to get all over Berry, play him like an all-court press in basketball, get in his face . . ."

Collier was just like Weeb Ewbank. He kept things sound, but simple. He had a few guns, and he knew how to shoot them. For example, Weeb decided what he was going to do from the few plays we had, and we ran them, ran them, and ran them until we could run them in our sleep. It didn't make any difference what the defense did, we could adjust. As I said before, I had grown up with a system like that with my dad, and I saw the power of it. You never had any indecision in a game about what you were doing.

Against the Browns our offense just couldn't stay on the field or create any points. The Browns had very good offensive personnel. Frank Ryan was at the top of his game as a quarterback, and they had this fullback named, um, Brown, or something. Jim Brown was a fairly good running back, I'd say!

Joking aside, at the age of twenty-eight, Brown was in his eighth (and next-to-last) season, and was still in his prime. Over his career he would lead the NFL in rushing in every one of his seasons except 1962, when his 962-yard total was fourth-highest for rushing yardage. In 1964 he ran for 1,446 yards, an impressive total, but he was capable of much more; the season before he set a personal high with 1,863 yards on runs. In five of his nine seasons, he ran for 1,400-plus yards, and for almost half of his career he played a twelve-game schedule. One year he accounted for a total of 2,131 yards gained from scrimmage. In five of his seasons he led the NFL in touchdown runs, and he averaged 104.3 rushing yards per game for his entire stint in the league.

The Browns also had this wide receiver who made a name for himself over the years: Paul Warfield. He only caught one pass in the championship game, but he was headed for fame. Actually it was Gary Collins, a big guy, who stole the headlines that day. He hauled in five of Ryan's eleven completions for 130 yards and each of Cleveland's three touchdowns in their 27–0 win. His three touchdowns on receptions set a new championship record.

They didn't need to throw much with Brown—Ryan threw eighteen times. When you're hammering people on the ground with big Jim Brown, it tends to give your quarterback a whole lot of time to throw. Ryan could throw when he wanted to.

If I was coaching that day, I tell you what I would have called: Jim Brown right, Jim Brown left, Jim Brown right up the middle. By this time Moore trailed only Brown and Don Hutson on the all-time list for touchdowns scored, but that day our ground game was stymied. Take away the 30 yards Unitas had to scramble for, and we managed only 62 yards on the ground. The Browns ran the ball forty-one times, twenty-seven times by Brown, who rambled for 114 of his team's 142 rushing yards. Cleveland put up 339 total yards to our 181, and twenty first downs to our eleven.

The second-largest crowd ever to watch a title game went home happy, but we returned to Baltimore dejected. My three catches gave me twenty in championship games—I'd end my career with those twenty total receptions tied for the third most in title games ever, but there was nothing that could salve our feelings after the defeat.

One bad thing Ryan did during the game was open his mouth at the wrong time, and it fell on the ears of the wrong guy. That guy was Gino Marchetti. Here's what happened. Already winning 27–0, and with maybe a minute or so to play, the Browns had the ball on about our 15-yard line. Ryan tried to add one more touchdown to the scoreboard. He threw a pass to tight end John Brewer, later saying he did it because Brewer hadn't caught a pass all day. After he had time to think things over, he said he regretted making the call.

Recently Marchetti said this is how he recalled the situation. "They got us by about four touchdowns, and he throws a pass on the sideline. And then the referee comes up to me and says, 'I'm going to call the game, you guys can't win it.' I said, 'I know we can't win.' Ryan heard that and he came running over, busting into the conversation and says, 'You can't stop the game, I got 45 seconds to go.' I said, 'You son of a bitch.' I was really upset."

After that, Marchetti said he "had one goal in mind—I was going to make him pay for that. I think he was trying to make his stats better, trying to score another touchdown, and he was throwing, he wasn't putting the ball down on the ground, letting the clock run. He was trying to build up the score and he says, 'Well, dammit, you guys [have done the same].'"

Two weeks later Marchetti and Ryan met in the Pro Bowl. On the first play of the second quarter, Ryan was sacked by Roger Brown, a three-hundred-pound tackle from the Lions, and Marchetti. Ryan was knocked out and had a shoulder separation on the play. Marchetti said Ryan was the only player he ever intentionally "went after. I did it because he deserved it."

Ryan still played well after that injury, but said he believed his arm was never quite the same. He was no dummy—he held a doctorate in mathematics from Rice—but he came to realize what a stupid call he had made against us in the title game and said he had nobody to blame but himself.

Later when I was on the Browns coaching staff, Collier was there as a coach emeritus, a consultant. I sat down and talked with him one day. He told me about their game plan for the championship game. "We decided we were going to run these six running plays and about ten pass plays." He was just commenting on the game, but I thought, "That's exactly what Weeb did with Unitas." And Collier trained under the same guy Weeb did, Paul Brown.

The 1965 season featured another outstanding Colts team. Though our running attack was limited—we finished ninth in the league for yards gained on the ground—at the age of thirty-two, Unitas was still a star. The Colts put up the league's third-best total for yards gained through the air. Those yards were spread pretty evenly, with Jimmy Orr's 847 leading the team, followed by John Mackey's 814, and my 739. I finished sixth in the NFL with my fifty-eight receptions, and ninth with seven touchdowns on catches. Cornerback Bobby Boyd, Jim Parker, Unitas, and Orr were first-team All-Pro picks, while safety Jerry Logan and Mackey were Pro Bowl selections.

The season started on September 19 with a win over the Vikings, which was followed by a loss to the Packers. After that we reeled off eight straight wins before the Lions tied us and the Bears beat us.

Unitas had been out of action for a short time with a leg injury, so we were playing with Unitas's backup, Gary Cuozzo, at quarterback. However, when he separated his shoulder late in the next-to-last game of the season, against the Packers, Tom Matte, a halfback, was suddenly thrust into the role of quarterback. Of course it was an unexpected situation, and Matte wasn't prepared for it, but how he would perform would largely determine if we'd make the playoffs. At Ohio State he had been an All-American at quarterback, but he was an option quarterback, more runner than passer. He went back to his Woody Hayes Ohio State years, and you know how little Woody threw the ball. His offense was based on the old line, "Three yards and a cloud of dust."

We were losing by 8 points to Green Bay when Matte took over, and he only threw three times with one pass resulting in an interception. We lost 42–27. Paul Hornung scored five touchdowns that day. So, going into the season's last week of the regular season, Green Bay's record was

10–3, and ours was 9–3–1. The Packers played to a tie versus the Lions in their finale, so we needed a win to pull into a tie with Green Bay for first place in our division.

Shula again turned to Matte to try to nail down a win to send us into a tie-breaking playoff game against the Packers. Matte had little time to prepare for his start and, unfamiliar with play calling, he needed the help of a rigged-up wristband Shula and Unitas had devised. It listed the plays we'd run that day.

Despite such handicaps, we defeated the Rams 20–17, with Matte throwing only two passes, both incompletions. He basically ran the ball, and he did it well, gaining 99 yards on sixteen carries. He did one heck-uva job, turning in a miraculous performance under tough conditions. His performance was absolutely one of the most remarkable things I think anybody's ever seen in the NFL. We ran for 214 yards to 57 for the Rams, but they outthrew us 233 to 81. Ed Brown threw five passes for us that day, hitting on three. The win over the Rams took our record to 10–3–1. Then it was time to meet the Packers again.

On a blustery day at Lambeau Field, Matte went five-of-twelve passing, for 40 yards in the tie-breaker versus Green Bay. We led 10–0 at the half on a 25-yard return after a fumble recovery by Don Shinnick and a Lou Michaels short field goal, but Paul Hornung scored a third-quarter touchdown. Then, with 1:58 to go in regulation, Green Bay's Don Chandler kicked a field goal to send us into overtime. Many witnesses say the refs missed the call, that the kick soared high and wide of the uprights, which, back then, did not extend up as high as they do now. In fact they were lengthened due to the controversy that swirled after this kick. About thirty years later, Chandler confessed that he thought his 22-yard kick had not gone through the goal posts.

Unlike our 1958 title game, this overtime contest didn't end up on a positive note for us. Green Bay won on that day after Christmas in 1965, 13–10, on a 25-yard Chandler field goal late in overtime. I was on the kick-blocking unit, and a picture that ran in many newspapers said Lenny Lyles and I came the closest to blocking the kick, but no such luck. The Packers racked up 250 yards on passes to our net 32 yards through the air. We ended up throwing twelve passes and rushing forty-seven times. Going into the game, head coach Vince Lombardi and his players knew we had to run the ball a lot. Planning accordingly, they held us to 3 yards per carry.

Counting the playoff game, our season record stood at 10–4–1, with three of the losses coming against the Packers. They would go on to defeat the Browns for the NFL championship. We had to return to Baltimore, our season over.

Still, I came away from that experience, the time when Matte took over, with some lasting impressions. I still think that what happened over those several weeks was probably the most improbable scenario I have ever seen in my years in the game. That had to be Shula's finest hour, I'd say, including his 17–0 season with the Dolphins.

When Shula first decided to go with Matte, he addressed us. "This is what we are going to do," he said. "Defense, you shut them out. Tom is going to be our quarterback and I want the offense to get the ball in field goal range." He turned to our kicker, Michaels, and said, "Lou, you kick the field goals." That was the essence of it. Our plan worked until the Packers game, and remember, the 3-point margin of their win came on what should've been a missed field goal. A referee later admitted he blew the call. So we came within 3 points of playing for the world's title with a running back as our quarterback.

There are lessons for all of us in that. One is that we all have untapped capabilities. In this case, adversity and leadership brought out a level of performance none knew was there. Our defense, in particular, took it to another level. Shula's refusal to be deterred by adversity was the catalyst. It's just a shame we fell a bit short.

In 1966, the adjutant general of the state of Maryland was George Gelston, a man I met when I first went to the Baltimore Colts and joined the National Guard. There were racial problems in Cambridge, Maryland, and Gelston wanted a prominent Maryland figure to be a buffer, or a bridge, to reach out. He was looking for some way to cool off the escalating fireworks. So, to calm things out, I met with all the parties involved and told them why I was there. One group of African-American protestors seemed to want to change society, and they were met with resistance. I was there for about six weeks in the off-season.

Newspaper writer John Steadman wrote that I served "as a peacemaker, a one-man monitoring station, between the black and white communities after the fires of racial unrest had inflamed the city." I really have no idea what I accomplished. But for me it was an insight and introduction about the racial tensions that were going to dominate the news for quite some time. Integration was going on across America, and we saw this on our team more and more as time passed from our eye-opening trip to Dallas.

The Colts season featured another streak and several broken records. After splitting our first four games, we won five in a row, but we couldn't stay hot. We dropped three of our final five games to end at 9–5. That was only good enough for a second-place finish. Green Bay went 12–2 and wound up winning Super Bowl I.

As for the broken records, on September 18, Unitas entered the game needing two touchdown passes to break Y. A. Tittle's record of 212 career touchdown throws. He ended up with four. The pass to tie the record was a 40-yarder to me, while the tiebreaker came on a 26-yard strike to Mackey. On October 9, 1966, I took over the number one slot on the all-time list for yards gained on receptions. I surpassed former record holder Billy Howton and ended the year with 9,108 career yards. Three weeks later, Unitas broke the record held by Tittle for the most career yards passing (28,339). I was honored to be on the receiving end of that historic pass. He hit me on a 31-yard pass, and I pulled it down on an over-the-head fingertip snag. Unitas would go on to throw for almost 12,000 more yards before he retired—he finished with 40,239 yards. After the game he modestly said, "Everyone could set records if he threw to a guy like Berry. That man can do everything as an end."

That was the last season in which I ranked in the top ten in a major category. My fifty-six receptions placed me seventh in the NFL, and my seven touchdown catches put me eighth best in the league.

A strange thing happened to the Colts in 1967, the year the NFL expanded to sixteen teams split among four divisions. The Colts tied for the best record in the entire NFL and, get this, we did not make the playoffs. We went undefeated until the last game of the season, all the way through our first thirteen games. Incidentally, in 1968 the Colts went to the Super Bowl having put together a two-season stretch in which they lost just two regular season games.

We ended the 1967 season with a record of 11–1–2 to finish in a tie for first in what was then called the Coastal Division. The Rams had a record identical to ours, but they were declared the division winners. The key was this: After tying the Rams in Baltimore back in October, we lost to them in the final game, 34–10. Therefore, they had a better record against us and had the edge in point differential in head-to-head play, and for some reason that was how the tiebreaker rules were set up for 1967.

The other three division winners each had nine wins, so only one of the two best teams in the league advanced to the playoffs. Before this season the rules stated two teams tying for the top of a division would play another game to determine who was the conference champ.

If only we had defeated the Minnesota Vikings instead of tying them in October, one week after we had tied the Rams, we would have won the title outright. Those Vikings were 1–4 coming into their game against us, and they would win just three games all year long. So, despite the fact that the Colts remained a team of great talent, I missed out on playing in the postseason for one last time.

One good thing occurred during the tie with the Vikings, however: Unitas broke yet another Tittle record, the one for the most career completions. The record-breaking throw, John's 2,119th completion, came on a pass to me. He would go on to finish his career with 2,830 completions.

Chase Stuart wrote a blog for the *New York Times* in which he stated, "Such a heartbreaking finish was the inspiration behind the Colts' scorched earth run in 1968: Baltimore would beat every team it faced and end the season with the third-greatest points differential in league history (since surpassed) before losing Super Bowl III to the Jets." The Jets win under Ewbank made him the only coach to win titles in both the NFL and the AFL.

The Colts were nearly perfect in 1968, going 13–1 in the regular season. Unfortunately, however, I was removed from all of it. Health issues had plagued me all year long in 1967. It started in training camp with a thigh-muscle pull and a problem with a knee cartilage. The thigh was the tip-off. Had I known that these kinds of things were going to happen, I never would have come back for my thirteenth year. Never. I did though because I had a heckuva good twelfth year, setting a record by catching 40-plus passes in ten consecutive seasons. So in 1967 I kept playing on the bad knee, and then kind of got over that to some extent. Then I got banged up some more. I told the press that I had reached the stage in my life where I was more prone to injuries and that it wouldn't be fair to the Colts to keep playing when I didn't think I could give them the kind of performance the team had a right to expect from me.

My body told me it was time to quit, so 1967 marked the end of my playing days. I played in our first two games, then missed the next three. In the sixth game versus the Vikings in October, I suffered the worst injury of my career when I dislocated my shoulder. I got into a real awkward situation—I caught a pass and was running up the right sideline with my left shoulder facing into the field. Then a guy came over to tackle me and hit me on the upper arm. That knocked the shoulder out of joint. My body was just over the hill.

I've been told the average length of any NFL player's career is around three years. Some say it's more like six. I guess I beat the odds. The fact of the matter is I was born with a body designed to do just what I did. That's a big part of my story. The length between my hip and thigh area is a little bit longer than normal. I had a long stride, and I had a real ability to leap and stretch out. I was very limber, and I had strong ankles and feet—running pass routes is a very strenuous thing to do with your ankles and feet. You're planting and cutting and making extreme movements. My body was different from a lot of people's. So I had all the physical tools to do what I was doing.

I had tremendous endurance, I had the ability to bend and bounce and not break. I mean, I took a lot of hits, but I knew how to absorb them, and I was floating in the air most of the time when I got hit hard. I also had football instincts, and I had learned that absolute, maximum conditioning was your best insurance against injury. I never stepped onto a field in the NFL without being ready to play sixty minutes of football. Still, age catches up with everyone.

I came back for the last three games but caught just one pass in each of those contests. My last touchdown came on December 3 in our twelfth game, a 23–17 win over Dallas.

Later, when I coached in other organizations, I realized to a greater extent that what I had in Baltimore had been so special.

When I left the game, I held the records for career catches with 631, and for the most yards on receptions with 9,275, although Don Maynard soon broke that record. Just as I broke Billy Howton's record for career catches the season after he retired, Maynard surpassed my yardage record in December 1968, the year after I retired. That was also the season Maynard and his Jets won the Super Bowl over the Colts.

Interestingly, Maynard, who went on to become the first receiver to top 10,000 receiving yards, began his career as a member of the Giants in 1958. That meant he had also played in his first championship game against the Colts—he returned two punts and two kickoffs. That's mainly what he did in 1958, but he also served as a backup flanker behind Frank Gifford. Even though he was said to be the fastest player on the Giants, and even though he would wind up in the Hall of Fame, the Giants cut him after the 1958 season, and nobody picked him up until 1960 (he spent 1959 in the Canadian Football League).

There are quite a few parallels between me and Maynard. He was born in Texas, about 350 miles due west of Paris, and began his college days at Rice, a school just 45 miles from my college, SMU. Most of his college career was spent at Texas Western College. He only caught twenty-eight passes over three years there, but he also ran track. He went low in the NFL draft—in the ninth round at number 109—and as a rookie he caught just five passes. He was another case of talent being overlooked—just like me and Unitas.

At any rate, when I hung up my cleats, only Don Hutson, Tommy McDonald, and Art Powell (who played mainly in the AFL), had scored more touchdowns on receptions than my total of sixty-eight.

But back then I wasn't as conscious of all that as I am now, writing this book. I think it had a lot to do with the fact that I was concentrating on being the best I could be and winning football games;

accomplishing statistical things was not really on my radar. All those things were happening in a sort of "outside the house" way—I wasn't really thinking about it, and I wasn't concerned about it. What was really important to me was getting my job done and doing what I was supposed to do—winning football games.

Later in retirement, the accomplishments definitely did mean a lot to me. I'm not sure exactly when it all started to soak in, though. Aside from being elected to the Pro Football Hall of Fame, the thing I'm most proud of in my career is leading the league in yardage gained and touchdowns. That was a tremendous thrill and accomplishment. You can't get too much better than that as a receiver. I was usually high up there in the stats. If I wasn't leading, I was second, third, or fourth several years in a row. That was very satisfying. In 1957 I ranked second for total receptions, led the league the next three years, then finished second again in 1961. From 1957 to 1960, I led the NFL in receiving yards three times and ranked fourth the other time.

It wasn't until I'd been in the pro game four or five years before I began to be aware of the tremendous gifts I had to be able to do what I was doing—like a body that could take all those hits without ever getting hurt, hands that could catch like I did, jumping ability, and the ability to think football.

As for my single best highlight ever, it's an easy pick. It's when we won the championship in overtime against the Giants in my fourth year. That was the peak of my NFL career. That game being played in New York with us winning the first sudden-death championship game ever, and with me having the best game you could possibly have with twelve catches for 178 yards and a touchdown, made it a dream come true.

Forty years after that game, I gave an interview and commented, "The longer I live, the more amazed I am by what an absolutely special time it was." I still feel that way.

Chapter Seven

Remembering the Colts

The Baltimore Colt teams of my era had a tremendous balance of personalities. Now, I wound up coaching a lot of years with a lot of different teams, but I don't think I've ever been around a team that had the mix like our team in Baltimore. You had comedians, like Art Donovan and Jim Parker, who kept everything loose, and you had a few serious ones like me, and you had great, unselfish, team-oriented guys. You had a lot of *highly* intelligent guys. You had some who were well educated and some who barely graduated college, but they were smart football guys.

Take L. G. Dupre, who was a great halfback for us. He had dyslexia before anybody understood what dyslexia was. So he had a hard time passing from one grade to the other in school, but he was a tremendous competitor and had great natural intelligence and instincts.

We had a lot of fun together. We were pros, doing our jobs in different ways, but we knew we could count on the guy next to us to do his job on game day. The personality mix, when you put it all together, just balanced into a tremendous team spirit.

How about the two Hall of Famers, Gino Marchetti and Lenny Moore? When someone asks me for my thoughts on Moore, I ask, "How much time have you got?" He was probably the greatest all-around athlete I ever saw in all my years in pro football. In fact I played in high school, junior college, college, and at the professional level for thirteen years as a player, and I put in around twenty years coaching, and of all the talents I've seen on a football field, Moore has to be in the top three. He once set a record by scoring in eighteen consecutive NFL games.

In 1961 Moore led the NFL with his average of 7.0 yards per carry, and that still ranks as the seventh-best average for a single season. By the way, his average per rush in 1956 was 7.5, and two years later, when we won it all, he averaged 7.3 per carry. But for some reason the averages from those years don't qualify him for mention on the all-time list—maybe he didn't have enough rushes to make the list I recently saw. Moore also led the NFL in this department one other time (5.0 yards per rush in 1957). In 1960 he led the NFL with an average of nearly 10 yards every time he touched the football. Of course in our 1958 championship season, he averaged 11.9 yards per touch.

Over the years there have been very few players who can do it all: running back, flanker, and punt and kick returner. Hell, if you put those guys on defense, they'd still be All-Pro. I call those men like Moore the "elite group," and during the years I played I can name only these athletes in that category: Elroy Hirsch with the Rams, Hugh McElhenny, and Moore. Frank Gifford and Kyle Rote were like them also.

Lenny had speed, he had power, and he could run the football inside and outside. He could run pass routes and catch well. I definitely think he was one of the best offensive weapons I've ever seen on a football field, right there with Jim Brown and Unitas. He was a total team-oriented player. Self-centeredness and selfishness were not a part of his makeup. He was not "I, I, me, me," *at all.* Actually, that unselfish attitude was one of the great characteristics of the Colts teams, one of our great assets that was pretty much universal, and not something you could plan. We were just a group of individuals who came together and had this mentality.

Moore was also one of the great personalities you'd ever hope to be around, an extrovert who enjoyed life and was full of laughs. He had a great sense of humor and was as loose as a goose.

The type of player he was is rare, too, because it was all natural. Everything he did was God-given. He didn't have to think much about it or practice it. He was just the best. The only thing that rose up to bite him was that because he was such a gifted athlete, it seemed like he never had to work at anything. I was able to help him with his fumbling because he went through a stage where he was coughing it up too much, and it was costing us big time.

He came to me and asked me what I'd recommend. I told him, "Now, you're going to have to break your mold here, Lenny. You're going to have to move into the arena of drill and discipline. You've never had to do that because you do everything so naturally—running and catching, dodging tacklers or running over them, returning punts and kicks. You got it all. The one thing you're going to have to work on through repetition and by thinking about it is protecting that football."

I showed him how to put that ball away, how to grip it in the front, pressure it in the back with the elbow and the inside of the arm, and, when he was running, to keep that ball in tight, not swing it out there. And, when he got in real heavy traffic, to get that ball up in the middle of his body and put both hands on it. He quit fumbling.

As for Marchetti, he was just a rare combination of tremendous competitive spirit and great ability. He was so athletic, quick, and strong. He was the whole package. When you think about the Baltimore Colt defense from those days, you start with Marchetti, because he provided the pass rush that limited the opposing quarterbacks' time in the pocket. Therefore, it affected everything about our pass defense and how long our guys would have to cover in the secondary. As for the run, the other team's ability to run sweeps and off-tackle plays his way wasn't all that great. He was just a dominant, outstanding player, our number one defensive force during our championship years.

If I had to highlight one thing about Marchetti, it would be his quickness. It was a case of, "Woe to the right tackle who had to try to block him because when the ball was snapped, he was lightning fast." Trying to keep him off the quarterback was nearly impossible.

Marchetti's intensity as a competitor was probably greater than any other defensive player I've seen. He had those inner qualities, plus he had his physical abilities. I remember seeing pictures of him when he broke his ankle in the 1958 championship game. He refused to be taken into the locker room until he saw us tie the game and send it into overtime. He actually would have stayed out there in pain for the rest of the game, but the people in charge insisted he be taken off the field for his own safety at the end of regulation play.

Marchetti was a combination of great competitive spirit and tremendous football instincts along with great strength for his 245 pounds. He had such great foot quickness and balance, two things to behold. I don't know if he ever got knocked off his feet. He had this amazing ability to use his hands. An offensive tackle trying to fool around with Marchetti was in for a long day at the office.

I watched him many times when the ball was snapped. His first move was to grab the tackle's shoulder pad on the right side, and he would slip opponents with his quickness. He was practically unblockable.

Marchetti was tough, but he was a real nice guy, too. He was also smart enough to run a successful business. One year in the off-season he and Alan Ameche got a hamburger business started, and it ended up becoming a chain called Gino's, which was all across the East Coast. It featured 15-cent hamburgers. Both of them became multimillionaires when they eventually sold the chain after starting from scratch. They had that mentality that makes the United States of America what it is, and that is the ability to put entrepreneurship into action, create businesses and jobs, and make money.

Ameche and I were rookies together. He was the first player I met when I reported to the Colts training camp. It was on the first day I was in camp, because a few of us reported a day early. He was the reigning Heisman Trophy winner out of Wisconsin. All he did as a rookie was lead the NFL in rushing en route to being named Rookie of the Year by United Press International and *The Sporting News*. In fact, his first run from scrimmage in a regulation NFL game was a 79-yard touchdown.

The movie *Diner* has a character quizzing his girlfriend on Colts trivia, and one of the questions he asks her is, "What was the longest run from scrimmage by a rookie in his first game?" The answer is, of course, the 79-yard ramble by Ameche in our season opener in 1955.

Ameche came from an Italian-American family, and he was the first Italian I ever met, because there weren't any in Paris, Texas. His IQ must have been off the charts—he was extremely smart. He also had the greatest sense of humor you could ever hope to have. He had a great personality and was very friendly. We were teammates for six years.

Of course Ameche was also a tremendous football player. He had speed and quickness, size and power. Plus, he could catch the ball, especially on the flare and swing passes that we used. He was the whole package. The defense could not completely blanket our wide receivers, because that would turn him loose on a flare, and he'd take it and kill you running after the catch. He was multitalented, one of the most talented people I've ever been around. In one respect what ended his career was an Achilles tear, but I think he could have recovered from that.

Ameche had been our number one draft pick, and Weeb had a thing about money—he almost resented players who got paid a lot. It was a funny psychological situation, but he was on Ameche's butt from the time he got there. For someone with a sensitive nature and the intelligence of Ameche, it didn't take long for him to think, "This just ain't gonna' fly." So there was not good blood between the two of them at all. It was one of the most destructive things I ever saw Weeb do. As a matter of fact, I think it's the *only* destructive thing I ever saw him do.

Weeb alienated Ameche to the point where Ameche just up and quit one year. He was only twenty-seven years old. He didn't have to quit, because he still had the ability to play, but he was fed up. Plus, he and Marchetti had ventured into that hamburger business while they were both still playing.

We had had great balance with Ameche, but then we went through a long period when we had to throw too much; and I think it was all because he wasn't there.

The tackle who played next to Marchetti was another Hall of Famer, Art Donovan. He was right there in the middle of the line most of the time in our 4–3 defense, but sometimes they put him at nose tackle. What Donovan brought to the job was 265 pounds of player, but he also had great quickness and tremendous upper-body strength. He was built in a kind of squat way. The scouting report on him was always, "You just can't trap him." Teams like to run traps against tackles to create a crease up the middle, a hole. But they gave up trying to trap him, because he had instincts and such outstanding quickness; a pulling guard trying to trap him would simply run into a concrete wall. On the pass rush he was quick and put pressure on the quarterback up the middle.

Donovan was a laugh a minute. He was always up to something. He could be frowning and angry, then two seconds later laughing like crazy. Just listening to him talk was enough to get you laughing because of his accent and expressions. He even became a popular guest on television shows such as Johnny Carson's *The Tonight Show.* He became famous for his sense of humor, which was often aimed at himself. Some say he weighed as much as three hundred pounds, but he wasn't too concerned about it. He claimed that in his thirteen years of football training camps, he did a total of thirteen push-ups. For most of his career his helmet had no face mask, and once Norm Van Brocklin, in order to get retaliation, fired a pass right into Donovan's face. Donovan later quipped, "I couldn't believe he'd just wasted a play like that. I guess he was mad. You have to respect a guy like that."

However, Donovan was much more than a guy who could tell great, funny stories. After attending Notre Dame for one year, he enlisted in the Marines and fought in the South Pacific. He became the first pro football player to be inducted into the Marine Corps Sports Hall of Fame. Because he was serving his country, he didn't begin his pro football career until he was twenty-six years old, and yet—as the *New York Times* reported in his obituary—he still became "the first pure defensive lineman inducted into the Pro Football Hall of Fame."

Donovan's grandfather was a middleweight boxing champion, and his father was a boxing referee who officiated fourteen heavyweight title fights and twenty Joe Louis bouts, including both fights against Max Schmeling.

We had another big force on defense, "Big Daddy" Lipscomb, a huge asset to us. We got him in a trade from the Rams. How in the world they let go of him has only one explanation: They had so much talent in those days, they didn't realize what they were doing. He was 6 feet, 6 inches tall and weighed about 290 pounds. He was quick, had great upper-body strength, and was a heckuva defensive tackle.

But Lipscomb was an early victim of the drug culture, dying of a heroin overdose. It happened in Baltimore during the off-season in 1963. I don't think all of the circumstances of his death became clear, except he got a hold of something that just stopped his heart.

We often had Don Shinnick play middle linebacker. He was a natural, instinctive defensive player. Very few of our defensive players studied film much. That was sort of new in those days, but Shinnick studied. And he inspired other Colts players to start studying film too, because they saw how he knew what other teams were going to do on various downs and distances, what quarterbacks' tendencies were, and so on.

That was something Shinnick and I had in common. We were probably two of the first players in the NFL to start studying game films. We were always looking for every edge. He was looking to understand his opponents and to figure out who they were, what they were, how they did things, and how to anticipate what they were going to do.

By the way, I even studied other receivers—tried to learn what they were doing to get open, how they caught the football, the moves they had, and what they did in general to be successful. If I saw them do something that really bothered a defensive back, then I got that in my head to try to duplicate it.

I studied films during the season, and I studied them in the off-season—and so did Shinnick. He studied more film than all the rest of the defensive players put together.

One of the famous jokes about Shinnick stems from a game we played against, I think, the Packers. The ball was snapped and the Packers started to run a play, and Shinnick hollered out, "They don't have that play! They don't have that play!"

One time we played the Rams in the Coliseum in Los Angeles. We were on defense and one of our defensive guys hit the quarterback. The ball went up in the air and Shinnick, who had taken on a blocker, had gone down. He was on the ground when the fumble or interception return began by Dick Szymanski. The camera caught Shinnick as he sat there watching a 30- or 40-yard run back, and he was clapping, giving Szymanski an ovation while he was running. That was Shinnick—always doing something unique.

Shinnick and I became close friends. We both seemed to just drift into each other's company. He had a great sense of humor, and that played to one of my chief interests, so we had a lot of fun together. He had a reputation on the Colts as being hilarious, and he was one of the most popular guys on the team. He was just such a positive guy who loved people, and he played his guts out.

He's probably the number one all-time character who ever played in the NFL; nobody could ever top him. His sense of humor and the lines he'd come up with were incredible. He was such a likable, positive guy. No profanity with him, either. Yet he had a competitive heart. He was one of my closest friends on the Colts. We had this in common: Football was the game for us, 100 percent, and we didn't have any interest in doing anything other than winning football games—and doing whatever it took to do it.

I also liked to hang around with Andy Nelson, who lived close to our neighborhood. He was a very competitive defensive safety and a tremendous athlete who intercepted a lot of passes. I don't know that I've ever known anyone tougher than Andy Nelson. Like Marchetti and Ameche, he started his own business, a successful barbecue business. He was a great guy, very down to earth.

Milt Davis was one of our corners. He led the NFL in interceptions in 1957 and 1959. He was out of UCLA and was highly intelligent. He and Shinnick played on the same side of the field, so they were a combo, working together with Shinnick underneath and Davis back on the corner covering people.

Jim Parker and I played side-by-side for eleven seasons. He was one of the best offensive tackles who ever came into professional football. His ability to pass protect Unitas's blind side was without comparison. He was such a force there on pass protection, and on run blocking, too. He was able to move people out of the way and create holes for Moore and Ameche.

I'm not too up-to-date on the modern era of offensive line play, but usually if a guy can do either pass or run blocking well, he does the other one well, too. The two skills pretty well go hand-in-hand. Of course any coach would've been happy with the way Parker protected and gave time to a guy like Unitas, but he did it all. That's one reason why Parker's in the Hall of Fame.

Jim Mutscheller was one of the best people you'd ever hope to be around, the kind of guy you'd want your daughter to marry. He had character oozing out of every pore. He was from Beaver Falls, Pennsylvania, the same home town as Joe Namath. Mutscheller played at Notre Dame under Frank Leahy, and he was on their 1949 national champion team. He was the team's captain in his senior season. Mutscheller was in the Marines and came out as a captain after serving in the Korean War. He joined the Colts a year before I did.

Mutscheller weighed about 210 pounds, and he had fine hands, intelligence, quickness, and speed. He was a typical Baltimore Colts player from those years, totally team oriented and unselfish. The skills he brought to the job of tight end made him an explosive, tenacious blocker—he could handle linebackers and defensive ends and was unerring in his ability to block on sweeps and off-tackle plays that went to the right. He could also catch the football and run well. He ran good routes, and he was physically tough.

For several years we had a system where an end would be considered a tight end or a flanker. As our system evolved, I was split out on the left side and Mutscheller was on the right as a tight end around 70 percent of the time, with Moore the flanker on the right. But Mutscheller would split out every once in a while when I would be a tight end on the other side. So he had blocking and pass-route assignments.

Of course there were two great Colt tight ends who played during my time. John Mackey was the other one, and he had it all. To have a tight end who could be a power-punching blocker and have the speed to beat people deep and the hands to catch the ball is special. He did not have natural hands—he just caught the ball anyway. And he was a Bronko Nagurski after the catch. Trying to bring the guy down? Good luck. There's film after film of him catching the ball downfield, breaking one tackle, breaking another, running, breaking another one, and scoring after people were hitting him from every angle, but just not bringing him down. That was because he had strong legs, hips, and shoulders. He was explosive. When you watched Mackey over a period of time, you saw explosion—as a blocker, as a runner. And he had a heart like a lion, even though by today's standards, at 6 feet, 2 inches and 225 pounds, he was far from being huge.

As tough as he was, Mackey was a walking time bomb, because things would frighten him. It was a well-known fact that you had to be careful to not surprise him. People would play jokes on him to get him to react, and they never had any problem getting him to react. They'd put something like worms in his locker and watch him go to the locker and let out this yell. Everybody would laugh. That was Mackey.

I think there's real strength in variety. As a matter of fact, I think the classic example of that in world history is the United States of America, a melting pot of determined people. Of course Weeb was the man who dealt with all of these people, and he did it well. All in all, the Colts of my day were quite a team, filled with great personnel and great personalities. Remembering the Colts? How could I forget?

Chapter Eight

From Cleats to Canton to Clipboards

After my retirement was announced in March 1968, Tom Landry called me the next day. We were living in Baltimore at the time. He asked me if I would be interested in joining his staff in Dallas, coaching receivers. I really hadn't thought about what we were going to do, so I told him I would call him back. Sally and I talked it over and thought coaching was a good move.

We moved to Dallas, where I coached with the Cowboys for two years, 1968 and 1969. Before I actually joined the Cowboys, I worked that spring with the receivers at Baylor for my ninth year.

The NFL had twelve teams for a lot of years. Then, when the pressure for expansion came, the league granted the Cowboys a franchise, but the "generous" NFL owners gave them absolutely nothing. They gave them the bottom three players off the rosters of all twelve teams. So when Landry started in 1960, he basically had no talent whatsoever. Their ability to compete was very low. The pre-expansion teams didn't want anybody to compete with them, but they wanted the money they'd get for the new franchise. They took the money and gave the Cowboys nothing.

I believe there is no way to succeed without persistence and perseverance, and Landry is a perfect example of this. Do you remember how long he had to hang in there before the Cowboys won their first championship? How many close ones they lost? How many disappointments they had to overcome? It took a lot of mental toughness to go through such experiences. You can't allow yourself to get mentally defeated. You have to learn to deal with defeat and learn from it.

Landry not only had to overcome adversity, he started by inheriting a situation with an empty arsenal. It also took a lot of years of going through the draft to finally put a team together that could compete. They didn't win many games early on, and their record for the first five years showed they were struggling to get personnel to compete. In their first season they went 0–11–1, and they never topped five wins until 1965.

Landry had one of the simplest offenses you could ever imagine. That's one reason why he was so potent. The main impression you got when you played the Dallas Cowboys was that they used multiple formations, something Landry had learned as a defensive coach with the New York Giants. There, one of the things he had discovered and dealt with was the effectiveness of formation changes. For example, an opposing team would line up in the I formation, then shift to spread backs, or they'd motion the flanker, and the defensive guys had to discern what was going on, and that interfered with their concentration on where the point of attack was going to be.

What Landry explained to me was that the Cowboys were very basic in plays, very fundamental, but they might run their off-tackle play off of six different looks. The Cowboys would shift the split backs, motion a guy, and use "trips" and double wings, but he had only a few plays.

This stopped the enemy from marshaling their forces at the right point. If they wanted to hit the right-tackle area, Landry didn't want six guys being there, because defensively that's what he did—he studied other teams' offenses and knew from their formations what they liked to do from given formations. So he taught his players, "When they get in this formation, these are the two plays they like to run." He was ahead of his time and ahead of other teams that used computers to learn such things. He'd have people at the right spot to stop those plays. And that's what he neutralized against other teams with his own offense.

See, Landry was a military man. He flew in World War II as a copilot on a B-17, flying over Europe. I think he flew around thirty combat missions. One of the things he said he had learned in the military was that if you're going to attack the enemy, then do a lot of stuff to disguise the point of attack.

He said the classic case of this was the invasion of Europe when the Allies built up all their forces in England. The Americans sent planes and tanks and trucks and men, and the British were getting all their people together, too. So Britain was the staging ground. Well, Hitler knew that, and he knew an invasion was coming sooner or later, so German forces were situated to stop that invasion. The Allied strategy was to disguise their point of attack, so they did a whole lot of trickery and faking with false signals and commando landings all up and down the European coast. The Germans didn't know where in the hell they were going to hit. Then, when the Allies launched the attack across the English Channel, the German forces were dissipated.

In Dallas I worked with Don Meredith, who had come out of SMU. Like me, he spent his high school and college days in Texas—he was from Mt. Vernon, about a forty-five-minute drive from Paris. In his case, though, he wound up also spending his entire pro career in Texas. With the Cowboys he got his butt handed to him over and over and over in the early years—I mean, he got beat up. Craig Morton was there as the other quarterback. Meredith got beat up so bad at first that it took its toll on him physically, and it affected his long-term career and production. Still, he was a tremendous talent—he could throw that football and hit the target, and he had great leadership ability. Players loved him. He was an extrovert from the word "go" and a great competitor. He just got there at the wrong time.

In my second year with Dallas, Roger Staubach came out of the US Navy after his enlistment, and he joined the team as a third quarterback.

Meredith was the starting quarterback, and he was a typical NFL quarterback: —He was a tremendous natural athlete. Those guys are born with an ability to throw the ball accurately, and Meredith could throw any type of pass there was. On top of that, he was one of the most interesting extroverts you'll ever be around. When you're talking about Don Meredith, you're talking about a multitalented guy. He was loaded with personality and football talent. He even became an actor and, of course, gained additional fame working on ABC's *Monday Night Football* with Howard Cosell during the program's first four seasons.

Meredith played with the Cowboys when they were just building a team, and in his early years there, the pass protection was not top-notch. They were building an offensive line, but it wasn't there yet. And an injury to his knee eventually affected his career.

Bob Hayes was in his prime at that time, and Lance Rentzel was there, too. Dennis Homan was a number one draft pick out of Alabama in 1968, and Pete Gent was another real good receiver for Dallas. I worked mainly with Hayes and Rentzel.

Hayes was one of the most talented natural athletes around. You just couldn't find a guy with Olympic speed that could also catch the football. This guy could. Not many sprinters could convert to the gridiron, but Hayes was one of the rare exceptions. He brought speed to the game that nobody in the NFL had.

Hayes was nicknamed "Bullet Bob," and he was a blur on the football field from 1965 through 1975. In four of those seasons, his longest touchdown catch went for 80 or more yards. In 1965 his longest touchdown reception was 82 yards; in 1970 his longest score went for 89 yards, tops in the NFL; the next year he scored on an 85-yard pass play; and his longest touchdown reception ever, during his second season in the league, went for 95 yards. Amazingly, that wasn't good enough to lead the NFL that season. Detroit's Pat Studstill scored on a 99-yard pass, and Homer Jones of the New York Giants hauled in a 98-yard touchdown catch.

In Hayes's rookie and second season, he led the NFL in touchdown catches with twelve and thirteen respectively. In both of those seasons he also had more than 1,000 yards in receptions, with 1,003 and then 1,232. Then, during the next two seasons, he went over 900 yards on catches.

The one thing that seems strange is that he wasn't effective while running the ball. He ran the ball just twenty-four times over his eleven years in pro ball, and he gained just 68 yards. The longest run he ever broke off was only 13 yards, and he averaged only 2.8 yards per run. You might think he could spring long runs on some kind of reverse plays, that someone with that kind of speed would have had a much higher yards-per-carry average than that. I have no idea what the reason was.

Still, over his entire career he averaged 20.0 yards per catch, and in 1970 and 1971 his averages of 26.1 and 24.0 yards per reception led the

Southern Methodist University picture, 1953 COURTESY OF SMU

Photo session at SMU COURTESY OF SMU

SMU, intercepting a pass playing defense. SMU versus Notre Dame, 1953.

ALL PHOTOS ARE COURTESY OF THE AUTHOR UNLESS SPECIFIED OTHERWISE

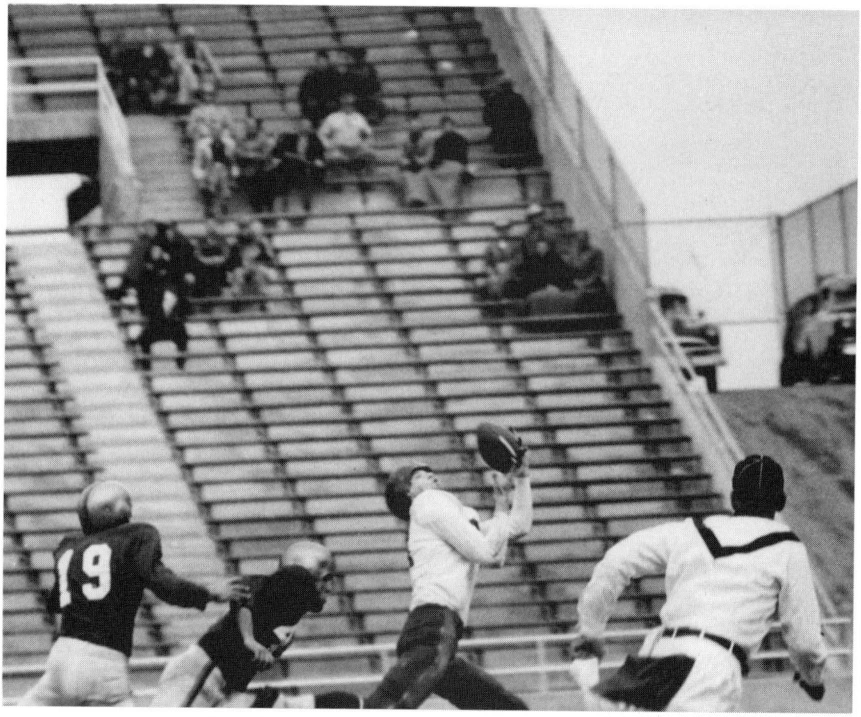

Over-the-shoulder. SMU versus Baylor, 1953.

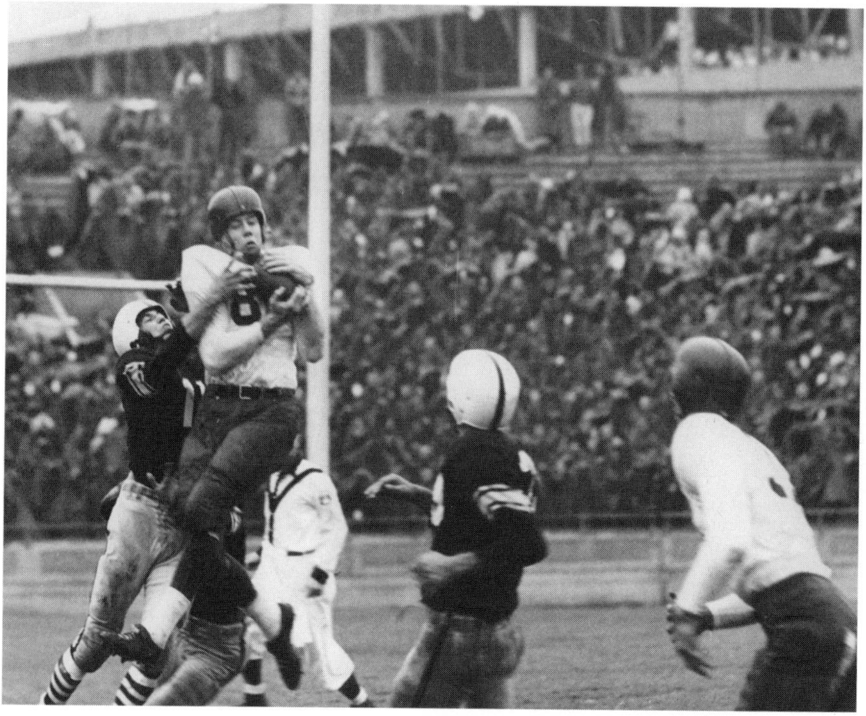

SMU versus Texas, my senior year

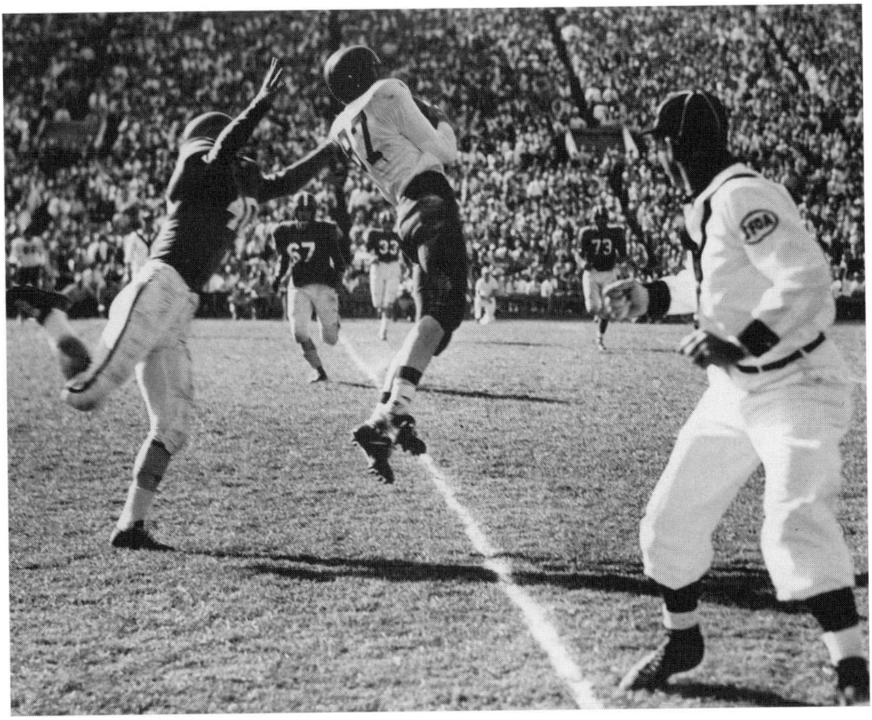

SMU and A&M, leaping catch

With Forrest Greg at SMU when my alma mater retired my jersey. Greg and I played side by side on varsity. COURTESY OF SMU

The whole Baltimore Colts team

After the NFL's first sudden-death overtime championship. We beat the Giants 23–17, on December 28, 1958. Alan Ameche, our fullback, scored the winning touchdown. Fans lifted him on their shoulders.

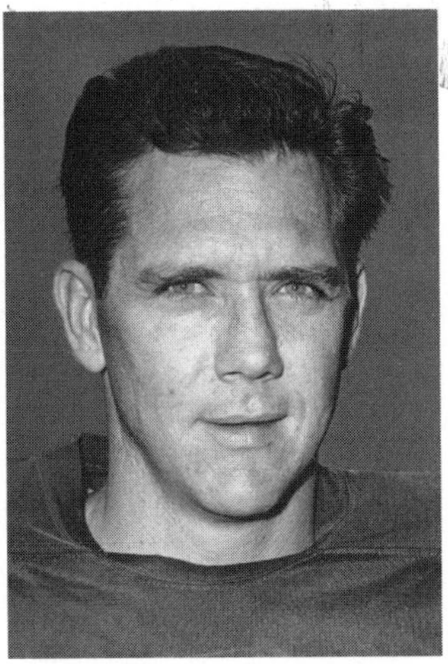

A couple posed shots with the Colts COURTESY OF THE INDIANAPOLIS COLTS

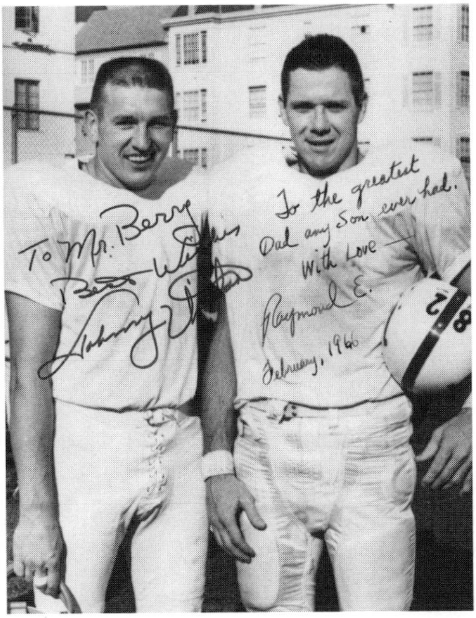

With my quarterback, John Unitas

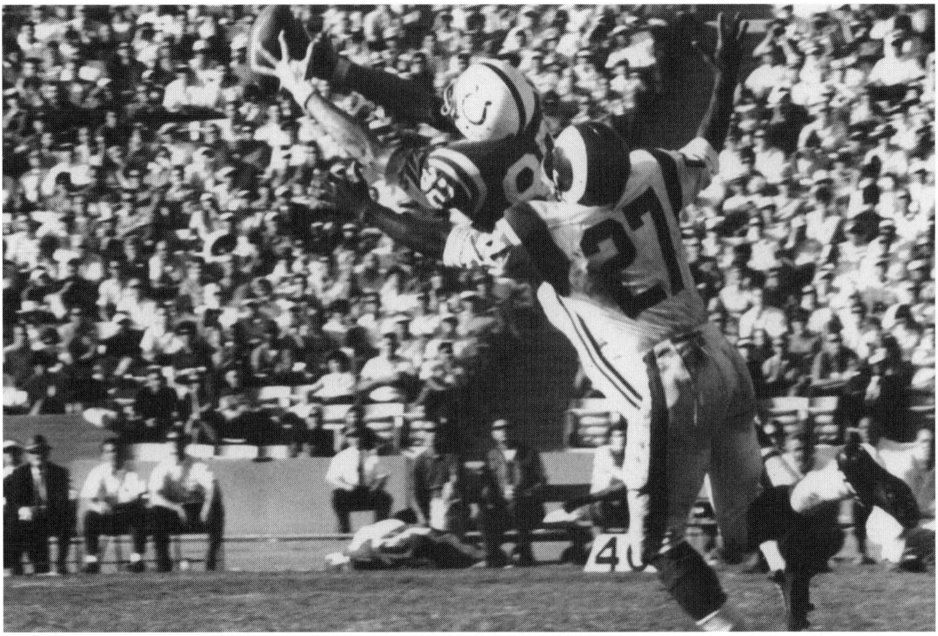

One of my best all-time catches in Los Angeles versus the Rams, defended by number 27, Irv Cross

Sideline catch versus the Washington Redskins

Touchdown versus the Rams

A sideline toe dance

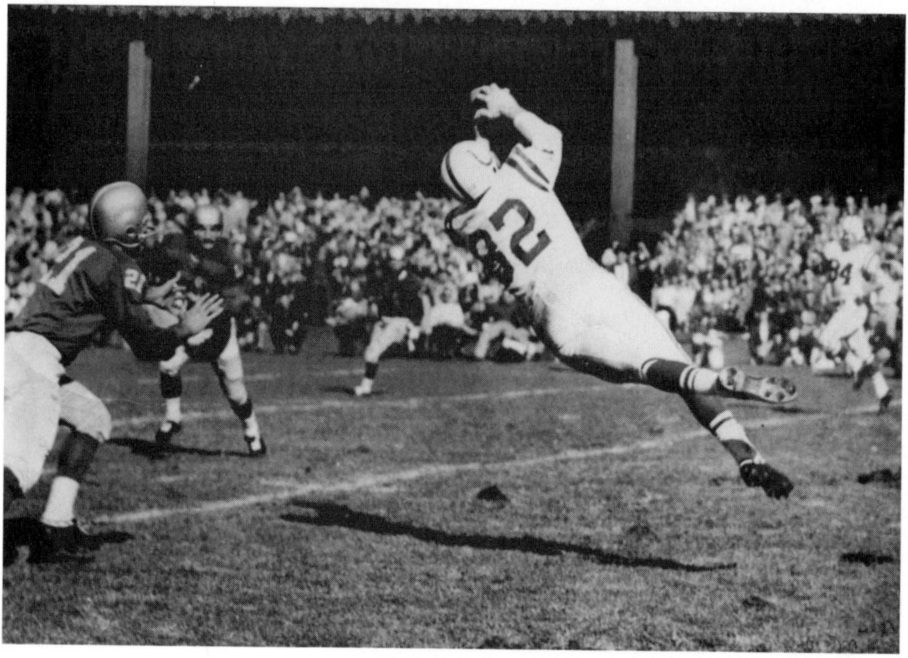

Against the Detroit Lions

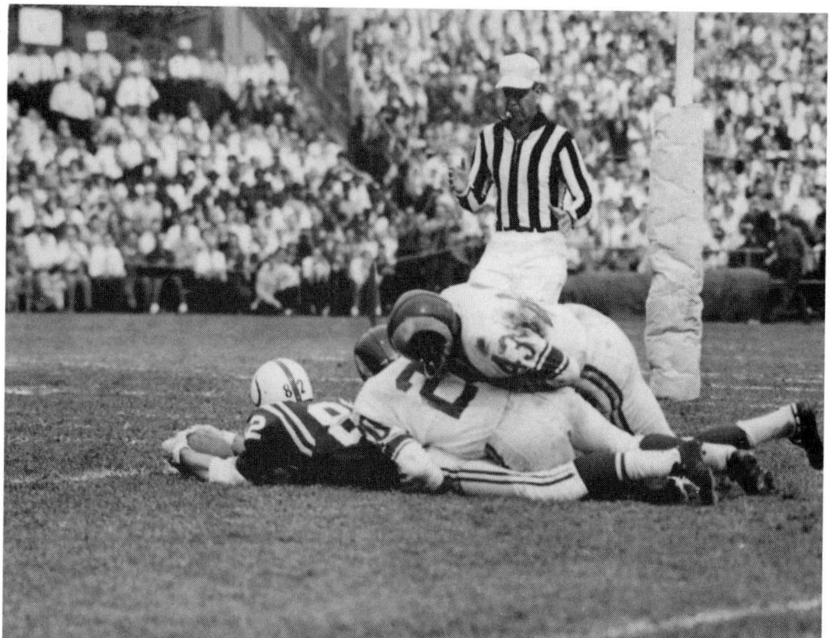

Stretching for that extra yard

A catch versus Detroit COURTESY OF THE INDIANAPOLIS COLTS

At the Los Angeles Coliseum COURTESY OF THE INDIANAPOLIS COLTS

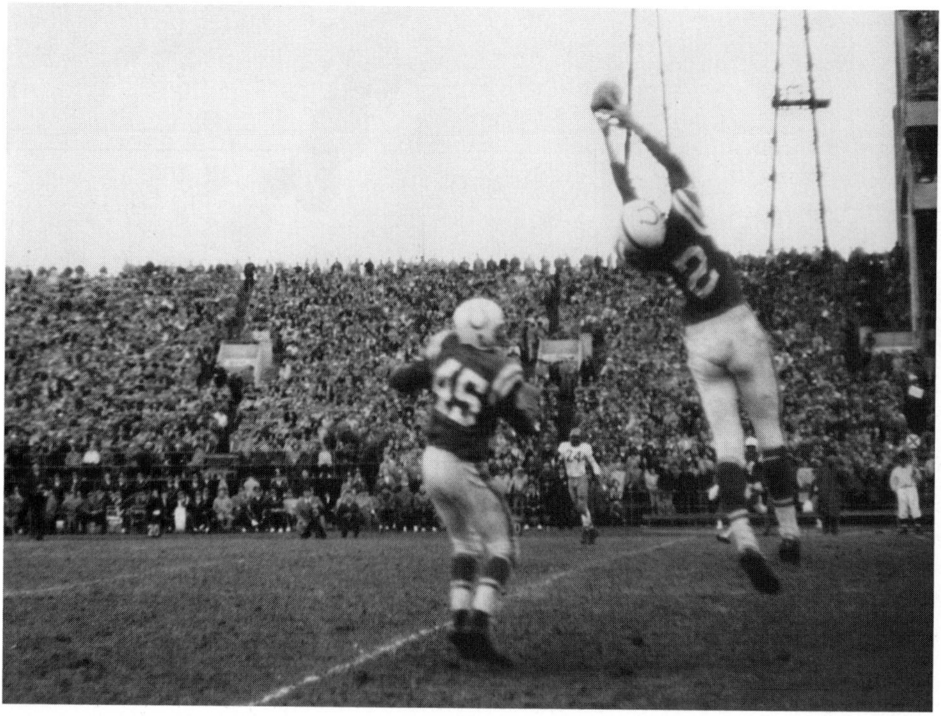

One of my best catches ever. A high, hard one.

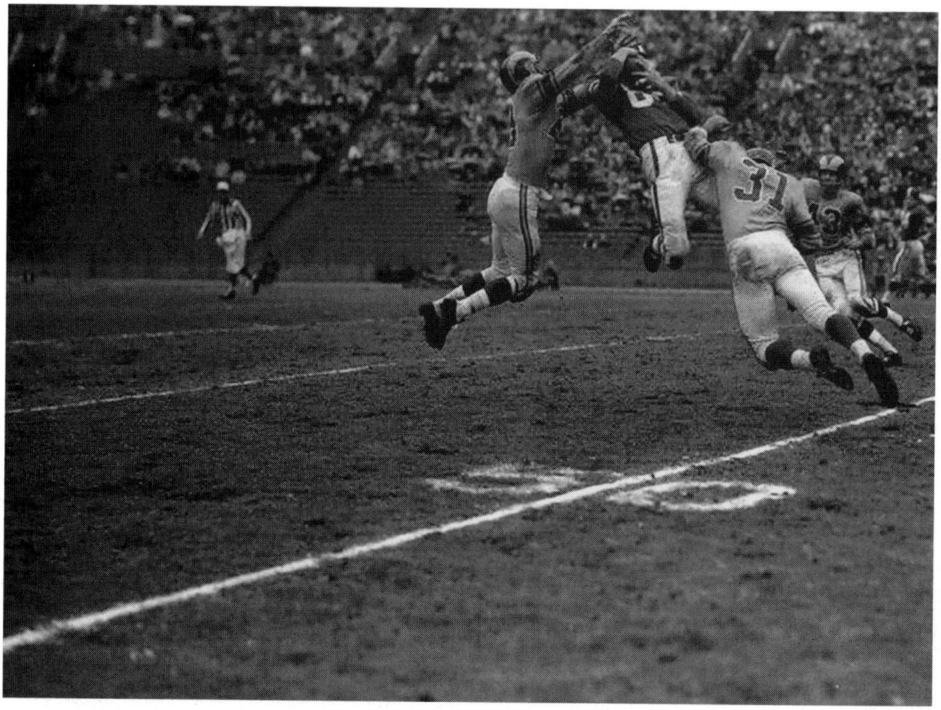

A catch against the Los Angeles Rams

At the Los Angeles Coliseum making a leaping catch in 1965

Versus the 49ers

Touchdown versus Green Bay

A catch in Baltimore
COURTESY OF THE INDIANAPOLIS COLTS

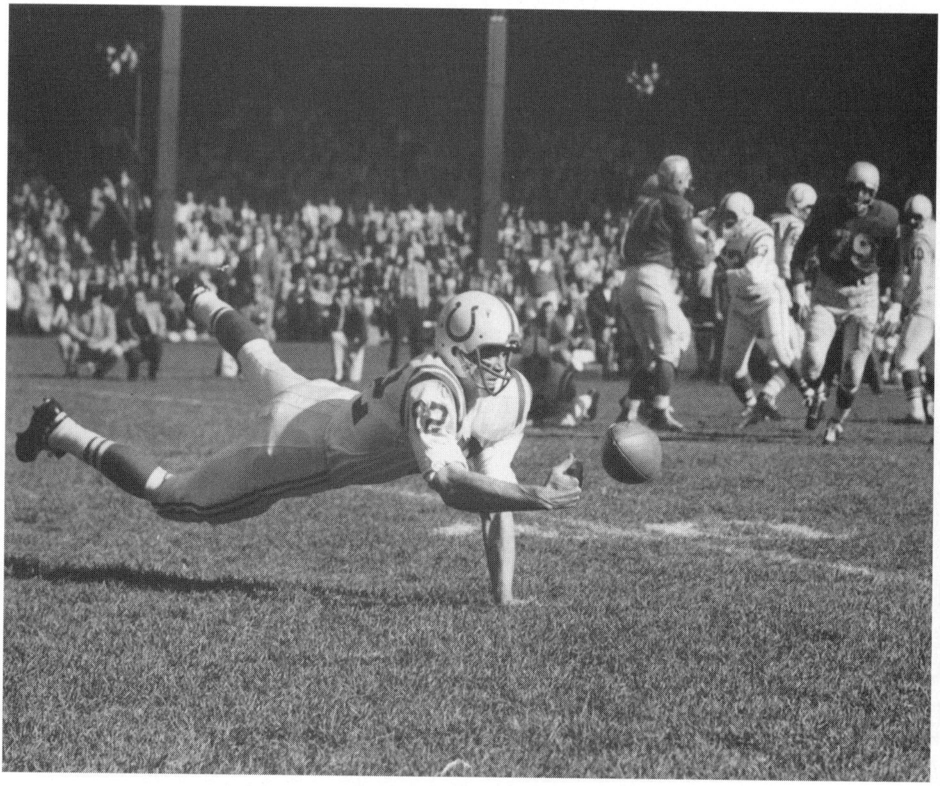

Diving, as I did a lot

Me and Peyton Manning COURTESY OF THE INDIANAPOLIS COLTS

At the Hall of Fame ceremony. Weeb Ewbank, my head coach, was my presenter.
COURTESY OF THE INDIANAPOLIS COLTS

My dad and mom, Raymond and Bess

My dad, my mom, and my children—Suzanne, Mark, and Ashley

With Sally the week we got married 1960. She is my best all-time catch.

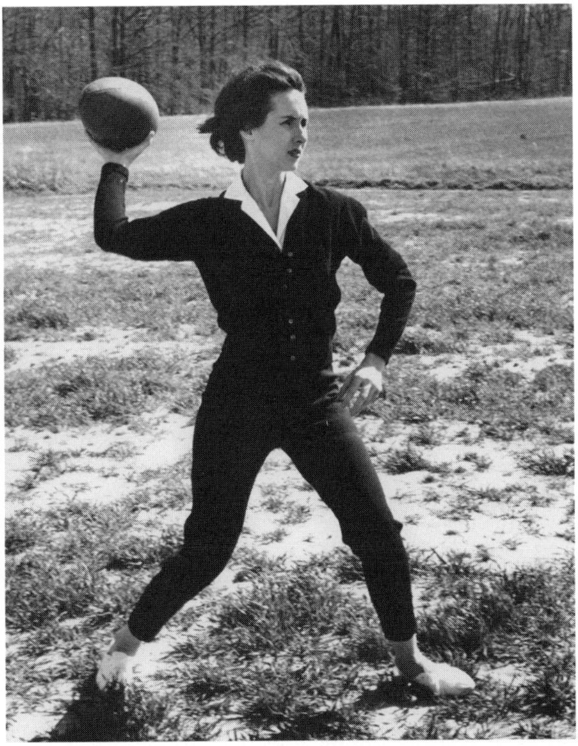

Sally threw to me before training camp in Baltimore.

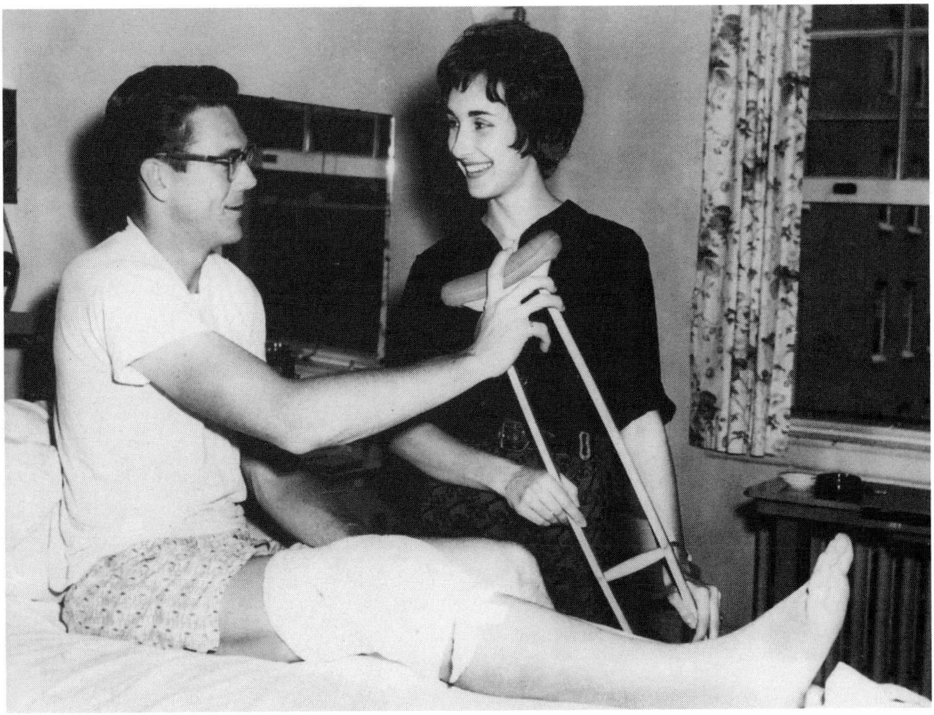

Knee surgery, 1961. Sally visiting in the hospital.

With Sally

NFL. He even led the NFL one year in punt-return yardage, and another time he led for yards per punt return at 20.8.

The fly pattern was perfect for Hayes. I've heard that he was even responsible for a change in the NFL, as teams soon realized they couldn't guard him man-to-man, so they changed to zone defenses. That's a huge impact made by one man.

Early in training camp Coach Landry timed all of his players in the 40-yard sprint, and Hayes was a blur. Landry laughed about it. He said, "Raymond, he's not even running all out—he's just kind of gives you part of it because he's not interested in trying to set any records here." So they never could clock him, never really did find out how fast he was, because he never ran full speed, and he didn't need to. He just kind of waltzed, not really trying to impress anybody.

How fast could he have run the 40? Let's put it this way: Being the world's fastest human, and having won medals in the Olympics, by today's way of timing it, I'm sure he'd be around 4.3, in that category.

I operated in the NFL with 4.8 speed, and here's Hayes, the world-record holder in the 100 meters. In the 1960 Olympic finals in Tokyo for the 100-meter dash, he turned in a record time of 10.06. That earned him a Gold Medal, and he won another one that year as a member of the 100-meter relay team. He was also the first man to run a 100-yard dash in 9.1 seconds.

Now there I was, a "move" guy working with a "speed" guy. I analyzed how I could help him, but I didn't fool with him as much as I studied him. As I got to a certain stage, I realized I could help him with some techniques and a little bit of finesse that would add to his repertoire. So I introduced him to a thing or two, especially concepts about routes, but not too much, because when he came off the line of scrimmage, he was open. Defensive backs guarding him gave him space, all the room in the world, because they were so afraid of his speed and how he could catch the long ball. All he had to do was run down the field and break out or in or hook, and he was open on the short routes. When I was playing I had to make every move in the world to get open, and he had to do nothing. It was humorous to me to see such a contrast—we were at total opposite ends of the spectrum.

In my first camp with the Cowboys, Landry said, "Berry brought a new concept to the game when he started faking with his first step. He would never run straight down field like most receivers and save his fakes for the vicinity of the defenders. Now, he's going to incorporate into our receivers the faking ideals he has developed. Bob Hayes hasn't even started to fake. He uses his speed to do almost everything. When Berry gives Hayes two or three moves, there's no way you can cover him with one man."

Sometimes a pro football receiver can get information from a veteran coach and absorb it mentally and then, and I know of more than one case like this, once the coach leaves his job, the receiver actually starts processing it. Hayes may have implemented some of my lessons after I left, but I don't know that he really needed too because, again, his speed was all he needed to get open. He wound up in the Hall of Fame, and I hope I was of some help to him.

As for Rentzel, he was a guy I could help the most because he had less speed than I did. He was a tremendous athlete and had great hands and quickness, but in the 40-yard dash he was around 4.9 at best. He could catch anything, and he was a strong, physical guy who was as smart as he could be—off the board intelligence. He would have been a strong halfback if they had put him back there, because he had a real powerful build. I started talking to him about fakes and double fakes and inside and outside approaches. He absorbed and applied what I taught him and it helped him.

One of the most interesting events that took place when I was with the Dallas Cowboys involved a practice session. The story got around that I had discovered that we were practicing on a field that was not of the correct dimensions. Writers said they were amazed that *somehow* I just *knew* its dimensions weren't right. Years later there were even some people who thought the story was made up or exaggerated, but it is true. It happened not while I was playing, as I think some people said, but it happened during my first year of coaching the Cowboys. I had played thirteen years in the NFL, and I lined up on the left side of the field a lot. We went out to Thousand Oaks, California, to the training camp, and the Cowboys had already been going out there, I don't know, six to eight years at least.

Some of us always stayed after practice, working with the quarterbacks and the receivers. So one day in 1968, I was out there working with, I think, Roger Staubach throwing to Dennis Homan. It was just the three of us. We were running a sideline route of some type, I don't know if it was 10 yards or 15, but we kept throwing it, and something about the thing just wasn't right—it just clicked in my head.

So afterward I went over and said something to Landry about it. He got somebody out there to measure the field, and sure enough, it was too narrow—from the hash mark to the sideline was a yard, maybe yard and a half off. I knew something was wrong, because I was demonstrating a pattern with Homan and it just wasn't right. You get such a feel for the fine points, so I was aware of it.

On December 1, 1968, I was able to leave the Cowboys briefly. We had played three days earlier on Thanksgiving, so we had the Sunday off. I traveled to Baltimore to have my uniform number officially retired by the Colts on Raymond Berry Day. The Colts crushed the Atlanta Falcons that afternoon, 44–0. After the game the players decided to award me with the game ball, a very considerate and appreciated gesture.

By 1970 Frank Broyles had been a fine coach at Arkansas for a long time. He decided to get away from a T-formation, ground-game offense. He wanted to go to a pro throwing game, so he recruited Joe Ferguson, who had a great rifle arm. Broyles offered me a job to work with his receivers and put a passing offense in.

Early that year I went in and told Coach Landry, "There's not really any reason I'm leaving here except I just feel that God is leading me to do this. As a Christian, you can understand the fact that we have to be sensitive to what such a leading is, so I'm going to go to Arkansas." He understood.

I was in Arkansas for three years when Broyles brought in former NFL quarterback Don Breaux and Joe Gibbs to work with the offensive line. Gibbs had worked under Don Coryell in San Diego. So both of them had this great passing background, perfect for what Broyles wanted and kept in his offense for several years.

Ferguson was a sophomore when I went to Arkansas, out of the same Louisiana high school Terry Bradshaw came from. His high school coach really knew how to throw the ball, so Joe had been passing for four years. When he got to Arkansas, he was well trained fundamentally—his footwork, drop, accuracy, and delivery of the ball were flawless. We wound it up and aired it out a lot when I was there.

In 1970 we went 9–2 and ended the season ranked eleventh in the AP poll. The next year Ferguson led the Southwest Conference in a ton of categories, and we finished with a record of 8–3–1 after losing to Tennessee in the Liberty Bowl, 14–13. However, in 1972 our record was just 6–5.

Then Frank decided to go back to the running offense, and that's when I left. Fortunately I got a call from the Detroit Lions, asking me if I was available. They had hired the ex-Baltimore assistant coach who had been there when I was, Don McCafferty. Later he was named as the Colts head coach, and his team won the Super Bowl in his first season there, 1970.

As you go through the coaching business, there are coaches who subscribe to the simple-approach philosophy, and then there are those who prefer the multiple-formation, multiple-play philosophy. I've worked under both types.

McCafferty was into the multiple-play philosophy, which was used in the Baltimore system after Ewbank, who liked simple play selection, left. I played under the McCafferty type of multiple-play offensive philosophy for my last six years or so in the NFL, so I was familiar with his offense in Detroit.

The Lions had Charlie Sanders, one of the greatest physical tight ends I've ever been around or worked with; he was just a super athlete. Ron Jessie and Larry Walton were the two main receivers, both tremendous athletes with great speed and two of the greatest talents I've ever worked with. After a game in December 1974, during which Jessie scored a touchdown and set up a late game-winning touchdown with a 45-yard reception, he was kind enough to present me with the game ball, which he had been awarded. He told the press the reason he gave me the ball was because I had worked so much with him and, as he generously put it, "taught me everything I know."

The Lions also had Lem Barney, a cornerback. He was another one of the greatest athletes I've ever been around. There was tremendous talent there.

The team also had veterans Bill Munson, who ended up having a sixteen-year career in the NFL, and Greg Landry at the starting quarterback position. When I first got there, Munson was backing up Landry. When Landry got hurt in late October 1973, the Lions were 2–4–1. Munson came in and led Detroit to four wins over seven games.

One of the most interesting things I ever learned working with quarterbacks happened when I was in Detroit. At one point in the 1973 season, I was analyzing things and studying the games, and it dawned on me that Munson wasn't throwing interceptions. In 1968 he led the NFL with the lowest percentage of his passes being picked off at 2.4 percent, and in my second year with Detroit, he repeated the 2.4 percent stat, which, this time, ranked second in the league.

I asked him about it, and this is how I learned one of the all-time classic lessons about interceptions. I said, "Bill, you just don't throw interceptions. How is it?" He said, "Because I got benched four years for throwing too many." That says it all. All it indicates is that it's a mind thing. You make up your mind you're not going to throw them, and you're not going to throw them. Here I was talking to a guy who had been there and done that. He was referring to his career when he was with the Los Angeles Rams and got benched. In his first two seasons as a pro there, he threw 6.7 percent and 5.2 percent of his passes to the other guys. After that he never started again and played in only ten games over his final two seasons with the Rams.

One thing I saw in Detroit was the introduction of a very complicated offense to a new group of players. That was a big problem, a big mistake. It was a learning experience, a great insight for me to see that a too-complicated scheme can neutralize athletic ability. The players just couldn't digest it, and we were basically a .500 team the three years I was there. This is one of the principles that I believe in: You have a great talented athlete and you give him just enough to really let his abilities take him to the maximum—that's what you want to do. If you overload him with too much stuff, you end up neutralizing his natural talents. He's hesitant; he's not going to operate on all cylinders. This is a big mistake in the coaching business that's going to go on forever, because there's now a tendency to get too complicated.

During the time I was with Detroit, I received word that I was being inducted into the Pro Football Hall of Fame. I was inducted in my first year of eligibility, being labeled the first genuine wide receiver to earn Hall of Fame honors. To me, going in on my first try was the most significant thing. I was going in with Joe Schmidt and Jim Parker, a longtime teammate of mine on the Colts, so I was especially glad to be inducted with him.

I was absolutely floored, blown away by my induction. It's a tremendous honor. At the same time, I wasn't surprised. I knew what my numbers and my track record in the NFL had been. So I knew it was very logical, but when it actually becomes official, you're aware of the fact that it's such a huge honor. You can hardly comprehend it.

I picked Weeb Ewbank to be my presenter. He had a special place in his heart for me, because he had a special place there for any football player who was totally dedicated to the game, men who would set aside everything in order to focus on football. That was me, so I was on his good list. That's probably one of the reasons why he kept me when nobody else would have. He saw something in me as a rookie that he liked. I was a raw talent, but he recognized it, and he kept me when, if I had gone to any other team, I'd have been cut within a month. In Weeb's speech he said, "If I had a son, I would want him to be like Raymond."

He pointed out that the Colts scouts had said I:

> *had none of the characteristics you normally attribute to a great pass receiver . . . It is true also that he wasn't blessed with blinding speed, he wasn't physically overpowering, and he didn't stand several inches taller than the defenders trying to stop him. However, Raymond's pass patterns were so minutely perfected that he was almost unstoppable. I don't believe that he had in his career thirteen dropped balls. There were many years that he never dropped the ball. Raymond had many other things going for him. Unusual jumping ability, a pair*

of fantastic hands, I mentioned, and a dogged sense of purpose that allowed him to become nothing less than the very best . . . The very best is exactly what he did become . . .

There may be pass receivers blessed with more natural ability than Raymond, but few have ever approached the standards of proficiency that became a weekly habit for Raymond. And it should be emphasized that Raymond and Raymond alone made himself into the super star he was. He combined his dogged determination to succeed with the keen football mind that perfected the scientific approach to the art of pass receiving that was far ahead of his time. Many of Berry's techniques are now more or less common place in football. But when Raymond first started to employ his methods of preparedness he was truly a pioneer in perfecting and specializing a pro football skill.

I think he was correct about my determination being more important to my success than my physical skills. I had the ability to catch the football and run routes, and I had a durable body, but it was the concentration on learning the game and the fine details of it that really paid off. The small things are what separate the ordinary from the extraordinary. In other words, little things, in some situations, get *very* big.

And a little thing can be like the one that happened in the 1958 championship game when we ran the linebacker slant. That came from my studying film week after week after week and seeing Harland Svare walk out on a split end one or two plays, then using that information to help win the NFL title. We had no way of knowing for certain that he was going to defend us like he did, but then it happened, and it happened in one of the most crucial times of the game. That's a prime example of why no detail is unimportant.

In my induction speech I mentioned that at no time during my playing days did the thought of making any kind of Hall of Fame cross my mind . . . All I was hoping to do was stay around for more seasons and win. I mentioned how if a player wants to play at his best, he needs to be surrounded by the best, and I surely was with Ewbank, Unitas, and so many more.

Another honor came in the year 2000 when my college retired my jersey number—it was number 87 at SMU, not the number 82 I wore with the Colts. That jersey number just happened to be assigned to me by Baltimore, but I preferred number 87. Earlier, in 1974, I was inducted into the Texas Sports Hall of Fame. That was a surprise to me. I didn't even know they had such an honor, but you have to have been raised in Texas to understand the football environment—it goes back to the 1920s when it all got started. It's just a huge deal down there, and to get that kind of an honor in the state of Texas is tremendous.

In 1976, after coaching for the Lions, I moved on to join my good friend Forrest Gregg, who was the head coach of the Browns from 1975 through 1977. They had just average talent there; they weren't a top-ability team then.

Mike Phipps started the season opener behind center in 1976. He led the Browns to a win, but would start only one other game all year long, another victory. However, Brian Sipe emerged as the number one signal caller, and Phipps was traded to the Bears the following season.

Sipe was sharp—a very smart quarterback and an accurate passer who got the most out of what he had physically. He was a thirteenth-round draft pick, the 330th player picked overall, out of San Diego State. When he came in to play, he threw bull's eyes. He was hardly ever off target on his throws, making him one of the most pinpoint passers I've ever been around.

Working with Sipe was an interesting experience, because he didn't have a fastball, but he could throw that ball like a pitcher who knows how to hit the corners and throw the curves, change ups, sliders, and all that. I guess he's an example that there's more than one way to get it done.

When I was with the Browns coaching staff, we won fifteen games and lost thirteen, finishing third and fourth in the AFC Central Division. If Sipe had been playing with a real strong overall football team, I think he could have gotten the job done real well in his own way.

Watching him throw, because he did not have the fastball, I noticed he had developed anticipation when it came to releasing the ball. A quarterback who throws hard can wait for his receiver to break and then throw the ball. Sipe would anticipate a receiver's break, and he had the ball in the air quickly, sometimes just as the receiver was going into his move or when he came off the break. He didn't wait because he couldn't. It was a classic case of learning how to compensate, to structure your talent to the need that you have.

Reggie Rucker was the number one receiver, and he was very good, but the Browns didn't have a whole lot of top-tier talent. We went 9–5 in 1976, but it was a struggle to win games. I lasted there two years. Gregg and I got fired in 1977.

As a coach I felt there was a vital lesson that quarterbacks had to learn. The number one thing they need to get in their heads—and I realize how simple this sounds—is, "Don't throw the ball to the other team." Actually, some of them have the ability to do it and some of them don't. They have to think, "I'm not going to make a dumb throw." It's better to make no throw. Another way of saying this is—and I used to tell them this—"Hey, we can punt, but you throw the interception and you just donated the other team 30 or 40, 50 yards."

I think this lesson is essential at the beginning of quarterback training. I know one thing for sure, if you have a quarterback who throws too many interceptions, you give that guy a bus ticket. It's exactly like having a running back who puts the ball on the ground. He does it too many times, and you give him a bus ticket, too, because you can't win like that. Turnovers will beat you.

Most quarterbacks have a lot of confidence and/or big egos, so I don't think there's any question that some of the foolish passes that lead to interceptions come because the guy's thinking, "I can get this pass through the defense." But you know, Unitas was the classic case of a confident quarterback. I've never worked with a quarterback who had more confidence in his ability than Unitas, and he didn't make dumb throws.

Joe Namath threw more interceptions than he had touchdown passes in his career. It really is inexcusable. Speaking of interceptions, I heard a quarterback who I was working with one time say, "Oh, I think I can make the big plays to make up for the interceptions," and I just thought, "Good grief!" That's when you want to plant a size fifteen up his butt.

It's an attitude, a state of mind, and as a coach you have to take your choice. If you want to go with a guy like that, good luck to you. I wasn't going to go that route myself.

Not long after leaving my job with the Browns, I was at the Senior Bowl game in Mobile, Alabama, and, if I remember right, Chuck Fairbanks was down there. Fairbanks was the head coach of the New England Patriots, having been hired there in January 1973. He had come out of Oklahoma University, and he had been a very successful college coach. He approached me saying he had heard that Gregg and I had gotten fired, and he offered me a job with the Patriots. It was a great opportunity, so my family moved. Fairbanks brought me to New England as a receiver coach, and we ended up being there for a lot of years.

Fairbanks was one of the smartest coaches I've ever been around. He was a college football coach who was trained and an expert in run-the-ball and split-T football. He didn't know his butt from first base about the professional passing game, because he'd never fooled with it, never been interested in it, and never needed it when he coached college football. Billy Sullivan, the owner of the Patriots, is the one who hired Fairbanks. I don't know what Sullivan knew before he decided to hire Fairbanks, but going with Fairbanks turned the history of the Patriots around.

When Fairbanks arrived there, he brought along a knowledge of how to hire people to do what he didn't know. He brought in the best brains he could to run a professional offense and defense. And he was the one who understood that you win football games with players. Schemes are all well and good, but schemes don't win, players do. Fairbanks knew this principle when he came there and hired people to run the football part of it.

Then he went to work drafting. I mean he went to work structuring and devising the entire evaluation process for the draft. It all came out of his brain. His system considered all these different factors for evaluating the players—their competitiveness, intelligence, effort, and skill.

Then he drew up charts and forms, and in the off-season all the assistant coaches sat in our offices with a projector and started getting college game film of players. Fairbanks had us watch all the films and fill out forms on the players. Every factor we examined was rated from zero to nine. So if you looked at a guy on film and saw him giving great effort all the time, you gave him a nine for effort. And if you saw a guy doing some stupid things, you'd put down a zero or a one. Anyway, you had to nail every one of these characteristics with a number, so there wasn't any room for wavering; you had to make a decision on each factor. Then he took the forms on all the players and went through an analysis process. That all funneled into a rating system, so when their names came up in the draft, you were sitting there in the drafting room armed with information.

Of course there were a whole bunch of teams drafting, so you didn't know who was going to be available. All of these big names were up on a big board, and as soon as one guy got drafted by somebody, that guy went off the board. When it came our time to pick, we looked up at that board. We looked at our ratings and rankings of the guys, and Fairbanks would take the player who was still available who had our highest rating. This is what he did, and this is why he was able to start funneling great players into the New England Patriots. Some coaches draft to fill needs at certain positions, while others go for the best athletes available. Fairbanks didn't care what position they played. He turned that whole organization around, and the success of the organization still exists to this day. He did it by the careful analysis of talent.

The Patriots won eleven games in 1976 and nine games in 1977, the two seasons right before I got there. He had started putting the team together that would eventually start winning championships. He was the guy behind it.

A classic example of Fairbanks's astute drafting was Stanley Morgan, a player who wound up with more than ten thousand career receiving yards. He was in his second year with the Patriots when I got there. The following season, 1979, began a three-year stretch in which Morgan led the league in average yards gained per catch. He was one of the greatest talents I've ever been around. He had everything Bob Hayes had, but with better hands. He was just a tremendous player and a great kid.

Fairbanks was also astute at trading, and he ended up being able to get Harold Jackson off the trade market from the Los Angeles Rams in 1978. Jackson had already put up two seasons in which he totaled more than 1,000 yards on catches, both times leading the league in that department, and in 1979 he topped 1,000 yards again for the Patriots. He was named to five Pro Bowl teams, one more than Morgan. So the two main receivers I had, Jackson and Morgan, were both super talents and great players.

Fairbanks also got Steve Grogan in there as quarterback, and he was one of the greatest quarterbacks I've ever worked with. He was the whole package: intelligence and competitiveness and strength of arm. He was as tough as nails. He was John Unitas reincarnated.

When somebody would break through the line and hit Grogan in the face, he'd come back and throw a touchdown pass on the next play. He was as much a duplicate of Unitas as any quarterback in the area of intangibles like leadership, competitiveness, and toughness that I've ever worked with, and that's the greatest compliment I can pay him.

You could not intimidate either Unitas or Grogan—they were immune to intimidation. It didn't make any difference what you did to them physically. Grogan was 6 feet, 4 inches and weighed about 215 pounds, and he could run. In 1976 he scored twelve touchdowns himself and threw for eighteen more, but his best season as far as throwing touchdowns goes was 1979, when his twenty-eight touchdowns led the NFL (tied with Brian Sipe). In 1978 Grogan ran for 539 yards, averaging 6.7 yards per rush, both personal highs. So he was a heckuva talent.

Now, when Billy Sullivan first approached Fairbanks about being the head coach of the New England Patriots, Fairbanks had one condition before he'd take the job. He told Sullivan, "I'll take the job here, but I don't want any interference about the way I run this football team, about the way I draft players, the way I sign players, or whatever."

But eventually he got into a conflict with Sullivan, because Sullivan did start interfering with him, violating their agreement. When that happened, Fairbanks said goodbye and walked out.

I don't really remember Fairbanks being suspended by Sullivan, but I've since heard that he was suspended for one contest. I believe it was the last game of the regular season, a 23–3 loss to Miami. Before that defeat, we had rolled to an 11–4 record under Fairbanks. Sullivan was angry because he heard that Fairbanks had agreed to coach the next season for the University of Colorado.

Fairbanks did a good job, though. He led the Patriots to the playoffs in 1976, and he wound up setting a franchise record, since broken, for coaching the team to the most wins in team history. However, in the 1978 postseason we lost to the Houston Oilers 31–14. Earl Campbell rambled for 118 yards and a touchdown, Mike Barber caught two touchdown passes, and Dan Pastorini threw for three scores.

Then Fairbanks left to coach college football, and Ron Erhardt took over. He had been the offensive coordinator with the Patriots, and I stayed with him as an assistant. We kept the same offense and pretty much went on the same way as Fairbanks had. The 1979 and 1980 seasons were winning ones at 9–7 and 10–6. But we struggled through the 1981 season, losing a lot of games, many of them close ones, so they fired Erhardt.

I was with the Patriots for four years, from 1978 through 1981. When they fired Erhardt, our entire coaching staff got fired, too. At that point I got out of coaching, because my three kids were all in school in Massachusetts and I didn't want to move them. Fortunately the day after I was fired, I got a phone call from Steve Alpert, a man I had met in Boston. He was an entrepreneur, a very creative business man who had a variety of interests in different businesses. He said, "Raymond, I've got a project up in Vermont, a time-share operation. I'd like to hire you to oversee this thing."

He had bought property up there and had built a beautiful housing complex. His dream was to make it a place where people could come on a one- or two-week basis, buying the time. That's what he wanted me to help promote. So I went to work for him for three years, taking my first job not related to football. He hired me at the same salary I had been making with New England, so I went from working with the Patriots to working for Alpert. Working in Waitsfield, I was introduced to the state of Vermont, which was a great bonus.

Meanwhile, the Patriots hired Ron Meyer as head coach in 1982, when a fifty-seven-day-long strike cut the season to nine games. He lasted another season and a fraction.

Then in October 1984 after the first eight games of the season, Pat Sullivan, Billy's son who had taken over as the Patriots general manager in 1983, fired Meyer. At that point the Patriots had a record of 5–3, with eight more games left on the schedule. They let him go right in the middle of the season when Pat became unhappy with him.

I had been out of coaching for several years at that point, away from the Patriots organization, and I really wasn't even keeping up with pro football. With my job outside of football, I didn't have time for it.

Billy Sullivan called me and said, "We'd like to hire you as the head coach." This was on a Thursday, I think, and they had a game coming up with the New York Jets on Sunday. I told Billy, "I'll call you in the morning."

Now the reason why I didn't say yes immediately was that I really didn't give a flip about getting back into coaching, to tell you the truth. I did not want to be a head coach. It was just such an unstable business. You're somewhere for a few years and you get fired and have to move somewhere else. That didn't appeal to me.

And the head football coach doesn't have as much control over things as you'd think. You're at the mercy, at least most coaches are, of the drafting process, the signing process, and owner decisions. All these things affect your ability to win games. And they design it that way. They want the head coach to take the rap for all their stupid mistakes, so that's the way it works, and I knew it, so I didn't care about getting back in it.

But, I'm a Christian, and soon I felt a calling. I talked it over with my wife, and I prayed about it. What I prayed was, "God, what is your will?" He knew I didn't want the job, but after praying, I knew what he was telling me to do was to coach, and then I had a clear conviction that I needed to take the job and go to work.

The way Sullivan offered me the job, along with a contract that would run through 1987, was unusual. I had been out of coaching for a while, so it was totally out of the blue, a total surprise. For the first time in my football career, I got an agent, a young man named Robert Fraley. Joe Gibbs, a future Hall of Fame coach, had told me, "Raymond, you need to get him to guide you through your contract negotiations." I took his advice.

Fraley had been a quarterback at Alabama in the early 1970s. He died in a 1999 airplane crash, which also took the life of golfer Payne Stewart. Fraley was a great person and one of the most honest and competent people I have ever met. I counted him as a great friend, and his death was a real tragedy for me.

Unlike the hiring of so many coaches and baseball managers nowadays, I basically got the job over the phone, and in a very short period of time. You don't become a head coach in the NFL that way. It just doesn't happen. It was a hand-of-God type of situation—a lot of things happen when He's in charge.

The NFL head coaching job is rare enough, but it's even more rare to be asked like I was. One head coach called me and asked, "Raymond, what did you do to get Billy Sullivan to hire you?" I said, "Well, I picked up the phone and answered his call." He said, "Are you serious? He called you? You didn't call him?" When I told him that was exactly right, he was startled and said, "That just doesn't happen." I realized that.

There wasn't even an interview with Sullivan or anyone else. He had observed me being an assistant coach several years with the Patriots. He knew what he wanted, he offered me the job, and I went over to the stadium and signed the contract. It was so unusual. I never had a contract longer than one year as a player. Now I had a long-term contract, which was good for the team, giving them, and me, a sense of stability.

Meyer had coached college football at SMU, and his staff was pretty much a college group, also out of SMU. They wanted to know what I did, or what kind of contacts I had to seek out the head coaching job. When I told them that I hadn't done anything, they thought I was lying, that surely I had been maneuvering behind Meyer's back to get myself in position for being hired.

I went to the team and reported in, but here's the situation I found myself in: I didn't know their offense or the defense systems. I didn't know the defensive coordinator. I didn't know but about two guys on the staff, and as for the rest of them, I didn't even know their names. I didn't even know two thirds of the players. I knew only a few veteran players who hadn't been replaced since I had been there before.

So I'm the head football coach having to prepare to play the Jets in a few days, and I'm walking the sidelines, and I don't know my butt from first base about most of the things going on. I just told all of the coaches, "The train is going to run the way y'all have been doing it. The only thing I'm going to do on the day of the game is make decisions on whether we punt, kick a field goal or go for a touchdown, go for it on fourth down when we were near the goal line—things like that." Other than that, I left it to the coordinators to run the game. And that's the way we went.

You can't make any changes during the season, so I just rode things out. You can't take over a ship in midcourse and change. You'll screw everything up if you do.

I started studying the personnel over the next eight games, looking at films and evaluating players and the depth of position talent that we had. The light bulb went on and all of a sudden I started realizing, "Good grief! This football team is drastically underperforming. This team has got everything it takes to win a world championship." For a coach to be given the job without even looking for it, and for him to inherit a team that is that deep in talent was just unheard of.

Naturally I had my own philosophy on coaching and how to best get the job done, and it was all based on personal experience. For example, in all my years of playing at every level I think I was inspired by only one locker room talk. It was when I was in junior college, and my coach's big talk really got my attention, carried over into the game, and inspired me, even though I don't recall the gist of it now. So when I became a coach, I didn't give any locker room talks. I just stayed with the facts, pointing out what was at stake and what the significance of the game was, such as where we were in the season, and maybe a point or two about how we were going to approach playing an opponent.

When it comes to coaching and how to win, I came up with a list of what it takes. Start with wanting to succeed, make up your mind that you can do it. Number two is to learn and master the basics. Then be sure you have the knowledge of your business, be it coaching or whatever. Have confidence and, finally, hook up with the right people—a top organization gets that way because it has top leadership.

In most fields you're up against top competition, so the tougher it is, the more you need all of the above plus persistence and perseverance. You can throw in welcoming constructive criticism and accepting corrections as absolutely essential parts of the journey, too.

Coach Landry once told me about his introduction of a new defensive system to his Cowboys. It was a sound one, better than what they had been using. He said he wanted to get to "level ten," moving up from what was in place, which was only working at about a level five. When he installed the new system, they went through a period at level two. Landry didn't panic. He believed what he was doing was right. As a result his defense soon got to level ten and beyond. He had dogged determination. He stuck to it and hung in there. He never gave up. He faced things without panic, and he maintained a belief in what he was doing.

During my six years as the Patriots head coach, Dr. Armand Nicholi, a man who had taught at Harvard and had a private psychiatric practice, was our consultant. He was a very valuable asset. During one of our conversations he told me, "Trust is the most important factor in a successful organization." I found out that when trust is in place, you can handle anything; and, from my experiences as a player and in working with many coaches, it was clear to me that players can handle your telling them the way it is. They may not like it, they may get angry at you, they may even stay mad at you. What they can't handle, though, is smoke and mirrors—that's a mistake because then trust is damaged.

Now, a lot of what I had to do as a coach was probably instilled in me by the effect my dad had on me as a player. He was always very positive, believing we were going to go out and beat these people, and that was obvious from listening to him make his comments before the game. I believed, like my dad did, that there was never a team that we ever played that we couldn't go out and beat if we played our game.

I learned a principle from Landry about defense when I was coaching with him. He used the phrase "recognizing and anticipating the point of attack." He was speaking from the philosophy that as a defensive player or coach, if you can predict the point of attack, then you can get your forces there to stop it. If you cannot do that, then you've got to spread your forces to cover all possibilities. Applying that to offense, when running routes with multiple moves the objective is to disguise the point of attack so an opponent can't anticipate where you're going to go.

I was also armed with an insight into people, like Unitas, who studied the game. So I knew that there's a whole lot more to football than meets the eye. Being aware of this carried over into my coaching. When you've got players who think, you've got a better chance of winning. As you pick your players, you need to be on double alert to locate players who can think. You may get impressed with somebody's 40-yard dash speed or how much they weigh, but at some point you better weigh in on how these guys can think, because there's more to it than just the physical.

Here's a perfect example. During the final game of our 1986 season, we had to beat Miami in order to make the playoffs. It was all or nothing. My starting quarterback was Tony Eason, but he got hurt early in the game and Grogan had to come in. The fourth quarter rolled around and we were tied at 27–27. On a third-and-3 with little time left, Grogan came over to the bench and asked me, "What do you think, Coach?" I just said, "Win the game," and I let him take charge. He went into the huddle and said, "OK, guys, we can run a couple of times and get the first down, or go to Stanley [Morgan] who said he thinks he can beat his corner on a slant and go. What do you think?" And he took a vote. The guys liked Morgan's idea, and Grogan hit him for a 30-yard score and we won.

Because I played on a team that permitted players to have input on what we did, when I was a head coach I was able to cash in on Grogan, a unique quarterback, the smartest player on the Patriots. When he was in there, I wanted the dynamic of him communicating with our offensive line and our receivers, just like we did in Baltimore. I felt that gave us our best chance to win.

Another example of this from the 1985 season comes to mind. Our offense was struggling against the Dolphins. Film study revealed their defense was vulnerable to a special flea-flicker play we had for short-yardage situations. We wanted to give the appearance of running on a fourth-and-1 situation with our fullback going up the middle. We'd take out our two wide receivers and our two running backs and put in our 290-pound right tackle, Steve Moore, at fullback; Mosi Tatupu, our second fullback at tailback; Greg Hawthorne, our backup tight end, at close flanker; and Art Plunkett, a reserve tackle, in at Moore's normal tackle position. We also had our third tight end, Derrick Ramsey, line up as the weak-side tight end.

Obviously, all this was not a simple personnel change. The idea was to fake Mosi up the middle behind Moore's lead block. When Mosi got near the line, he would turn and flip the ball back to Grogan. If all went according to plan, the Miami defense, especially their safety, would react and come up to tackle Mosi. In the meantime, Hawthorne would fake a block, slip unnoticed down the middle, and take off for a Grogan pass.

I explained the play and all of the personnel changes involved on Wednesday. We rehearsed the play from then through Saturday. Now, on the day of the game, we trailed 13–3 in the final quarter and faced a fourth down with a foot to go inside the Miami 30. I felt a tug at my arm. It's Plunkett. "Coach, are we going to run that play?" I looked at him and realized that I had forgotten all about that. I called a time out. Grogan came over to me and said, "Are you sure you want to run this play? We can run and get the first down." I said, "Steve, we're going to score on this play."

We executed it just like it was drawn up, and we scored on a 28-yard throw to Hawthorne. We went on to win 17–13 in what was a turning point in our season. Plunkett may have been a backup player, but because he had his head in the game, he was responsible for us winning the game. In understanding the power of a team, you have to understand that everyone has a role, and each role is important. Plunkett could think. He carried out his role, and the season, which ended up with us going to the Super Bowl, turned around.

My study of film was intensive as a player, and now, as a coach, I spent a lot of time trying to figure out how to beat our opponents—looking for weaknesses in personnel or tendencies on their calls and what they do in situations to make them vulnerable. As you study, something may come up about the way a player does something and how he's predictable in certain situations. That gives birth to a special play, to an opportunity. That's what you're looking for as you study every play. The only thing that keeps such study from being exhausting is that you don't have much time. The week goes fast and the clock doesn't stop, so you have to make decisions based on time constraints.

Furthermore, a lot of coaching maneuvers came into play from the stuff I had learned from my dad. It was an interesting psychological experience, because I realized when I became head coach that so many of the things I had absorbed from my dad were all stored in my mental library, waiting to be used.

And I'll tell you this: One of the most important things I learned from him was when an individual player has a capability, he needs to be told about it over and over. My dad used to say, "Not one kid in a thousand has any idea of what he's capable of doing until he makes up his mind to do it." I heard him say that many, many times growing up, and he learned it from a Texas high school football coach he served under as a young assistant in West Texas. My dad learned that these kids need to hear it. Verbal reinforcement, I guess they call it, is so important.

So when I started seeing the talent on this New England team made up of men who just didn't have any idea of what they were capable of doing, my dad's lesson started to kick in. I started telling these players individually and as a team, "You're capable of doing this—we can beat these people." I kept telling them, and I think they began to believe it, because we started to see a turnaround mentally. We went 4–4 over the last half of the season.

In the off-season I got my own coaching staff, which was absolutely necessary, because I had more competent people to bring in. To establish my own systems on offense and defense, I needed my own staff, coaches I had known over my thirty years in the league. However, I did keep the special teams coach, Dante "Scar" Scarnecchia, because he knew his business and I didn't want to change the kicking game; and, not wanting to change our defense, I kept Rod Rust, the defensive coordinator. Actually, shortly before I was hired, Rust was fired by Meyer, and the next day the Patriots fired Meyer. When I got the head coaching job, I had him reinstated. Later, ironically, Rust would replace me as the Patriots head coach.

For 1985, I brought in three veteran defensive coaches—Don Shinnick, Jimmy Carr, and Eddie Khayat—to give Rod the heavyweights he needed. I had a staff to run the defense, and it was like I never went back into the defensive meeting room the rest of the year, not caring what they were doing because I knew they knew what to do.

The players involved in the kicking game and on defense didn't have to learn a new system, but the Patriots didn't have an offense that could win.

I totally threw it out and started over, designing an offense based on the Colts' system and what I'd learned under Landry. I brought in Harold Jackson to coach the receivers and Les Steckel to work with the quarterbacks.

I wanted to make as few changes as possible, though. Where I could get by with what the team had been doing, I wanted to do, because I knew this team had the talent to win if we didn't screw them up by making too many changes. I kept it simple, because I knew that the first year you put an offense in, you're going to have a learning curve, a big learning curve. It affects the players' capabilities. They're hesitant and operating at three-quarter speed, unsure about what they're doing.

Some coaching, meanwhile, goes beyond the Xs and Os. For example, perhaps it's a relatively little thing, but I thought it was important to teach my players to respect the referees. Sure, they miss some calls, but over the long haul they'll make mistakes that benefit you as well as the calls that go against you. It'll all even out. It's not worth getting frustrated about. My rules were these: "We're not going to argue with any referees. We're not going to be talking to them or insulting them. We're going to just let them do what they've got to do." The level and degree of competency among officials are very high.

I stressed communication, concentration, and consistency. One United Press International story wrote of how I also demanded that everyone associated with the team be treated with respect. The article stated I had snapshots taken of all of the ball boys during training camp and had their names written on the pictures so the players could memorize and identify them.

We even worked on intangibles, like dealing with the difficulties of playing on the road and dealing with crowd noise, which I'll get to later in this chapter.

We started the 1985 season tentatively, at 2–3. Then we won six in a row as we began to get a feel for the offense. We beat the Green Bay Packers in the season opener, a home game, 26–20, then got beaten on the road by the Chicago Bears, 20–7. We then defeated the Buffalo Bills on the road by three points, 17–14, but lost at home to the Los

Angeles Raiders, 35–20. The defeat to the Cleveland Browns in Cleveland Municipal Stadium on October 6 by a score of 24–20 would be our last loss for quite some time. We gelled and didn't lose again until November 24, when we dropped a very disappointing overtime decision, 20–13, to the New York Jets in Giants Stadium.

The big hurdle we had to overcome was how early we were in our system. We put it in place that year, and we kind of bumped around early in the season. Then the players started getting the hang of it, and we kept it basic. We had talented players, so we didn't need to try to fool anybody. The simplicity of what we were doing matched the talent we had. We didn't have more than about six or so running plays and eight or nine pass plays. That is one of the reasons we went so far.

As my players gradually started getting the grasp of the offense, a feel for the system, their talent started flowing, and we went on a hot stretch. We rattled off six straight wins to raise our record to 8–3. Over that winning streak we were very stingy on defense. We gave up just 3 points to the Bills, 13 to the Jets in an October home game, 14 to the Tampa Bay Buccaneers, then 13 to the Miami Dolphins, 15 to the Indianapolis Colts, and 13 to the Seattle Seahawks.

I remember when we flew to Seattle in mid-November. They had a fine football team. They had Steve Largent, a future Hall of Famer. That season he led the NFL for the most receiving yards with 1,287, which was 50 yards more than the previous time he led the league in that category. In fact he went over the 1,000-yard mark eight times in all. The Seahawks also had a great running back out of Penn State, Curt Warner, who would run for 1,094 yards that year, one of four seasons he went for 1,000-plus yards on the ground.

We were starting to click at that time, and we won the game 20–13. Flying back on the plane—it was about an eight-hour flight from Seattle back to New England—I was thinking that this victory was a launching point for us. Our players started realizing what I had been telling them—that they were capable of playing anybody in the league, because Seattle was one of the top football teams in the business around that point, coming off a 12–4 season in 1984. So to go out there on that field and match up with them and beat them, I don't think there was any question that my players started to realize they were really good.

Not only did I have talent on this team, I had a ton of it. Start at the quarterback position. I had inherited two quarterbacks who saw a lot of action. Tony Eason, the young starter, was a great, accurate passer who was at his best in the clutch. And Steve Grogan was an old vet coming out of the bullpen. Having them was a big plus, because in the NFL it's very difficult to get through a season without a quarterback getting injured at some point. I knew Grogan because I had coached him when I was an assistant with the Patriots, but I didn't know Eason. Still, I was thinking, "We can win a championship with both of these guys. We're two-deep at the quarterback position, and that's very unusual."

Grogan was in the mental and competitive mold of Unitas. He had toughness, fierce competitiveness, football instincts, and of course, the ability to throw the football. Both of them were great leaders who inspired their team. Their teams had tremendous confidence in them. And what Grogan added to it that Unitas didn't was Grogan was a very dangerous runner.

You couldn't have come up with a better quarterback for that team than Steve Grogan. The players loved him. And he was just like Unitas in that neither was a "me, me" guy. They both were team oriented, not self-centered at all, and that's huge.

When I took over the team in the middle of the 1984 season, Tony Eason was the starting quarterback. They had drafted him number one and he had been there a couple of years, so they made the decision to make him the number one quarterback and use Grogan as the backup.

One of the first things I did was sit down with Grogan. He had been in the league since 1975. I said,

> *Steve, you're a starting quarterback, without question. Tony's a starting quarterback, too. Now, I want to give you this angle on being the backup—at this stage of your career, you're at the high point of your salary level. If you remain as a backup quarterback and Eason plays a year, two, three, four, you're going to stay healthy. You'll get paid top*

salary and you're not going to get hit, so you've got a good deal. What you're going to end up doing is extending your career maybe as much as four years because what eliminates quarterbacks eventually is knee and shoulder injuries causing them to retire. And I've got a good deal because I've got you coming out of the bullpen if Eason gets hurt; and you can go out there and win because you're the caliber of a starting quarterback. I want you to think about it because that's the reality of the situation.

Being the type of guy he was, he knew I was telling the truth, so that's the way we operated. And it worked out. Eason played well and then, boom, got hurt, and Grogan went in there and we don't miss a beat. Grogan started six of our regular-season games in 1985, and he won five of them. Then, when Tony got well, I put him back in there and Steve went back to his former role.

I did another thing with Grogan, because he was a veteran who really knew football and our offense. I had seen him calling his own plays under Fairbanks, and I knew from my experience in pro football that every once in a while you run across a quarterback you just know is smart enough to call the plays. There are a lot of advantages of having a quarterback on the field doing that, if he's got what it takes, and I had prepared him for that. So I knew I had in Grogan the perfect guy to do that, and we weren't running a complicated offense anyway. He was a leader and he had instincts. I knew our best chance of winning when he was playing was to let him call his plays.

One day when Eason was starting and got hurt, Grogan came off the sidelines. He walked over to me to get ready to go in and I said, "You go in and run the show." He looked at me and calmly and simply said, "OK." Of course later he got hurt, and Eason had to go back in and play, which he did throughout the playoffs, even though Grogan did see some action in the Super Bowl. That was the way we operated, and Grogan was one of the reasons we got there.

As for our ground attack, our fullback, Craig James, ran for 1,227 yards, which was ninth best in the NFL in 1985, and he made the Pro Bowl team. He was instrumental in my first win ever as an NFL head coach, and coincidentally, he played his college ball at SMU, just like me. He was one of the most talented all-around running backs I've ever been around. He had power and great speed, and he was a very intelligent player. He could catch anything and he could even throw. He got some big plays in our offense on the halfback pass. He was very accurate when he threw it. In our Super Bowl season he threw two passes and both went for scores in the regular season, and he was one-for-one in the playoffs. He was a great offensive weapon.

That season Irving Fryar was our second-leading receiver with 670 yards, 90 yards less than Morgan. To have Fryar and Morgan, two great athletes, was just unbelievable—I mean, they had it all. Fryar was bigger than Morgan. He was around 190 or 200 pounds, but he had this tremendous explosion, power, and speed and he had great hands. He was a competitor and a great blocker, too. He and Morgan were team players, carbon copies in that they were both great athletes and team oriented all the way.

Fryar went on to have five 1,000-yard seasons on receptions, and he made the Pro Bowl five times. He's still in the top twenty-five for career catches through 2015, and he's number nineteen for lifetime receiving yards, as well as number eighteen for touchdowns on receptions.

We had a great defense that year, too. It was made up mainly of guys who were all at about the same caliber. They were all really outstanding, a whole passel of them.

We had one of the best all-around defensive backfields you'd ever hope for. We had Raymond Clayborn, who made the Pro Bowl, at one corner, and Ronnie Lippett at the other. Those two guys could shut down any receiver in the league. And we had two safeties who could cover and tackle in Pro Bowler Fred Marion and Roland James.

We also had three great linebackers. Steve Nelson, who also made the Pro Bowl that season, was one of the leaders in the middle along with Larry McGrew. And we had two outside linebackers, Don Blackman and future Hall of Famer Andre Tippett, who was a combination defensive end and linebacker.

Man, these guys could do everything—stop the run, pass rush, cover the pass.

Tippett was a *force.* When it came to pass rushing, as the season went on, we started sending him more and more and dropping him back less and less, because he was so disruptive—they just couldn't handle him. He made first team All-Pro with his sixteen and a half sacks.

We also had an outstanding defensive line with great pass-rush ability. Kenneth Sims was our left defensive end, Dennis Owens was our primary nose tackle, and Julius Adams was at the right defensive end position.

We had an outstanding offensive line. That's one of the reasons why we were able to run the ball like we did—we just ran it at a tremendous level. One game when I was calling the plays, we started hammering somebody, and I think we reeled off fifteen straight runs. They just couldn't stop us. That bunch up front was something, and we had a great blocking tight end, too, named Lin Dawson.

There's great significance to what I'm describing here, something that's overlooked by people who are not professionals: Whenever you can run the football and run it well and run it a lot, you're actually playing defense. That is to say, you're keeping the other offensive team off the field. And they can't score if they're not on the field, so that's a great way to play defense, so to speak. That was another one of the reasons we got to the Super Bowl. In one game that season we let the other team's offense have the ball for just about thirteen minutes or so.

Our offensive line featured men such as future Hall of Famer John Hannah at left guard. He was so good, he was named to the Pro Football Hall of Fame's second team on their All-1970s Team, then first team on their All-1980s Team. The 1985 season was his thirteenth and final one, and he was still good enough to make first-team All-Pro and earn his ninth selection to the Pro Bowl.

One of the most interesting pieces that fell into place—actually, it was already in place when I was hired as the head coach—was the organization's recognition of men like Hannah. He was the total package. He was powerful and competitive to the nth degree. His middle name was Competitor. He gave total effort, and he was one of the most intense football players I've ever been around. And, actually, at 6 foot, 2 inches and 265 pounds, he was a heckuva athlete. When he blocked, there wasn't any stopping him.

I think the Chicago Bears defense that we met in the Super Bowl had Hannah going up against William "The Refrigerator" Perry, who was 6 foot, 2 inches and 335 pounds. That was pretty much a standoff, and Hannah was thirty-four years old. Perry was just twenty-three. When he and Hannah were butting heads, I don't think there was too much give on either side.

After that game, Hannah decided to retire. I think losing that Super Bowl, and by the score we lost it by, was too much for him to handle. He just decided to call it quits. I seem to remember him telling me earlier that year, "I'm nearing the end of my career and I don't want to play at a lower level than I'm used to." So I think that's why he retired. Still, there's no question about it: He could've played quality football for at least a couple more seasons.

Our place kicker, Tony Franklin, was one of those rare players who kicked barefooted. I'm told there have been nine such kickers, including several men who punted exclusively, in NFL history. Of course the most famous barefooted kicker was probably Rich Karlis, who kicked an overtime game-winning field goal in the 1986 AFC title game versus the Browns to allow his Broncos to advance to the Super Bowl. They say a man kicking with a bare foot carries more force than one kicking with a shoe on, but I have no idea. I do know that the style worked for Franklin, who lasted ten seasons in the league. He scored 112 points for us in 1985 and led the NFL the next year with 140. His longest kick was a 59-yard field goal in 1979, but he kicked a 65-yard blast one year in college at Texas A&M.

I think Franklin was the best money kicker you could ever hope to have. His temperament was such that pressure didn't bother him at all. He was such a tough competitor that I think he actually would have made a great defensive back.

We even had depth on our squad, with great backup people at all positions on both defense and offense, so we could handle injuries. Of course when you win championships you don't get many injuries. That's one of the characteristics of a championship team—you go through the season without getting hurt too much.

The drafting process that had put those guys together was, of course, all in place when I came there. That was the team that I inherited.

Getting back to our great 1985 season, earlier I mentioned our last regular-season loss, the 30–27 game versus the Dolphins, which was decided by a fourth–quarter 47-yard field goal by Fuad Reveiz. I remember Eason threw an interception at the wrong time in that contest. He was so angry with himself, just livid. I could tell that he was in danger of harming himself almost, but I consoled him. He hated to throw interceptions, and he normally didn't, but he threw a critical one in that game that cost us. In 1984 he threw the ball 431 times and had just eight passes picked off, which gave him a league-low interception rate of just 1.9 percent. It teed him off to a huge degree. That was one of the great things I liked about him.

Interestingly, we would soon wind up playing Miami in the Orange Bowl again, for the AFC title. We were able to shake off the regular season loss to Miami and win our season finale against the Cincinnati Bengals. Our 11–5 record was the best in franchise history, but only good enough for a third-place finish in the tough AFC East Division. The Dolphins won the division at 12–4, and the New York Jets put up the same record as we did. Luckily we made it to the playoffs, as did the Jets, both as wild card teams.

During the season we knew that we had to get hot and stay hot to make it to the championship game. We won nine of our last thirteen regular-season games, then won three playoff games on the road, an NFL first.

It was rewarding to work hard and make it to the playoffs The wild card system officially began in 1970, and we were just the third wild card team of ten (through 2015) to make it to the Super Bowl. Only four of those ten wild card teams earned a trip to the Super Bowl by winning three postseason road games. We accomplished that by defeating the Jets, the Los Angeles Raiders, and the Dolphins (more on those games later). As a wild card team, we had no choice: We were required to play all of our postseason games on the road, never an easy thing to do in the NFL.

One important thing that happened that year—at least I think so—comes under the heading of the head coach and the importance of his teaching concepts, ones that he communicates well to his players. A concept I emphasized with our players from the word "go" was, "Look, I don't care if we play on the road or at home. It doesn't make a flip. What matters is how we play, and whether the people in the stands are yelling or not is immaterial. This business about on-the-road stuff is all a myth. The main thing about playing on the road is you play good football and you win."

From the very beginning I tried to erase the home/away distinction. And when we were on the road, our players were mentally prepared, very confident that we could win. And we did that, winning three post-season games in a row. I think as the season went on, our team got more and more confident about playing on the road, because we worked on it and they began to realize that they could operate away from home and make adjustments.

Playing on the road in those days, and it's probably still true today, means you've got to learn to deal with the crowd noise. From the earliest part of training camp, I started training our team to do that. We were about thirty or forty minutes from our stadium in our camp, so we'd go up there at least once or twice a week and run our entire practice on the field where we had a press box and loud-speaker system available. In those sessions, we practiced with noise pumped in so loud that it was deafening, and we did this over and over and over, because that's exactly the way it would be in the Miami Orange Bowl. You could be there standing on the sideline and you'd have to shout to the coach right next to you. You simply had to learn to operate with no ability to hear. I told the players, "I'm not going to say one word to you about what you're going to do and how you're going to do it. We're going to put you in situations and you're going to figure it out. We're going to learn how to operate our offense and our defense and our kicking game in deafening noise. So go out there and go to work."

And we did. They started learning how to compensate for the deafening noise. As a matter of fact, I never asked them what they did, but one of the players commented about it once, saying something about reading lips. I wasn't interested, because I knew they'd figure it out and come up with something. But later I finally did ask about what they did in such deafening conditions, and they said they had worked out a system to communicate with each other. Our offensive line told me that they developed a technique that began when they came up on the line. They held hands, all but the center, and the guards were right next to the ball so each guard, out of the corner of his eye, could see the ball when it first moved. The tackles were too far away to see the ball, so the guard would drop his hand as soon as the ball moved to let the tackles know the ball had been snapped. That way they could keep their eyes on the defensive ends on the pass rush and still communicate the start of the play—they didn't really need to hear.

One of the things that struck me as funny that year was when we went down to Miami to play Don Shula's Dolphins in the conference championship game. Now the Miami crowd had learned about how noise can bother a team and how they could really screw up the opponents. They were all of one mind, and when that opponent was out there, they turned it up to all the decibels they could muster.

Well, they started their act against us, and our team just went along, operating smoothly as ever. We didn't miss a beat. We were already trained. What was so funny was that the crowd just shut up and sat down. When they found out they couldn't do anything, the noise just started to drop off, and finally, by the last part of the game, they weren't making a sound, because they knew it didn't do any good.

We actually began the postseason, though, with a 26–14 win over the Jets, three days after Christmas. It was the first playoff win for the Patriots since 1963, when the team was known as the Boston Patriots. In fact over its twenty-five-year history prior to the 1985–1986 season, the franchise had won only one other playoff game ever. The first-round win was also the third time we played the Jets that year. Tony Franklin kicked four field goals for us and accounted for 14 of our points, and Morgan hauled in a 36-yard touchdown pass from Eason. It seemed to me like he was throwing darts for bull's eyes. He hit on twelve of his sixteen passes. Our final touchdown came on a 15-yard return of a fumble by Johnny Rembert.

Our second postseason game was on January 5, 1986, when we defeated the Raiders by a score of 27–20 in the Los Angeles Memorial Coliseum. The Raiders finished the season with a win–loss record one game better than us at 12–4. We trailed 20–17 at the half but rallied, scoring 10 points in the third quarter and shutting them out the entire second half. Our scores came on a 13-yard pass from Eason to Lin Dawson; a 2-yard run by Craig James, who ran for 104 yards that day; two Tony Franklin field goals; and a fumble recovery by Jim Bowman for a touchdown to close out the scoring, putting us ahead for good.

We hammered them on the ground, big time. I was calling the plays again, and they had Mike Haynes at one corner and Lester Hayes at the other corner. And I can tell you right now, going into that game I had no intention of throwing against those two. We only threw the ball fifteen times, with one of them being a completion thrown by Craig James, who wound up leading our team with just three catches. Morgan caught one pass, and Fryar caught none. We basically threw to James and a few to our tight ends, and that was it. We found a weakness in their defense, and we just kept hammering them over and over and over, keeping the ball on the ground. We didn't gain a whole lot on most of the forty-nine rushes, but we had possession of the football for a second shy of thirty-seven minutes. Naturally, that kept their offense off the field and kept the clock moving.

The other thing about running the ball is field position—maybe they stop you and then you punt, but you make them go 80 yards. Teams don't go 80 yards for touchdowns very often. So if you can keep them backed up and make them go a long way, you're going to win games. Of course you also do that by not making turnovers. Against the Raiders we did lose two fumbles, but we didn't throw any interceptions.

Turnovers were a huge part of our playoff run, and, for that matter, of our season. See, at Paris High School, under my dad as coach, he had us take a water break midway through every practice. Texas heat in the summer is unbearable, so he would stop for us to get water. But when we came back, we would go to a position coach who had several footballs. We'd have three or four groups out there and they'd throw the ball on the ground and we would have to get it. It was a fumble-recovery drill, and during all the years I was in Paris High School we were trained to recover loose balls.

If you've ever stopped to think about a bouncing football on the ground, you cannot predict the way it will go. It has a screwed-up design to start with, and when it hits the ground and starts bouncing and rolling, it goes everywhere. So whenever you are faced with recovering a fumble on the ground, you've got yourself a challenge. My senior year at Paris High School, we won ten games and lost one. The ball went on the ground twenty-nine times on fumbles, and we got twenty-seven of them. And we won one close game after another. The difference in those close games was two or three fumble recoveries every game. Those experiences would later help my coaching record.

As a matter of fact, when I got to be the head coach of the Patriots, I explained the same story to our team every year. And I told them, "That's why we're going to work on recovering fumbles every day." At one point one of the players said to me, "Coach, why don't we work on picking the ball up, too, once it's fumbled." I agreed, and we started to do that. We'd throw the football on the ground and have them pick it up and run with it. On the entire season, our opponents recovered a total of twelve fumbles while we recovered thirty-seven. That's a huge difference, one that made an enormous contribution to our cause all year long.

Well, getting back to that division title game against the Raiders, our guys forced the key fumble that Bowman secured for a touchdown. That was typical of what was happening that year. It wasn't any accident. They were trained that way. They believed in their ability, because they started seeing those plays happen. And once players realize that what they're practicing works, then, boy, they really get after it—they take pride in it.

We forced five fumbles against the Raiders, adding to the three fumbles New York made when we played against the Jets earlier; and in our next game, we recovered four of the Dolphins' five fumbles. That was in the conference championship game. In all, we recovered nine out of thirteen fumbles. That was often the difference in the games. On the way to the Super Bowl, the turnover ratio was absolutely off the charts.

One of the things that started to happen late in the season was that our running game got cranked up. When Grogan got hurt, I took over the play calling. I began to realize we could hammer people, and the thing that I learned about the running game was that one way to defend a great quarterback and a great offense is to not let them play. And, as I mentioned regarding how this worked in our win over the Raiders, one of the ways you don't let them play is you run the ball, make first downs, and run the clock. That was one of the formulas we used when I was calling the plays for Eason.

If you look back at the statistics for some of those postseason contests, we ran the ball a lot. We ran nearly fifty times against the Raiders, almost forty times versus the Jets, and in our playoff game versus Miami, we ran the ball fifty-nine times for 255 yards and threw the ball just twelve times. Of course Eason hit on ten of those passes, and three of the completions were for scores. They couldn't stop us on the ground. And when you can hammer, hammer, hammer, then sneak throw them, you got them—they're sitting ducks.

Miami had gone 12–4 during the regular season. They were tough, but that day things went our way, and the win was a relatively easy one. That gave us twelve wins over our last fourteen games.

Miami had a weakness on their defense, and I realized it, and we kept hitting the "4" hole and the "5" hole, and back to the "4" a couple times. Good for 3 yards, 5 yards, 4 yards, and 5 yards. We just kept making first downs, and we kept Dan Marino on the bench—that's where you want him. That's the best place for him, because Dan Marino can't hurt you when he's sitting on the bench.

That was the Miami Dolphins Achilles heel—they didn't have a defense that could stop the running game, and we had a good running game. That was the main reason we beat them. We had the ball for forty minutes and we let Marino play twenty. In that time he threw forty-eight passes, trying to play catch-up football. He did throw two touchdowns, but he also threw two interceptions.

Anyway, we led 17–7 at the half on short passes to Tony Collins and Derrick Ramsey and a field goal, then we tacked on a touchdown on another short pass, a 2-yard toss to Robert Weathers from Eason in the third quarter. We wrapped it up with a 1-yard touchdown run by Mosi Tatupu in the fourth quarter to win it, 31–14.

So it was on to the Super Bowl to meet the Chicago Bears. This was the season the Bears rolled to an undefeated start to their season—going unbeaten deep into the season and virtually unchallenged in almost all of their games. Going into their Monday night game of December 2 against the Dolphins, who were then 8–4 on the year, Chicago was 12–0, and there was a lot of talk about them going the entire season without a loss. Miami beat them, though, 38–24. Still, it would be the Bears' only loss of the nineteen total games they played.

They not only went 15–1 during the regular season, they won five games by 20 or more points. They played six games versus teams that ended the year with 10-plus wins, and they won five of those contests, outslugging those opponents by a combined score of 178–71. In the post-season they shutout their first two opponents, then continued to prevent touchdowns until the final quarter of the Super Bowl.

We got our ass handed to us by the Bears in the Super Bowl at the Louisiana Superdome. We were humiliated 46–10, and the main reason wasn't differences in player talent or coaching. There wasn't one thing I could have done about the fact that we had enough talent to match the Chicago Bears, but they had a tremendous defensive coach named Buddy Ryan who had spent eight years installing that Bears defense. I had only one year to start our offense, so we put a first-grade offense on the field against a PhD defense.

With this being my first year with the offense, I had to keep things A, B, C simple and not go any further. You can start adding a few "letters" later on, but I still think the simplicity of what we were doing by design was a great strength. We were able to execute what we were doing well because we weren't doing too much.

However, that put us at a real disadvantage against the Bears. We didn't have any secrets, so to speak. The simplicity of our system hurt us because we were A, B, and C, and they were the full alphabet. As a matter of fact, in this comparison we were only A and B. I still believe that if our team had had as much time as Chicago had to install our offense and defense, the game wouldn't have ended with a 46–10 score. It would have been very close. We had enough talent to match them. Who knows? Maybe Walter Payton would have been the difference or maybe even

Ryan, or Mike Ditka, who was the Chicago head coach and an outstanding leader and competitor. Still, it would have been close in my opinion.

Their defense certainly was packed with standout players, including linebacker Wilber Marshall; defensive end Richard Dent, who had seventeen sacks that season; another linebacker who had ten and a half sacks in Otis Wilson; tackle Steve McMichael; strong safety Dave Duerson; Dan Hampton, who was mainly used as a defensive end; and middle linebacker Mike Singletary. Dent, Wilson, Hampton, Duerson, and Singletary all made it to the Pro Bowl that year. Plus, McMichael, Dent, and Singletary were all first-team All-Pro selections. The team was stacked. In fact, along with Walter Payton, three of their defensive players later became Hall of Famers: Dent, Hampton, and Singletary. I felt their front seven defenders compared favorably to the great Steelers defense from their glory years. Speaking of defense, somehow we held Payton to 61 yards in twenty-two carries in the Super Bowl, but it didn't matter.

The Bears knew everything we were doing, and they were able to stop us. We were held to 7 yards on the ground on eleven carries. Our longest run from scrimmage was good for just 3 yards. We only scored a field goal in the first quarter and a meaningless touchdown on a Grogan pass to Fryar in the final quarter. We were limited to 177 yards passing, and their players teed up on us, racking up seven sacks, meaning our net passing yards as a team was just 116, giving us 123 total yards of offense.

Again, I have to say that if we had had a five-year offense against a five-year defense, it wouldn't have been a 46–10 game, because we did have the players to match them. But that was the way it was, so we weren't able to match them.

All in all, I was the head coach of the New England Patriots from the second half of the 1984 season through 1989. One of the rules of thumb that I had as a very young player, and I took it into professional football, was, "Full speed. Snap to whistle." I preached that in New England. Full speed—give me some reason why not. My players definitely knew what I expected, and there wasn't any waffling on that. You go 100 percent, or your butt is going to be in deep trouble and you ain't going to be around here very long. It's that simple.

The reason for this rule goes back to the fact that, and this was true in Texas high school football, the competitive level in the game is such that the margin of victory is razor thin. In the NFL you cannot afford to leave anything on the table. When the game is over, I want to know that we did not leave one stone unturned or one effort unexpended.

I think my credibility was definitely there because of my background. That was a great asset, but that only goes so far. Coming to work with that in my favor was great, but then I had to follow it up. That got their attention, but if I didn't have something to give them after that, forget it.

I was honored that the Vince Lombardi Committee selected me as the Coach of the Year for the 1985 season. United Press International named me the AFC Coach of the Year. I'm sure making it to the Super Bowl in my first full season as head coach was a deciding factor in my receiving honors that season.

Despite some problems, we came back as a unified team the next year. In June I was rewarded for our success in 1985 by being given a five-year contract. We started regrouping and going about our business again, and we came back and had a helluva year the next year.

We finished at 11–5 again for the 1986 season, and this time that record was good enough to win the East Division, one game ahead of the Jets and three ahead of the Dolphins, who slipped, becoming a .500 team.

On January 4, 1987, we met the Denver Broncos in Mile High Stadium. They also finished the season at 11–5, but earned the home field advantage. The Broncos won, 22–17, behind John Elway, who scored their first touchdown on a 22-yard scamper and later fired a scoring pass of 48 yards to Vance Johnson.

Morgan caught three passes for exactly 100 yards and two touchdowns from Tony Eason. However, Sammy Winder ran for 102 yards on us, and Denver kept possession of the football for more than thirty-five of the sixty minutes of the game.

You know, there's a lot to consider in coaching that goes beyond game strategy. I never studied psychology, and I'm not even sure when it became a part of my thinking, but certain concepts of psychology have applied to my coaching. Yet I never really linked the concepts of confidence and discipline to psychology.

There are many intangibles that go into making a good football player, and one certainly is confidence. It's not just quarterbacks; it's true for most any position. There's just a wide variety of personality types. I think you get more conscious of this when you become a head coach and you're working with forty, fifty, or fifty-five men on a squad.

Another principle about football that can take some time to learn is that there's more than one way to get it done. That is the number one fundamental—don't be looking to put everybody in the same category of playmaker. The only thing that really counts out there on game day is, do they get it done? And there are different approaches to it, different personalities to it, and different ways to go about preparing. It's very interesting to observe this phenomenon—it's one of the most interesting things in coaching, because you just never really know a guy until you get in a position to start learning about him. You wonder, "OK, how does this guy go about getting it done? We're going to put him in this position and this is his assignment and his job." And then you don't get too dogmatic about how to do it. Find out if the guy gets it done, and gets it done his way. Again, that's the object—to get it done. There are a lot of different personality types that end up being tremendous competitors and winners.

While I always admired Unitas and his ability to lead, to excel even when in pain, and to execute his game like a field general, I know not everyone can be a Unitas, especially when it comes to toughness. There's no question that different players have different levels of pain tolerance, and I think, basically, they're born with it. I don't think it has anything to do with their mental attitude or whether they want to play through pain or not. I think some guys are just not as tough as others, but it doesn't mean that they're not reliable football players.

Protecting the football is another, *seemingly* little detail, but to my way of thinking, it is something very important to do, and to coach. In my NFL career I handled the ball more than six hundred times over thirteen years and was charged with a fumble just once.

I learned to tuck the ball away the instant I got it. From then on, every single time I caught a ball, even in practice or just fooling around, I'd secure it. The thrill of being a receiver came with running with the ball. I always tried to explode the moment I had control of the ball, because that could often be the difference between making a first down or a touchdown, but you have to secure it first.

I've discussed that fumble already, but there's another story behind it, one that goes back to the value of a bad experience and a bad memory. I'm going to go back to my senior year at SMU. We were going to Austin, Texas, to play the Texas Longhorns before sixty or seventy thousand people. We were going to go back to pass plays twice in that game where I caught the football moving inside the Texas 20-yard line, scoring territory. I caught the ball and I fumbled twice and lost the ball. One time nobody even touched me—I caught it and I don't know what happened to the darn football. It just came out, slung on the ground, and Texas got it. On the other one, I caught the pass and a guy slapped my arm a little bit, and the ball came out again. Because we lost two fumbles, the game ended in a 13–13 tie. Had I not fumbled, but rather advanced the ball inside the Texas 20, we would have won the game. That tie game cost us the Southwest Conference championship and a trip to the Cotton Bowl.

Whenever the reality of that sunk into my thick head, I got so damned mad I could have bit a nail in two, and the more I thought about it, the madder I got. That kind of a waste—that kind of stupidity, that lack of fundamentals—branded that memory on my butt and my brain and wherever else, and I started catching the football in practice situations with that memory.

I started catching them no matter where they were—low, high, deep, short, inside, outside—and I'd slam that ball into my rib cage and grip it tight in the front, grip it tight in the back, with the elbow pressure into the rib cage. Every time, over and over and over. Hundreds and hundreds and hundreds and hundreds of times. That memory never left me. The anger never left me, and I swore it would never happen again.

It was what you would call a real, real valuable bad experience, and it led to correcting the problem. First of all, it led to identifying a problem I didn't know existed, and then the cost of it motivated me to never let it happen again.

When training an athlete for any particular skill, it's drill and repetition, drill and repetition, drill and repetition. Then in a game, that skill is automatic—you don't even think about it, you just do it, because you've done it over and over and over. It's discipline. And when I was the head coach of the Patriots, every year after I told our team the story about my fumbling, I'd say, "Now you know the background of why we're going to be very careful with this football in practice. Now you know why every player on this football team is going to carry a football during our warm-up drills. You're going to carry it tight and squeeze it in the front and squeeze it in the back, and you're going to learn how to carry a football. The centers, the guards, the tackles, the defensive linemen, the linebackers, the defensive backs, and, of course, all the receivers and so on." In my six years of coaching the Patriots, we led the NFL in the least fumbles practically every year.

In 1987 we dropped to second place with a record of just 8–7 in a season shortened one game due to a players' strike. That year Doug Flutie joined our team. He was a fine college player, a Heisman Trophy winner, in fact. In the NFL, though, he was just too small. He was listed at 5 feet, 10 inches and 180 pounds, making him the shortest quarterback I ever worked with.

The strike began after the second week of the season, after our September 21 game, and the games of the following week were canceled. Flutie had begun the season with Chicago. On October 4, the league decided to go ahead and play what would have been the fourth game of the season as well as the rest of the remaining games on the schedule rather than cancel any more contests.

So teams started signing players off the street, so to speak—free agents and guys from the United States Football League, the Canadian Football League, and so forth. In all, three games were played with replacement players before the strike ended.

The Patriots had quickly signed Flutie as a quarterback. He was a local boy who had played at Boston College, and Billy Sullivan was a Boston College and Flutie fan. Those factors would become a problem later.

Flutie started just one game for us, two weeks after we played our first game without our regulars. We knocked off Houston 21–7, and Flutie went fifteen for twenty-five for 199 yards and one touchdown pass.

However, by the following Sunday, the strike had ended and Tony Eason was under center again with Flutie as the third quarterback.

Despite that, I still think Flutie was one of the greatest athletes I've ever been around. He was as sharp as you could get, and he was a leader who had great charisma. He threw the ball very accurately with that good, strong arm of his. He had quick feet, and he was a scrambler who could throw accurately on the run.

His big handicap was simply his height. As you played game after game and studied the films, you saw unfolding in front of you the fact that he'd be back in the pocket and the guys would be breaking open, but he couldn't see him, couldn't see out of that pocket. So the ball wouldn't be coming out, and that was really a tremendous handicap.

Nowadays I don't think he would even get drafted because, for one thing, his playing gave the NFL a confirmation about the fact that a height disadvantage like his just can't be overcome. I'm just theorizing here, but after the Doug Flutie experience, people who were in the league at that time saw it and knew not to go that route because it's just not going to work.

I don't know if the height and size of defensive linemen have continued to increase or not to a *huge* extent over the years, but I have a feeling it has. Now you're up against more defensive ends and tackles who have height, and they put those hands up and you have a vision problem.

Take Johnny Manziel, *listed* at 6 feet. I watched him in college and when he was a rookie with the Browns. He is a fascinating case. He's the kind of guy many people wouldn't bet against. Having experience with Flutie gives me a real insight into what Manziel is going to deal with. If I was an NFL executive who was going to be held responsible for a draft pick, I would not have drafted Manziel. And I wrote those words more than a year before the Browns released him.

Eddie LeBaron, who was only around 5 feet, 9 inches, was another interesting case. He played from 1952 through 1963. There were a lot of similarities between LeBaron and Flutie. They both had quick feet and could run. Both were accurate throwers and great leaders. LeBaron was very effective, but I don't think there was any question that his height disadvantage was a real handicap to him and his teams, Washington and Dallas. Even in those days the defensive linemen were pretty big.

Getting back to Flutie, even when he was with New England, he fooled around with kicking. He was actually an excellent kicker. Percentage-wise he was perfect: one for one lifetime in games. In his final season in the NFL, 2005, when he returned to the Patriots under Bill Belichick, he was used sparingly as a quarterback—going five for ten on his passes for the year. However, in the last quarter of the final game of his career on January, 1, 2006, at the age of forty-three, he was sent in to kick a point after touchdown and *drop kicked* it successfully. I would have to say he had to be the last guy in professional football who even knew how to drop kick. The last time a drop kick had been successful in the NFL was way back in 1941.

In the 1988 season, four different quarterbacks got at least one start for us, never a great situation. Grogan started four, but lost three before Flutie took over. Flutie started nine, winning six. Eason's record at quarterback, in two December games, was 1–1, and Tom Ramsey got one start, a win. That adds up to a 9–7 season. We finished third in our division.

By 1989 I knew, and the team knew, Flutie wasn't the right man for the job, but Pat Sullivan was enamored of him and wanted me to start him. We had opened the season with Eason as the starter and went 1–2 in September. The following month, I started Flutie in three games and he hit on just fifteen of forty-one, then nine of eighteen, and twelve of thirty. He threw two touchdowns, but four interceptions, and he never threw for more than 176 yards in one of those games.

I had a problem on my hands. Even though I knew it would upset Sullivan, I had to do the right thing. I went with Grogan and Marc Wilson instead, again carrying four quarterbacks. The decision not to stick with Flutie would eventually help lead to my being fired. I was looking for a quarterback who could win for me and the one who is the best guy I've got. If you let the owner start making decisions for you, and your football team is going to know it, then, baby, you're in deep trouble.

With a record of 5–11 in 1989, my only losing year as a head coach is one I would like to forget. We were plagued with injuries, leading the

NFL with the most players on the injured-reserve list, with nineteen, eight more than the second-worst hit team, and fourteen more than the league average per team. We ended the year fourth in the East Division, ahead of just the Jets, who went 4–12.

Victor Kiam, who bought the team from Billy Sullivan in 1988 and retained Pat Sullivan as the general manager, wanted me to reorganize my staff, bringing in outside people. Those two believed making a drastic change in my coaching staff would solve the problem we were having, but the problem was that our draft had been failing for several years in a row—our number one picks had not panned out.

Kiam knew nothing about football. I'm not even sure he knew how to spell *football.* He wanted to come in and be the owner of an NFL team and make all the decisions, because it's his pride of authorship, it's, "I want to put my stamp on this." And that can be fatal.

What you had was a situation with amateurs meddling in a professional arena—that was the problem. Neither Kiam nor Pat Sullivan, who was under pressure from Kiam, knew their butts from first base about who was a good assistant coach. I basically had to tell them that, and that there wasn't any way they were going to fire my coaching staff. They could either keep the coaches or fire my ass, but I wasn't going to let them fire them. If you're a football coach like I was, sitting in a situation like that, you can't put up with it. I do things I believe in, and I'm not going to do things I don't believe in. When I was asked if I had ever wavered regarding my beliefs on this issue, I told them that I could not do that. I would not compromise my beliefs.

The main reason why I could never allow the front office to fire any of my coaches was the players and the coaches would know that I caved in to those people who didn't know what they were doing. As soon as that happened, the respect of both my coaches and my players would be gone, and I was not going to go that route. I would never lose my self-respect, either.

Under my contract, which still had a year to run, naming my staff was my prerogative, but when I said they could take the job and shove it, I was fired one day before my fifty-seventh birthday. Our record over my coaching tenure was 48–39, the best record any of the other nine Patriots coaches had ever posted to date. Going into my last season, only two active NFL head coaches had a streak going of never experiencing a full season in which their team did not finish with a winning record, Jerry Burns of the Vikings and me.

My next move had me in Detroit for the 1991 season, my second stint with the Lions. Their head coach, Wayne Fontes, called me about coming there as the quarterback coach, something I had never done before. We had a good season, going 12–4 while winning the NFL Central Division title.

Rodney Peete and Erik Kramer both started eight regular-season games that season. If you put Kramer in the educational field, he'd be a PhD. He had very strong leadership skills and a good arm. Peete was the starting quarterback to open the season, and he took the Lions to a 6–2 record before an Achilles injury ended his season.

Detroit drafted real well. There was great talent there. Barry Sanders was just twenty-three years old then, and he ran for 1,548 yards and sixteen touchdowns. I worked with him, but when I first met him, I said, "Barry, when you get the ball, the goal line is in that direction, so head for it and do a lot of juking along the way." He just carried it out to a tee. Obviously my advice was a joke. This guy didn't need any coaching. What you did with him was take him to the field on Sunday and give him the ball, and he'd take care of the rest. He was a totally unique talent; nobody ever used the same style that he did. Nobody could. He was born with that ability, to move like he did and jump here and there, explode, cut back, and do everything that needed to be done. He was a superb athlete going to work, worth the price of a ticket.

Defensive back Bennie Blades was a Pro Bowl player in 1991. So was linebacker Chris Spielman, who also was a First-Team All-Pro selection. Kicker Mel Gray, Lomas Brown our left offensive tackle, and our nose tackle Jerry Ball all were either All-Pros, Pro Bowl players, or both.

In the opening round of postseason play, we defeated the Cowboys 38–6, but the Washington Redskins beat us in DC by a score of 41–10 in the conference championship game. Two weeks later they would win the Super Bowl over the Bills, 37–24.

In 1992 Denver's head coach, Dan Reeves, called me about coming out there to work with John Elway, but not as a receiver coach, because they already had one. They gave me the title of quarterback coach. I took the job and moved to the Denver area.

Elway was one of the greatest physical talents at quarterback I've ever been around. He was the entire package you're looking for in a quarterback. He had that great height of 6 foot, 4 inches, and he had size, like 215 pounds. And he had speed—I mean, he could run fast. He had off-the-board intelligence, great charisma, heart, and leadership. He had good football instincts, a tremendous competitive spirit, and quick feet. And he had that tremendous arm. He was like Sandy Koufax and Don Drysdale—power. Speed on the ball and accuracy. And that's about all you could hope for.

When Reeves hired me to work with Elway there was one factor I had studied most about him: He was throwing way too many interceptions. I had learned from experience—remember what I said earlier about Bill Munson—that a quarterback can stop throwing interceptions if he makes up his mind to stop throwing them. I wanted to focus on only one thing with Elway: throw the ball to our receivers or throw it away.

I knew I had to be very careful dealing with him, because he was a veteran player and I was a coach who had replaced the man who was his favorite coach of all time. That coach had been fired, and it was a very unpopular move with Elway. So I had a hard situation coming in there, and I immediately sensed it, so I never tried to push any boundaries with him. Actually, he didn't need much coaching.

When I started working with him, I analyzed his career up to that point. I told him, "John, I'm not here to teach you how to throw the ball or work on your footwork and all that other stuff. I'm a pass receiver and I don't really know a thing about that stuff, and I couldn't care less. But there is one thing I can help you with. You're throwing too many interceptions for someone with your intelligence and your ability."

It was interesting because this was earlier in his career. Now, later on, when Mike Shanahan went out there, Elway had some great years with him. He wasn't throwing interceptions. I don't know what happened—he didn't buy into what I said—but he must have respected what Shanahan said about this. I think Elway really liked him.

Actually, over the year I worked with Elway, his rate of throwing interceptions was 5.4 percent. The next two years under new head coach Wade Phillips, that percentage plummeted to 1.8 and 2.0. Then, when Shanahan took over the job, Elway's percentages remained low at 2.6, 3.0, 2.2, and 2.8, even though he was then in his mid- and late thirties.

In 1992, when Elway started games, we went 8–4. Unfortunately he missed four games from late November into mid-December, and the team lost all four contests, so we wound up breaking even with an 8–8 record.

When Reeves got fired, his entire staff got fired. I was out of work after I had spent just one year there. That was my last coaching position. We were renting a house in the mountains west of Denver and, financially at that stage, I could afford to get out of football. So my family stayed there, because we loved living in Colorado. There was 7,500 feet of elevation where we were with three hundred days of sunshine and no humidity. We had beautiful scenery. It was a tremendous experience living out there. We stayed there about thirteen years.

My coaching days were over, but my days of continuing to watch and study the game of football were far from being through.

Chapter Nine

The NFL Then and Now

Before I give some thoughts on the game of football today, let me praise some of the great receivers from my era. I'll start with Elroy Hirsch. As I said previously, the movie about his life, *Crazy Legs, All American*, inspired me to want to be a wide receiver.

Gino Marchetti tells a story about Hirsch:

> *He was something. He taught me a lesson. We played the Rams in Baltimore, and he was playing in tight so they could get an angle on me on end runs and whatever. That's what good coaches do—they moved him maybe 3 or 4 yards to my left, I guess, and they would run this sweep toss, and I probably had my eye on the ball too much. Anyway, he was sitting out there and every time I'd go to hit him, he'd come from the side and just whack me. All through the game he kept saying, "Nice going, Gino. Nice going." and "God, Almighty, you really hit hard." Here I am walking back to my huddle feeling like a giant. There's a big man, a big name in the NFL at that time. I felt really great. They beat us 42–6, or whatever.*
>
> *Next day at the meeting the first thing out of Weeb's mouth—he's upset because we didn't show very well—were, "You know what? If anybody in this room would've told me that Crazy Legs Hirsch could block Marchetti, I would have never believed it, particularly because he blocked him all afternoon." So there's old Hirsch complimenting me, and I'm eating it all up, but all the time he was knocking me on my butt and I never realized it. I thought I was blocking him out, but he was*

blocking me. The films embarrassed me, and the coaches kept rewinding the film. "Watch this," Weeb or the line coach would say. "What were you doing there, Marchetti, huh? Sleeping?" So, big lesson learned.

Hirsch was a great receiver with the Los Angeles Rams, but his pro career started with the Chicago Rockets. When he wound up out there on the West Coast, the Rams ended up with one of the greatest offensive collections of personnel ever. The Rams also had Bob Waterfield and Norm Van Brocklin, two quarterbacks who are both all-time greats, Hall of Famers, in fact. Hirsch was in an environment in which his great athletic skills were being fully used. He was a halfback in college, and the Rams converted him to a flanker. His specialty, as it turned out, the thing that set him apart in his greatest season, 1951, when he led the league in eight categories, was the long ball. The way the Rams were going for it was unbelievable, and he was making these catches over the shoulder, directly over the head, with outstretched fingers, on the dead run. He'd catch it and run another 40 yards. He was spectacular.

The Rams also had Tank Younger and Deacon Dan Towler, a man who our Colts defensive players thought the world of. They said he was one of the toughest guys to tackle they ever had to face. Jon Arnett played for that team, too. They were just overloaded with talent.

Other great receivers back then were Max McGee and Boyd Dowler, two big guys who were really impressive and ran great routes for Green Bay. As I started coaching later on in pro football and I looked back over big receivers, they were the model for me, and I thought, "If you can get them big, get 'em," because they were hard to handle due to their size plus great athletic ability. The Packers also had Bill Howton, a premier receiver, who twice led the league in yards gained on catches.

The 49ers had a great receiver named Billy Wilson who was 6 foot, 3 inches and had tremendous catching ability and great hands. The Lions had Hopalong Cassady out of Ohio State; he was also one of their great receivers. Tommy McDonald was another great pro, mainly with the Philadelphia Eagles.

When I came into the league, Otto Graham and his Browns were in their prime. They had Dante Lavelli and Mac Speedie together from

1946 through 1952, two of the best of the day. Paul Brown handled that group, and he was a genius of a coach. Throw in Marion Motley at fullback, and the Browns had offensive firepower. Later Paul Warfield would become another great Cleveland (and Miami) receiver. He was poetry in motion because of his running style and the way he handled himself and made his cuts. He was just so smooth.

The Bears never really had a Pro Bowl–type receiver while I was playing, except for Harlon Hill, who had a very brief career in the NFL. While he was there, though, he was one of the most beautiful athletes I had ever seen. Our defensive backs said he was one of the most difficult guys to cover and handle because he was big for the time—6 feet, 3 inches and two hundred pounds—and he could run like the wind and catch anything. The Bears were very good at throwing the deep ball to him. He led the NFL twice in his first three seasons for the most yards per reception. In fact to this day his career average of 20.8 yards per catch ranks third, ahead of guys like Warfield and Bob Hayes.

When I coached, I worked with Dave Logan, a big receiver for the Browns. He was a natural athlete, and when he stuck his hands up in the air to catch, he was going to catch the football even though he never worked a bit on catching the ball. He was just born with that ability. You didn't have to train him to catch. My drills were immaterial to him.

When you look at some of the most important facets of receiving, for players of yesterday and today, you certainly consider players' hands. I spent so much time working on my hands each year. When you catch seventy, eighty, or more footballs a day for ten months, you really work on your hands.

As for who I think is the best in the game in more recent years, I have to admit that I mainly keep up with the Patriots. So when speaking of fine receivers, the first guy I think of is Wes Welker, who has led the NFL in receptions three times. I enjoy watching him operate. He's sort of a carbon copy of McDonald—small, but quick, and he can run like heck and catch anything.

Still, of all the players I've seen since I left the game, Jerry Rice remains in a class by himself in a lot of ways. He also had what I had in Baltimore: He came to a team that had great management, great coaching, great quarterbacks, and a great supporting cast all around. In that atmosphere, Rice flourished like nobody's business, because this guy could do it all—short, medium, deep, and running with the ball after the catch. And he had durability. I would say that if you were trying to come up with which guys in the NFL had the greatest work ethic, Rice is going to be in the conversation real quick. He not only had the physical tools to do it, he brought a work ethic that was second to none.

I think Jerry and I know exactly what it's like to be set on a goal. If I had to pick one player who reminds me the most of me as a player, Rice would be the guy. I don't think he dropped many passes, and he worked hard at his trade. When people talk about pro athletes, you don't often hear them talk about work ethic much, but with Rice, it's different. A strong work ethic and Rice go hand-in-hand. I think he was also one of those guys who, just like I did, worked out virtually year-round. I know when I played, I took two months off and then went back to work. That's one reason why he had such durability to accomplish at top level for so many years—he worked his butt off.

As for the best quarterbacks ever, let's start with today's elite: Peyton Manning and Tom Brady. They deserve to be compared to the all-time greats like Unitas. I put them right up in there with Unitas.

Remember how I told you how clever Unitas was at choosing just the right play to call, how he would elect to run something opposite of what our opponents were looking for? And how important it is to have players who aren't just physically gifted, but also mentally sharp? I can't prove this, but I think there are still coaches out there who recognize players who can think, and there are players out there today, such as Manning and Brady, who can think, players who coaches can give free rein to, free rein to use their natural talents. Human nature hasn't changed. Now that Manning has retired, unfortunately there is one less player in the NFL with that ability and the freedom to use it.

Sure, there are coaches who try to dictate everything, but you've still got coaches who know how to hold them and know how to fold them. One of them is up there in New England; his name is Belichick. You've got another one in the guy who handled Peyton Manning, and that's

John Fox. There's no question in my mind that what you're looking at in Manning and Brady is a whole lot of Unitas.

Maybe a lot of coaches don't let their quarterbacks call their own plays nowadays, but when you realize that you've got an unusual talent like Brady or Manning, you know what they bring to the game—and that's a knowledge of the game, an intense study of the game, an instinct for it—you get out of the way and let these guys play. I admire those two guys.

The team I used to coach, the Patriots, have been so successful lately, doing the right things. There are three fundamental, critical factors for a team to have success. First of all, the owners have got to have enough sense to hire a guy like a Belichick. Second, he has to have enough sense to take this low-round draft pick, Tom Brady, as a quarterback—the third critical factor. Brady was selected in the sixth round as the 199th overall player taken. So, you've got an owner, a head coach, and a quarterback, and you've got the ingredients to have a championship team. The same was true with Manning. I have to admire Bill Polian, the general manager of the Colts, for having had enough brains to get Manning. There are a lot of great throwing quarterbacks today, and that's what the game revolves around.

My experience in the NFL has shown me that if early on you put a guy like Brady in a different organization, maybe we wouldn't even know his name today. As I've said many times, based on my analysis of Unitas over the years, a player is the beneficiary of everything it takes for his abilities to operate at absolute full force. What it takes to begin with is an owner who's got enough sense to hire a head coach and let him get the job done. And the head coach has got to have enough sense—when he's got a player like Unitas, Brady, or Manning—to let him do his thing. It's like riding a great racehorse—unhitch the bit and let the horse run. This is what you're looking at with Brady and Manning. Their coaches put these racehorses on the track, point them in the right direction, give them some tools, and let them go.

This gives you the best chance of winning, because these guys know the game in depth; they have the instincts, the competitive spirit, and the physical skills; and they've been given talented players around them who they've got to have in order to move the ball with a balanced attack and protection up front. Even with skilled quarterbacks, if you start relying on throwing too much, you're going to get your butt handed to you sooner or later.

Take Peyton's father, Archie, a great college quarterback out of Mississippi, drafted as the second overall pick in the 1971 NFL draft by a poor New Orleans Saints team. At Mississippi, Archie finished fourth and third in the Heisman voting in 1969 and 1970, and he had thrown for 4,753 yards in twenty-eight games. New Orleans was coming off seasons in which they had won just three, four, five, and two games. So in just their fifth year of existence, they handed Manning the starting job.

The Saints won just four games, and Manning's record as the starting quarterback was 3–5–2. Throughout his career in New Orleans, his best record was 8–8, and he suffered through seasons where his team's records with him as the starter were 2–11, 1–8, and 1–15. Yet he was a fine quarterback. In fact in his second season, he led the league in both pass completions and attempts. But, again, that's not necessarily good. He *had* to throw the ball frequently, because, for one thing, his Saints were frequently playing from behind, forced to throw more than run to catch up to opponents. Perhaps more important, his team rarely had a strong running game. The year he led the league in pass attempts and completions (1972) the Saints' leading rusher had a mere 381 yards. No threat of a run means the pass rushers are going to tee off.

Watching great players over a lot of years, and with my perspective as a coach, I've said to myself, "If I was the head coach of an NFL team now and you gave me Peyton Manning, Tom Brady, or John Unitas, I'd win a world championship. Those three are in an elite group, without question." I don't care which one, I'll just close my eyes, reach into the hat, grab one of them, and I'll win a world championship. It doesn't matter which one because they can all do it, and they *will* do it. Among the stars of today, I also enjoy watching Drew Brees. He's a classic quarterback.

Of course in my day there were other great quarterbacks—give them to me, and I'd win a championship. Off the top of my head, some other greats from my era include Norm Van Brocklin and Bart Starr of the Packers, and I was in the league when Y. A. Tittle played with the 49ers. Here's a guy that didn't do anything but throw strikes. He led the NFL in completion percentage twice, at 63.1 percent and 60.2 percent, and that was in his next-to-last season when he was pushing the age of forty.

Then there was Sonny Jurgensen and John Brodie, who didn't play with great defenses behind them; the 49ers defenses were just so-so. They weren't like Starr, who got to play with great defenses, or Brady today. That's a big part of being a winning quarterback—you've got to be linked to a great defense.

Then there's Fran Tarkenton. He's a different type than most of the quarterbacks I've mentioned. That's the interesting thing about sports: There's more than one way to get it done. There are different styles that different people bring to their game. It's fascinating to see how different athletes have their approach, how they do their job and are hugely effective.

Now, Joe Kapp wasn't a great quarterback, but he played for the Minnesota Vikings when they were a good team. He was such a competitor. He could have been a great middle linebacker. A lot of the great quarterbacks had a heart as big as a lion. If you played them on defense they'd knock your head off.

I was coaching in Dallas when Don Meredith was playing for them. Some of his years there were when they were just building a team, and he got hit all the time as a young quarterback. But give me a Meredith, and I'll win a championship. In his final season, surrounded by some talent, the Cowboys were 11–2 in his starts. And I was with Dallas when Roger Staubach came out of the Navy. This is another guy you can win with. More recently you've got Dan Fouts and Dan Marino.

Obviously when you choose some of the greats, you're going to be influenced by your age, your time frame, and your personal exposure to players, as opposed to just watching them on television. Different people are going to have their favorites.

There are many fine defensive backs today, but we had some greats, too. In no particular order, I will name some who gave me the hardest time. Dick Lynch was a really fine man-to-man cover guy—and you have to remember, it was practically all man-to-man in those days. So, when you talk about defensive backs, you have to realize that their assignment was to cover some great receivers—and they didn't get a whole lot of help, either. Jesse Whittenton of the Packers was an excellent man-to-man guy, too.

Zones were developed later to give corners help. The team that introduced the zone defense, a three-deep zone, was the Colts when I was still active. They remained one of the few teams in the league that really used it back then. Charley Winner was our defensive back coach who put the zone in. When you stop to think about the simplicity of it, we played just that zone, but we would blitz every once in a while, sending two or three linebackers out of the man-to-man.

I played against Dick LeBeau of the Lions twice a year. He was one of the brightest corners you'll ever play against. He was bound and determined to keep you from getting a touchdown on him, and he pretty well carried that out.

Abe Woodson of the 49ers was tough. When he was at the University of Illinois, he was a track man as well as a football player. He won the 100-yard dash in track in the Big 10—that's the kind of speed he had.

Then there was Dick "Night Train" Lane, but he covered the other side of the field, on Lenny Moore when we played against him. They were two super athletes. I used to say to myself jokingly, "It's good they're up against each other. They deserve each other." I'm glad I didn't have to come up against Lane very much.

Author Dave Klein quoted Hall of Famer Lane as saying that guarding me "wasn't a question of staying with him. It was a question of slowing down enough so that he wouldn't stay clear in front of you. But then after you did everything you had to do, there he'd be with the ball in his arms. It got so I hated to hear his name." Of course I respected Lane, too.

When I watch the modern-day NFL, one thing I'm aware of about today's players is that there is some tremendous size and speed out there. These guys are super athletes.

People wonder if some of the great players of my day could star, or at least hold their own, if they played nowadays. Take our great defensive end, Gino Marchetti. Would he still excel against some of the huge offensive players in today's NFL? Well, he played against some big guys. A tackle for the 49ers named Bob St. Clair would fit in with the modern-day linemen without any problem. He was 6 feet, 9 inches and weighed in the 270 range, and Marchetti had to play him twice a year, even though he was only 6 foot, 4 inches and around 245 pounds—and it was always a battle. They had been college teammates at San Francisco. When those two went up against each other, you were looking at a classic match.

Marchetti was so quick and so powerful and athletic that to block him and try to keep him off the quarterback was a major job. They were holding him a lot, but he never did get all that carried away or upset with it—he just figured it was a part of what he was up against. And they really weren't all that successful against him anyway.

One thing you've got to remember is that there were twelve teams in the NFL in my early years. By 1961 the league had expanded to fourteen, then to sixteen teams by 1967, my final season. Today the talent is getting spread pretty thin. Expansion has seriously diluted the talent level of individual teams. You don't run up against the really great ones on a regular basis. Marchetti worked against great pass-blocking people—out of a twelve-game schedule I'm sure he had at least eight games where he was up against somebody who was really, really good. Percentage-wise, two thirds of the time he was up against a great one. Today, there's no way in the world you're going to come up with that many great ones.

Over a three-year span from 1957 through 1959, the last season the NFL had just twelve teams, there were seven future Hall of Fame quarterbacks playing—more than half of the teams had an all-time great on their squads. They were Len Dawson (even though he didn't see much action back then with the Steelers, where he broke in), Bobby Layne, Norm Van Brocklin, Y. A. Tittle, Sonny Jurgensen, Bart Starr, and Unitas.

In 1957, for example, we played seven different teams and faced a team with a future Hall of Fame quarterback on their roster in nine of our twelve games. That's a 75 percent Hall of Fame ratio. I would doubt seriously if you took any NFL team today and asked yourself the question, "Do any of these teams, 75 percent of the time, play a future Hall of Fame quarterback?"

When there were twelve teams in the league, each team had a maximum of thirty-five men on its roster. Now you've got thirty-two teams, and the rosters have also expanded. It's like the principle of inflation—you print more dollars, and the ones that you've got are worthless.

So, with so many teams in the league, I don't think you face a quality defense every week or face a top line defensive corner every week. But in my day, boy, you were going to have a hard time coming up with a team that's weak or with a cornerback who doesn't know his business. Now, there are sixty-four corners who have to get up there and cover. It's a quality issue that I think is demonstrated by that idea of inflation, and I don't think the United States is producing three times as many great football players as they used to.

So what you have today is a total inflation and dilution of the game of football as we knew it during the years I played. To put it another way, they've cheapened the game, and I find it hard to deal with when I watch what they've done. The players don't have any idea what they're involved with. What if they came up with a new rule saying they were going to reduce the league down to twelve teams? If that happened, the only players left standing would be the very best. The players just don't understand how the league has evolved and how there's been a multiplication of teams compared to my playing days—a dilution of talent.

I still enjoy watching football, though. There are great athletes, and I think the United States is turning out more of them than ever before. And, no, I'm not contradicting myself. To watch their skills is amazing. There are a lot of positives in the game today.

However, the game *is* different. It is not anywhere near what it was when I played, and what the owners of the league have decided to change is the offense. And the reason they have changed the offense, in my opinion, is strictly because they are concerned about television money. They are concern about getting people to watch the games, so they want more offense. It's marketing and selling tickets, and I don't agree with it.

They've changed the rules in football, and now they're allowing offensive linemen to hold, reach out, encircle, pull down, and grab. And they're giving quarterbacks double time to throw—receivers have *way* more time to get open. And they're giving running backs more and bigger holes to run through than ever would have been there in the old days.

All of this cheapens the game and changes it, skewing the history of the game. Modern-day records shouldn't be compared to the past. Unitas only had from 1.9 to around 2.4 seconds to throw. Today quarterbacks can get back there and hold the football for 3 to 4 seconds. They have much more time to look the field over, pick out a receiver, and deliver the ball to him than Unitas had when we teamed up. You've got a totally different game.

When I played, the offensive linemen couldn't extend their hands and arms. They had to keep them inside and use their chest to block. Any defensive lineman who played when the rules were strict regarding holding, but who also lasted into the era when holding rules loosened up, had to be upset. Modern defensive linemen don't really know anything about the history of the development of the rules, so they're probably not even aware of such changes. They probably think the way it is, is the way it always has been. I'm sure that they just accept the holding as, "That's the way it's done."

And today the defensive backs do a lot of grabbing and holding. In all the years I played, I never had anybody reach out and grab me, but maybe one time. Now you see it going on in every game. I call it the National Holding League.

Another thing that's quite different today than it was when I played is the way some players ask out of a game to take a breather. You see a receiver come back toward the huddle after running a long route or maybe after catching, say, several passes in a row. But instead of returning to the huddle, they gesture to the bench that they need to come out of the game.

Maybe they don't want to be in the game for the next play if they're not at 100 percent. I'm not really sure what the thinking is for these guys who wave a hand for relief. That never was the case for *anybody* in the days I played. Our conditioning was at an extremely high level.

I don't remember ever having total exhaustion at the end of any game when I played. I can't speak for other players, but my level of conditioning was off the board. I was so conditioned, I could run all day.

The 1958 sudden-death championship game against the Giants was a classic example of this. We threw the ball the entire doggone game, forty times in all. I was running pass routes all day long, and our condition level was so high that I don't think I was getting fatigued until maybe late in the game. The modern-day player comes off the field. I'm not sure whether or not they're taking advantage of a routine today—coming out is accessible to them. They probably just do it without thinking, but it wasn't a routine in the days I played. I'm thinking if they were playing in an era in which you just didn't do that, they probably would do just fine, too.

We did have tough players in my time, but I don't believe that football players of one era are any tougher than ones of another. However, when I played, guys would knock your ass off with a shoulder pad, and there were guys who would throw an elbow in your face or hit you with a fist. There were some dirty players.

We played a physical game back then, but concussions weren't a big topic. The first time I became aware of the reasons for concussions was in 1953 when I was a junior at SMU. I'm not going to name the college team that started it, because they should be ashamed, but they had a player or two who started using his headgear into the face. From that point on I started seeing it again, but just periodically. In thirteen years of playing in the NFL through 1967, I cannot recall a time when I saw an NFL player deliberately put headgear into somebody's face. I'm not saying it didn't happen, but I have no memory of it. It was not a part of the NFL culture then, even though we had some of the greatest, toughest defensive players of all time.

I did a lot of coaching through 1992, and using that tactic was very rare during my coaching years. However, one particular team introduced the deliberate, illegal use of headgear around the 1970s, I think. That's when all this business about concussions started happening. Then it started escalating and spread down to college football. Coaches began teaching it, and it became a part of the game with a great many players.

I've been around enough coaches to know there's a mentality among the modern-day coach who says, "Put your hat on him! Put your hat on him!"—meaning hit him with the helmet. It's an epidemic. And all these coaches who shout out that phrase never had a hat put on *their* face.

The Riddell helmet is an unforgiving blunt instrument. You might as well take a sledge hammer to somebody as a helmet. And the National Football League sat on their ass and did nothing about it.

You don't need any headgear tactic to make pro football a great spectator sport. It already was before that move came along. It's unnecessary and extremely damaging and dangerous, and it has long-lasting effects on multiple players today. I think the league is too ignorant to understand this. If that's not the case, then they understand exactly what it is and don't give a flip because of the amount of money coming in.

So, yes, I am totally against how defenders go about taking down the man with the football now. It seems there are a lot of times when defenders now don't so much try to employ the traditional skills of making a pure tackle as much as they try to maul whoever has the ball. I think the art of tackling has certainly deteriorated, but you know the emphasis is on trying to put the headgear on people and do damage.

The thing that concerns me more than anything is that at some point they decided not to throw flags too often when a player hits another in the face with his headgear. How many times have you seen a penalty flag thrown after a headgear to the face? The use of headgear to the face and neck area is an epidemic, and I think the NFL is not doing enough about it. That is the most disturbing thing about the modern game—the refusal to do much about it and the fact they're just allowing it.

One recent study revealed that 76 of 79 deceased NFL players who underwent postmortem examination had degenerative brain disease. Another study reported nearly 80 percent of the 128 men they examined posthumously who had played football at the high school level or higher tested positive for chronic traumatic encephalopathy.

It's no wonder injuries are so prevalent. So many of today's linemen are huge *and* fast. The average offensive lineman is around 6 foot, 5 inches and 310-plus pounds. As recently as 2011, there were 170 men who started at least one NFL game on the offensive line and only 28 of them weighed in at fewer than 300 pounds. Another recent survey showed the average defensive tackle weighed in the neighborhood of 305-plus pounds. In the 1950s, the average offensive lineman was around 6 feet, 2 inches and around 240 pounds, and the average weight of those players during much of my career never exceeded 260. Our line was probably typical—Jim Parker played at 270, and the rest were in the 255 to 260 range. That was the norm for the time. Today, I'd say four out of five of them are 295 to 310.

My dad had an interesting theory about the growth of players. He said that he grew up in the Depression era, when money was short, and then World War II came along and money flowed. Then when he was a coach, sometime around the late 1940s and into the early 1950s, he saw a change in the size of his high school players and realized it was because of the food families were able to purchase. The kids got better food, and they just got bigger and bigger.

Maybe, though, today's players aren't getting smarter—at least about some things. One of the things I look for and think about concerning the game today are the dumb penalties players get that are so costly and so unnecessary. I wonder, "Aren't these guys ever taught the rules?"

I think one of the best things I did as a coach was emphasize the rules all the time. While I was the head coach of the Patriots, I think we were the least penalized team in the league every year—either the least or second-least penalized. And we won a lot of close games. So much of it was because we didn't commit the dumb penalties and the other teams did.

Furthermore, another thing that bothers me today is players who thump their chests and gloat about making, say, a sack when their team is down by three touchdowns. They seem to have the look-at-me and the me-first attitude, rather than the team-comes-first approach. What I would like to do is line up all the owners and head coaches in the NFL and kick some ass. They're the ones who are responsible for this. All the owners have to say is, "We ain't having any of that crap. The instant you do that, your butt is out of here." Tell the coaches that, or the players, or both.

Those players don't have any concept or appreciation of the fact that the reason they exist and the reason that they're getting all this money is because of the football fans across the United States. They're the ones paying for all of this.

Players have become one of the biggest influences, most powerful forces, in the country, and look what they're doing with that power. They're thumping their chests and chanting "Me, me, me," and all that stuff. Yet I don't blame the players. It goes back into the home and then, right now, the owners and head coaches—they're the ones responsible for this stuff. I'd go up to the head coach and ask, "Why are you putting up with this?" Then I'd go to the owner and ask, "Why are you putting up with a head coach who puts up with this?" It's a shame that those actions have such influence over the young people of America. It's a total abdication of the owners' and head coaches' responsibility.

All of this is opposite to the small group of people out there across America who are my biggest heroes, and those are the members of the US military. They're spread all over the world, and they are holding on to the last parts of what this country's all about. These people not only put their lives on the line, they give them. So I still have a few scattered heroes left.

As for today's salaries, people ask me, "Don't you wish you were playing today, making the kind of money these guys make now?" Actually, if you want an ideal situation, I would like to have played *when* I played, but at *today's* salaries. That's *my* joking response.

In my day, the economic part of the game was not developed like it is today. The NFL was in the process of building tremendous popularity during the years I played. Baseball was still the king for most sports fans. Now, the television money that has come about as a result of the NFL's growing popularity keeps multiplying. If I played today I'd make so much I'd have to hire a financial guy. I heard Calvin Johnson signed a long-term contract worth about $16 million per year. By way of contrast, remember, I was paid $10,000 for my rookie season. My actual base salary was only $8,500, and I believe my top salary was $42,000 in my final season.

All that said, although my salary may not have been golden, my era was definitely a golden one, packed with talent, camaraderie, and fun. And my memories are as golden as the era itself.

Chapter Ten

Family, God, and Life Beyond Football

When 2012 rolled around, I had been retired as a player for many decades, but to my surprise the NFL decided to honor me at Super Bowl XLVI. They had me participate in the Vince Lombardi Trophy ceremony at the end of the game between the victorious Giants and the Patriots, two teams I had strong connections to. I presented the trophy to NFL commissioner Roger Goodell, who then handed it over to Super Bowl MVP Eli Manning. I joked that the only reason I was picked to carry the trophy out to midfield was that as a player I had good hands.

In 2006 they had expanded the post–Super Bowl ceremonies to include former NFL stars, and had previously saluted men such as Roger Staubach, Don Shula, and Bart Starr. It was a very unexpected honor, but it was one of the biggest thrills I've ever had.

There is a lot to life beyond football, though. I think Gale Sayers had it pretty much right when he chose the title *I Am Third* for his autobiography. I believe he was saying that the Lord was first, his friends and family were second, and then, and only then, did he himself enter into the equation.

We'll save God and religion for later and start here with my wife, children, and our nine grandchildren. I met Sally when I was playing for the Colts. John Bridgers was our defensive line coach in the 1958 championship game. After that game, John got offered the head coaching job at Baylor University. So he left the Colts staff and took that job. He called me in the spring of 1960 and said, "Raymond, I'd like for you to come down here. I'm going to put in a pro passing game. I'd like for you to coach my receivers in spring football." I didn't have anything else to do, so I went there. I had no idea that I was going to run into a lot more than I figured.

That's where I met Sally. She was a senior at Baylor University. There was a friend of mine from Paris, Texas, named Bobby Norris. He was at Baylor and was friends with Sally, and he put two and two together. He came to me and said, "I've got somebody, a friend of mine, that I think you ought to meet." He arranged for that blind date, and the rest is history because I fell for her that first night.

Earlier, when I had first become a Christian, I read a proverb one day that said, "A good wife is a gift from God." I started praying for a wife. God answered my prayers—this is who he led me to.

I coached at Baylor in April and May and stayed down there with Sally until I had to go to training camp with the Colts, to report in during the first week of July. At that point she stayed in Texas. We had decided to wait until the off-season to get married. But I got out on the highway to drive from Texas to Maryland, and a few days later I thought, "Man, I can't take this." Being away from her for a few days was way more than I could handle. So I stopped somewhere along the way, around Virginia, and I called her. I said, "Hey, we're going to go to Plan B. This isn't going to work. I can't live without you, so we're going to have to get married so you can be in Baltimore with me."

We had a trip to Dallas to play the Cowboys in a pre-season game, and that's when we got married. We had looked at the Colts schedule and knew that would be the right time. I asked Coach Ewbank, "Sally and I would like to get married. Would you give me permission to stay in Texas and not fly back after the game on the team plane?" He agreed.

So, after playing the Cowboys on a Friday night, I drove over to Tyler, Texas, and the ceremony took place the next day, on August 20, 1960, less than half a year after we'd met on that blind date. Then we went back to Dallas to fly to Baltimore, and I was back in training camp on Sunday night.

She came to camp with me in Westminster, Maryland, and brought absolutely no real understanding of the game of football. She started from ground zero, or maybe minus territory, when it came to football. She couldn't have cared less about it.

Then came her exposure to football in watching practices, exhibition games, and then regular-season games. To this day I don't really know what it is about her that enabled her to start absorbing football, but she got interested during training camp and found herself fascinated by the game.

Normally, no wives came to practice to sit there and watch us, but Sally lived in a motel about ten minutes away from our training camp, so she came all the time. I brought films home to study our opponents all during the week, and she sat there at the kitchen table where I had the projector. She watched films with me and asked questions. She loved football.

I'd go to the two-a-day practices, and we had meetings at night, but I'd meet up with Sally and we'd spend an hour or two together before I had to get back for room checks. So camp was actually where we started off our marriage before we moved into an apartment in Baltimore. Shortly after that, we bought a house and stayed in Baltimore year-round for about six or seven years.

When Sally went to our games, she made the comment more than once, "I don't care about sitting with the coaches' wives, because most of them don't know anything about football and they can't care less." She was interested in watching the games, not talking. That continued throughout my days of coaching. Sally probably knows more about football than most men. In fact, she is one of the sharpest people I know.

I had one of the greatest assets going for me when I was a coach, and that was a wife who loved the game, understood it, and didn't have any illusions about the nature of the game. In the coaching profession you have a shelf life of about four to five years at most, then you're gone. That's just part of the deal. So you move a lot, and that didn't bother her, either. Some women wouldn't be suited for that lifestyle. First of all, they wouldn't have any interest in football at all. It would be really boring to be married to a football coach if you didn't care anything about the game. Sally was a great coach's wife.

Sally and I still watch football together. I like to keep up with the college game as well as the NFL, so I watch as many games as there are on television, and we buy all the sports packages on cable TV, so we're pretty busy on Saturday and Sunday. I still have a real desire to see the Colts and the Patriots. When they're on television, I'm 100 percent go. When the rest of the teams are on, I'm at 90 percent.

The greatest accomplishment I ever did was marry Sally, and I'm serious about that. We are in our sixth decade of our marriage now. I said it before, and I'll say it again: She is my greatest catch ever. To get a woman with the qualities she has is a blessing. She is a diamond in every respect. I told her parents one time, "I don't know if y'all realize what kind of daughter you raised, but this young woman is something else." Her character, her honesty, and her intelligence, personality, and beauty make quite a package.

As for our children, one of the biggest influences in raising them was that at some point in my Christian life I ran across an organization in St. Louis called the Bible Memory Association, BMA. The essence of what I got from them was this: They had printed materials based on age groups, and what they had learned from dealing with children over a long period of time was that a child's ability to memorize is way, way better than what most people have any concept of. And what they memorize becomes imbedded in them.

So I got their material, and when our children were very, very young, I started them all on memorizing Scripture. I would read them a little story and then give them a Scripture to memorize. The approach was that the child had to recite the verse perfectly and then you rewarded them.

I think the first verse our oldest child learned was, "My God loves me," or something simple like that. But you'd be surprised how early a child can start absorbing it.

Another resource I had was a book called *The Bible in Pictures for Little Eyes*. As a child sits there in your lap, you open these books that have beautiful pictures and simple verses and you recite the words. The idea is that the pictures reinforce the words, the messages presented there.

One of the most significant things I've learned in life is the importance of raising children and understanding the healthy combination of love and discipline. And the classic example of this is God's dealing with us.

In raising our children, we explained this to them. I said, "If Daddy has to discipline you, it's because I love you and because you're doing something that you shouldn't be doing, like something that's harmful to you, or something that is going to be destructive to you." If a person loves somebody enough, he's not going to let him destroy himself. You know, there's a Scripture to back this up in *The Book of Proverbs* that says, "The man who loves his child will be quick to discipline him."

Our first born was Suzanne, who arrived when we were living in Boston. She ended up going to Boston College when I was coaching for the Patriots. The job she has now is right here where I live, in Murfreesboro, Tennessee. She and her husband, Doug Duross, moved here several years ago and now own an Italian restaurant called Marina's on the Square. He had been working in the automobile industry, and they went to that restaurant for a year or two. One day the owner approached and said he was selling the place. He asked if they would be interested in buying it. He got out of the car business, and they bought the restaurant. They have four children: Alexandra, Luke, Rebekah, and Lilly.

My son Mark, like Suzanne, graduated from Medfield High School in Massachusetts. When he was a senior in high school, he wanted to go to school in the South. He wrote to Vanderbilt University to see if he could get in. He did, and he played football there. He wasn't on a scholarship, but he went out for the team, and after being there for a year, they put him on a full scholarship. He was a receiver. When he was growing up, he was around the game the entire time, of course, because I was in it. He had natural hands to catch a football, and he was a very good receiver.

Mark got his master's degree from Vanderbilt, too, an MBA. He coached football as a graduate assistant in his sixth year there. During that time, he was going to a church in Franklin, Tennessee, called Christ Community Church. He got involved there and really felt God leading him to becoming a missionary, so he did that. He met Lori at that time, an Auburn graduate who was attending that same church. They got married and then went to Peru for seven or eight years. We visited them one time in Lima. They have five children: Emmett, Anna, Taylor, Abigail, and Madassah. They all grew up speaking fluent Spanish.

My youngest daughter is Ashley, born in Dallas before the coaching carousel took us to Boston. She also went to Medfield High and then on to Vanderbilt. While she was there, she started working as an intern in the country music field with a promising young performer named Alan Jackson. After she graduated, Alan hired her full-time and she worked for him for several years.

Ashley's married now, and she and her husband, Tom Bass, live in Nashville. They come and see us on a regular basis. Suzanne lives right next door to us, and Ashley lives thirty minutes from us. Mark and Lori get to come home from their missionary assignment about every four or five years and stay for a year to year and a half.

I had a lot of great accomplishments as a player, but as a human being I am most proud of my family. It's important who these people are, what they mean, and what they've done.

My family pride is also connected with my mother and dad. I came out of a home so good, I don't think you could ever design anything better. The quality of people my parents were and the atmosphere they created in our home was tremendous. To be around people like that growing up, well, you just can't equate the impact and power of that. I had both love and discipline.

I found religion with the help of a friend and Baltimore Colts teammate, linebacker Don Shinnick. He came to the Colts out of UCLA in 1957 as the twentieth overall player taken in the draft. He grew up in California and happened to be on the UCLA campus when one of the most important Christian events in American history happened—the founding of Campus Crusade for Christ. It's an organization that is still in existence as one of the most powerful forces for the Gospel of Christ ever in the United States. It was started by a man named Bill Bright.

Shinnick was one of Bright's first converts. Bright spoke and ministered to the UCLA football team on their campus. It was through Bright that Shinnick first became a Christian. Shinnick's the one that first turned my attention to Christ. That happened in August 1960. He said that he doesn't make decisions in his life. Through prayer, God does. I got a Bible and started reading it for the first time. I think I read it from cover to cover, and I don't know that I really knew about anything in it even when I got through reading it. A little later, though, I really started studying Scripture, in the off-season of 1961 at the age of twenty-eight.

I think getting to meet Shinnick was another case of God being the master of timing, and He understands everything that's going on. What was going on in the first year or two when I knew Shinnick was this: He never said one word to me about Christ, and I wasn't inquiring.

However, I was starting to become aware of the fact that I was getting to play professional football, to do what I love to do, have the ability to do it, and not be injured. All that was no accident. The fact that I ended up with the Baltimore Colts with the best football coach in the business and the best quarterback in the business was no accident. I said to myself, "What is the purpose of all this?" I began to realize there is more to life than chasing a football.

Shinnick was around, but what I didn't know is that he was praying for me. He had been watching me read the Bible for a couple of years by then. The timing of when he approached me was not accidental, either. He approached me one off-season and said, "Raymond, I don't think you've really ever accepted Christ as your Savior."

He didn't know what was happening, about how God was preparing my heart for his conversation, but I was prepared when he finally talked to me. He knew about my church background. I'd been brought up in the church, I was raised in the First Christian Church in Paris, Texas, a good solid church. I had gone to Sunday School, been baptized, made the confession of faith, and so forth. But the fact of the matter is, I didn't know anything about any of it. I had never experienced a spiritual birth, and that is where it starts. To put it another way: I was as lost as you could be and had no clue.

I asked Shinnick, "How do you go about doing this?" You can imagine two football players there—the conversation took about thirty seconds or less. He said, "Well, this is what I did. I said, 'God, I believe in your son Jesus.'" And that's about all there was to it. He also said, "If you trust Christ, He'll come and live in you, Raymond. He's the power to live the Christian life—you don't have the power to live it. Let him live it through you, and when you mess up, tell him." That was the theological explanation given to me that day.

The most significant thing about it was I meant it. When the spiritual birth happens to a person, it is the most significant event that can ever happen in a person's life, because you immediately pass from death to life. There's an interesting parallel between the spiritual birth and the physical birth. When a child comes into the world, do you think that child is aware of what life is? Does he even know he's alive? Absolutely not. He doesn't know anything, but he is alive. As soon as I meant business about Jesus Christ, He came in and I was born again. That's exactly what he promises: If you mean it, I will meet you there. And He did. I was a newborn Christian, and I was just like a newborn in a cradle. I had had no clue that I was alive. The awareness of life, that process began at that point, and gradually I began to become aware that I was spiritually alive.

One of the evidences that was a part of this awakening was when I became aware of my sin nature, of what was going on in my mind and coming out of my mouth. All of a sudden I had an awareness of stuff that had been going on there for years that I never saw. Well, I never had the spiritual eyes to be aware of it before. Now I was aware of my need for forgiveness, and that led me to ask, "How can you be forgiven?" I studied the New Testament and became aware of guilt, too. All that led to understanding what the cross is all about, that you could be set free because Christ paid for it. My sin had not been overlooked, it had been paid for.

I had had tunnel vision for years and years; I wasn't focused on anything but football—that was it. The 1958 championship game was such a turning point in my life. I didn't fully realize the spiritual impact of it at the time, but when I came off the field that day, it was like I knew what had just happened out there wasn't any accident. Unlike my teammates, who celebrated the usual way, I first isolated myself. I went in the locker room, went off by myself, and had my first experience of God revealing Himself to me right then and there.

Even though I didn't know anything about praying, I was so aware that what had just happened on that field was something God had orchestrated. The impact of that hit me right between the eyes.

I've read the Bible enough that I can recite verses and cite specific ones that fit certain occasions I come across. It's a funny thing about memorization—I never really consciously tried to memorize Scripture, but after studying it over and over and over, a lot of it you remember without realizing you've memorized it. Some of the Scriptures strike you so strongly that they stick. I also have 3-by-5 index cards on which I'd write the Scriptures that struck me, and then I started carrying them in my shirt pocket. I found myself driving around Baltimore or sitting on a plane, and I'd take them out and read them, just to study them, not to memorize them. They started taking hold.

The Bible itself says that there's a process that takes place where you get the Word down in your heart—it is there, and in different life situations it will come out.

A few years after I became a Christian, I got to meet evangelist Billy Graham. I was asked to speak at one of his rallies. His wife Ruth and his daughters were there at his place in Montreat, North Carolina, out in the country, a good retreat for him. The thing I remember being most impressed about was how real he was, and what a great family they were. This guy was one of the most famous men in the world at that time.

For many years I have spoken to various Christian groups, a lot of different churches and organizations like Campus Crusade for Christ, the Salvation Army, and the Fellowship of Christian Athletes. Basically I tell them how I became a Christian, my personal testimony. I don't enjoy public speaking. My personality is not geared that way, but I do it anyway. I see it as my duty.

Once, after I had been a Christian for a short time—maybe a year at most—the off-season came and I was a very prominent athlete on the NFL scene around the country, and word got around that I had become a Christian. So a lot of organizations jumped on that, and a phone call came to my house. The person said, "We'd like for you to come and speak, give your Christian testimony." As soon as he got as far as "come and speak," I shut him off and listened enough just to wait until he got through so I could say no, which I did.

I put the phone down, and then came my first real experience with the Lord taking a razor strap to me. Boy, did I get enveloped in misery such as I had never experienced, and I knew I had made a big mistake. I was really getting disciplined. I was overwhelmed and miserable, and I knew exactly what the reason was. I hadn't paid attention to the caller, so I couldn't call him back. I didn't know what to do.

About an hour or so later, the phone rang again and the caller asked me about speaking for *his* group. I didn't pay any attention again, because I was waiting until he got through so I could say, "Yeah. I'll come." That was to be my first speaking engagement. I had made a commitment to stand in front of a bunch of people and talk about Jesus and how I became a Christian. And I was thinking, "Good grief, what am I going to say? I don't know what to do."

I was a nervous wreck for the three months leading up to the event. I was trying to get prepared, but I came up with nothing. To this day, I don't know what I said to that group, but it had to be absolutely pitiful. Sally told me later that she was sitting with some people, and when I got through speaking, they kindly said to Sally, "Well, your husband is so sincere," but it was absolute misery for me. And I have felt that I have to do those speeches from then on. It gradually got better, but I still don't like to do it.

When one low point in my coaching life came up, I actually got so angry with God, you cannot believe. In essence I felt like, "Hey, why are you letting this happen? This is not some minor deal here, so, why? What the heck is going on?" I can't describe what it was like. I quit praying. I quit talking to Him. I quit doing everything for about a month.

One of the things I ran across in the Scripture years later, in one of Paul's letters recorded in the New Testament, was his hinting on this topic, a concept about the Christian life. The phraseology in this particular letter was basically, "We not only believe in Him, but we have the privilege of suffering for His name." Suffering for the name of Jesus. I read that and I was thinking, "Lord, you've got to be kidding. This is a privilege?" And linked with that quote is, "Be thankful in all circumstances." But He's not kidding—this is a part of the journey.

That's exactly what it was, though, I was suffering for the name of Jesus. It's easy to just roll those words off your lips, but to go through the suffering is another thing altogether. My suffering was absolutely brutal.

The other concept God began to teach me out of this was sharing the suffering of Christ. If you read your New Testament, it's like this is a part of the contract, a part of the deal. But it was like, "I didn't count on this when I signed up."

What I learned in later life, from reading the Bible, is the way God deals with His children. He loves them enough that you aren't going to get by with getting outside His will without Him laying the razor strap to your butt, so to speak. He loves you enough that he's going to jerk you up by the tail and one way or another get your attention. And if He doesn't get your attention one way, He's going to get it another way, and it's going to be painful.

In 2015 I made my most recent trip to Israel. It was one of the high points of my life. The experience of being there and taking in the history and being a part of the geography of the nations over there was just fascinating.

The first time I went there, back in the 1980s, there was a woman in Boston named Ann Kiemel who was one of the most successful Christian book writers of her time. Sally and I became good friends with her when we were living in Boston, and one day she called us and said, "Get your passports. I want to take you to Israel." She financed the whole trip, and we were over there three weeks. It was unbelievable.

On the negative side, the longer I live, the more I see in the present condition of the United States children coming out of homes in which they don't see anything but the wrong thing. We've got an epidemic in this country, and it all starts in the home.

I'm in my eighties now, and I've seen America at its very best. I was eight, nine, ten, eleven, twelve years old during World War II. I saw a country that was absolutely, totally united for the right reasons. And this country came out of a Depression, an economic hit-upside-the-head that was as bad as America's ever experienced, and we got up off the mat and came out, financed the war, and beat the Germans in Europe and the Japanese in the Orient. It's one of those phenomenal economic things.

It's a puzzle to me how this ever happened, but this was a generation of people who came out of a hard, hard school, the Depression, and then went into World War II, the biggest conflagration in the history of the world, and won it on two continents. That's our heritage. Then to see where our country has fallen, what you have on the scene today, is not just sad, it's tragic.

There's a thing I like to talk about, and I call it the American Mentality, or the American Spirit. It's a major part of our tradition, our national character. Nations are like individual people, none of us are perfect, but when our American Mentality is at its best, it's wonderful and it's worth our doing everything we can do to preserve it, to use it, and to pass it on.

This spirit had to have begun when the Pilgrims had the courage to get on those fragile little ships to sail from England. There truly was opportunity in America. People were set free from man-made restrictions, and the American Mentality began to emerge as people from all over the world eventually came to this country to be a part of it.

Then there's the matter of work ethic. Have a job, do it, and do it right. Take pride in your work—whatever it is. Someone hires you to do a job, give them his or her money's worth. If you sell something, give him what he's paying for.

When it comes to competition, Americans have learned it brings out the best in us. We look for every edge when competing. Ty Cobb may not have been a great person, but he was an American original. Someone once asked him, "I notice when you get on first base, you kick the bag, then take your lead. Why do you always kick the bag?" Cobb replied, "You notice I always kick it toward second base?" Cobb, always the competitor was looking for an edge—even 1 inch.

That reminds me of a story an Oakland teammate of Ken Stabler told me. The Raiders were behind in the fourth quarter, and they had the ball on their 2-yard line, 98 yards out. Stabler came into the huddle to start the drive and said, "We got 'em right where we want 'em." That's how Americans think.

Americans do their own thinking when the situation calls for it. After World War II ended, a German general was asked who the best soldiers in the world were. He answered, "The Germans, of course." Then he was asked, why had the Germans been beaten? He replied, "To answer that, consider who are the best fighters, the Americans." He elaborated on the difference between the best soldiers and the best fighters. "The German will do exactly as he is told, and do it well. That is a good soldier. But you never know what an American will do. He is not out there to be a soldier. He is out there to win, and he has the initiative and ingenuity to figure out all the best moves himself." Just like Cobb, just like Stabler, and just like another legend, John Unitas.

Unitas was one of the greatest competitors I ever saw. As I recall, in 1956, when our number one quarterback got injured in a game versus the Bears, back when Unitas had yet to establish himself, he came in to play in what was just his second NFL game. In that contest he threw a touchdown pass, but to the wrong team. His pass was picked off by defensive back J. C. Caroline and returned 59 yards for 6 points, putting Chicago up by 13. The Bears went on to rout us, 58–27.

Now, here comes a big tip-off as to why Unitas was going to become an all-time great. Even after mistakes, he went about his business. After the interception, I felt he played a very solid game. His type of response to adversity, to a setback, comes from being mentally tough. When I think of Unitas, that's what I think of. He had the American Mentality. Americans at their best can handle things when the going gets rough.

By the way, a *Baltimore Sun* writer, Mike Klingaman, came up with research indicating that the often-told story of Unitas's first NFL pass being the Caroline interception isn't correct. Klingaman reported Unitas's first pass actually came against the Lions, two games before the Caroline interception took place. According to Klingaman, the truth is Unitas's first-ever pass in the NFL was incomplete. He then scrambled for 23 yards before throwing an interception to Detroit's Jim David. According to something I saw recently, his first-ever completion did come on a pass to me.

At any rate, another strong point of Americans is their "find a way" mentality. Traditionally we have been innovative, unorthodox, and unafraid to try something new, to find different ways to get it done. Take the Seabees, a nickname for Construction Battalion. During wartime they had to build things such as bridges under all kinds of conditions. They really believed, "The difficult we can do immediately. The impossible takes a little longer."

The challenge to each new generation of Americans is, "Get back to *basics*." Doing that allows us to handle the good and the bad. There is a sure and certain result of neglecting the basics, though, whether it's for an individual, an athlete, a team, or a nation. To put it bluntly: Forget the basics and you will soon get your butt handed to you.

I guess I've taken care of the basics pretty well. For example, I think I am in good health. I've been under the great care of some extremely competent medical people since coaching with the Patriots and living in Boston. I had complete physicals every year there at one of the best hospitals in the world, Mass General Hospital. It was part of my contract for me to get a yearly physical. Now I live near Nashville, and Vanderbilt has got a great hospital with skilled people looking after me.

Our home in Murfreesboro, Tennessee, which we bought about fifteen years ago, had a building out back that's totally separate from the house. I was able to finish it off and remodel it. It has three rooms, and in one part of the building I've got weight-lifting equipment, an elliptical machine, and a treadmill. I can get tremendous cardiovascular work, plus all the muscle-building and toning stuff I need. It's got a bathroom and shower, too.

On the other side of the building, I've got my office with my files and memorabilia. It's just a beautiful arrangement. I handle a lot of mail from young boys, fans, and coaches—from a wide variety of people. I have materials that I've built up over the years that I've had printed, and I'll pick some of it to fit the needs of the people who write to me. I spend a lot of time writing letters, and I keep the letters I get and a copy of a lot of the ones I send back. I handle about sixty letters a month.

Even though I haven't played one down of a football game in nearly five decades, people often want to talk to me about my career and, in particular, the 1958 title game. You get used to it in a way, but then after the years go by, you add being surprised to being used to it. It doesn't really figure.

I think the proliferation of books and magazines on sports and television programs about NFL history has spawned an interest in a lot of young fans as well as middle-aged and older fans. It takes time to process that mail.

There are more than just autograph requests. There are young coaches who ask me questions, and young receivers who ask me something. I get some young quarterbacks who will mention something, too. I have different materials that I have developed over the years to address their needs, and I address their individual issues. I keep the letters as insights into these coaches and young athletes.

As I mentioned, another thing I do now is keep up with football and what's going on in the game and how it's moving along in different directions—like what's being emphasized and how it's evolving. I like to study that part of it. I really get a big kick out of watching the great players they've got today.

Having strong connections to the Colts and Patriots, I particularly like to watch them play, and it just so happens that they have treated us with two of the greatest quarterbacks you could ever hope to see in recent years. So it was extra special to watch the Colts play when they had Peyton Manning, and New England with Tom Brady. No, I don't like to miss any performance those guys are doing. Of course, because Manning retired after winning the Super Bowl in 2016, I won't get to watch him execute his craft anymore.

I know Unitas felt that the records set by the Baltimore Colts and those set by the Colts when they were in Indianapolis should be kept separate. To him, the *new* Colts were not the Baltimore Colts.

Now, I think, *without question*, it was a total mistake by the NFL to move the Colts' name out of Baltimore. It was just stupid. I think money clouded their judgment about it. I don't think they had any sentimental value involved in their decision—and it should have. The Colts' name should never have moved out of Baltimore. And the later arrival of another pro team in Baltimore proves that. The name should have stayed there, and when the next team came in there, they would have been the Baltimore Colts again. And Indianapolis could have their own identity. When Cleveland moved to Baltimore, they didn't call them the Browns any more. Nobody's perfect, but the NFL made a big blunder there.

As I look back on my life, I am very aware that I've been blessed with a wonderful life and a career in the sport I love so much.

I was very fortunate to team up with a man who loved football as much as I did in Unitas, and I was so glad to be able to be his receiver in twelve of my thirteen seasons in the NFL. When you think back on our relationship, you think, "How in the world could a free agent quarterback and a twentieth-round draft pick end up on the same team, under a coach perfectly suited for them?" I don't think that was a coincidence or luck. It was God's plan.

In my personal life, I've been so lucky to have been blessed with a wonderful family. Rest assured that I thank God for each and every one of my blessings.

Well, I guess there's only thing left to say for now. Catch you later.

Appendix One

Raymond Berry's Numbers and Records

by Wayne Stewart

- Raymond Berry was not only an integral part of the Baltimore Colts and one of just seven players from that team to have his number retired, he also set numerous records and accomplished incredible feats.
- Three years in a row, Berry led the NFL in receptions, from 1958 through 1960, and in 1957 and 1961 he finished second in the league for catches. That means he ranked first or second in all of pro football every season for five consecutive years. In eight of his thirteen seasons he was in the top ten for receptions. His personal high came in 1961, when he snagged seventy-five passes, one more than he had caught in the previous season.
- He was named to six Pro Bowl squads (1958–1961; 1963–1964).
- He was on the First Team All-Pro from 1958 through 1960. In fact he was a first- or second-team All-Pro selection from 1957 through 1961 and again in 1965 in his next-to-last full season.
- He led the league in touchdowns on receptions twice, with nine in 1958 and a sterling, personal high of fourteen in just twelve games in 1959. On two other occasions he was third in the NFL in this department.
- In 1959 only two men scored more points than Berry's 84. Paul Hornung led the NFL with 94 points, but 52 of those points

came via kicks; and Pat Summerall finished second in scoring with 90 points, and all of his scores came on kicks. Take away field goals and extra points, and Berry's 84 points would have dwarfed Hornung's adjusted output of 42 points scored. Cleveland's Jim Brown also scored 84 points (all on rushes), as did Bobby Joe Conrad, who scored the majority of his points handling the kicking chores for the Cardinals.

- During the 1958 championship game versus the New York Giants, Berry caught twelve passes, good for a stunning 178 yards—both figures established championship game records.
- In 1957, 1959, and 1960, he led the NFL in yards gained via catches. He topped 800 yards in receptions three times with highs of 959 in 1959 and a whopping 1,298 the following year, in a season that ran only twelve games. That yardage total was exceeded only twice at that point—by Elroy Hirsch in 1951 and in the old AFL by Bill Groman, also in 1960.
- Upon his retirement after the 1967 season, Berry held the coveted record for career catches, 631. He also totaled 9,275 yards on receptions, also the most ever at that point. In addition, only Don Hutson, Tommy McDonald, and Art Powell had scored more touchdowns on receptions than Berry's sixty-eight; and only eleven men, regardless of position played, had scored more total touchdowns than Berry.
- When his playing days ended, Berry also ranked twelfth for most receptions ever in a season with seventy-five in 1961, and thirteenth for his seventy-four catches in 1960. His sixty-six receptions in 1959 put him in a tie for the number twenty-one slot in the rankings in existence at the time of his retirement. Likewise, his 1,298 yards on receptions in 1960 stood at number thirteen all-time, and his fourteen touchdown catches in 1959 was tied for the seventh most ever. He was also number seven all-time for the highest average of yards per reception based on his 108.2 in 1960.

- Berry also established a record by catching forty-plus passes in ten consecutive seasons.
- In 1959 and 1960 he topped the league for the best average of yards gained per game played. In 1959 he was good for an average of 79.9 yards on catches per game, and he improved that figure to an astronomical 108.2 yards per contest the following season, the fourth-best average at that point and still the thirteenth best average (through the 2014 season). Reaching or topping an average of 100 yards per game over a full season has been done just thirty-nine times by receivers.
- Even today, decades after he last laced his cleats, Berry still ranks high in many categories. That fact is even more remarkable considering several factors. For example, the rules and playing conditions he played under weren't as conducive to putting up big offensive numbers as the ones quarterbacks and receivers enjoy nowadays. In addition, Berry played the bulk of his career when the NFL season ran only twelve games. Even when the league expanded its schedule to fourteen contests, Berry only played fourteen games in a season three times. In all, he played 154 games, yet still ranks thirty-ninth for touchdowns on receptions, fifty-first for receiving yardage, fifty-seventh for receptions, fifty-eighth for average yards per game on catches, and ninety-sixth for total touchdowns scored, regardless of position played.
- When based on seasons of twelve games, Berry ranks first through fifth for the most receptions in Colts history, ranging from his high of seventy-five catches to his fifty-six in 1958. His career yardage total through 2014 is still the third highest in Colts franchise history—the two men ahead of him, Marvin Harrison and Reggie Wayne, played in many more career games than Berry.
- Likewise, for virtually every team-receiving record, Berry ranks first for the Baltimore era, which ran from 1953 through 1983, and near the head of all of the lists that include the entire run of the franchise (through 2015). Furthermore, upon his retirement

in 1967, he owned outright a slew of Colt records. Start with his twenty-three 100-yard games, now third best ever for the history of the entire franchise.

- In 1960 Berry had seven 100-yard games, then a record and still fourth for the franchise.
- Only three Colts players have ever recorded multiple three-touchdown games—Berry, who was the first to do this (on two occasions), followed by Jimmy Orr and Marvin Harrison.
- Berry had eleven games in which he caught ten or more passes, another Baltimore Colts record. Only Harrison and Wayne have been able to surpass that record.
- For eight seasons (of his thirteen) Berry led his team in receptions, and five of those seasons, 1957 through 1961, were in a row, establishing two more Baltimore records. Only Harrison has led the Colts more times, and only Harrison and Wayne have topped the team in catches more seasons in a row than Berry (with six each).
- Starting from the eighth game of the 1959 season and into 1960, Berry chalked up seven consecutive games with at least one receiving touchdown, still an all-time franchise best.
- He was named to the Pro Football Hall of Fame 1950s All-Decade Team, their all-time great NFL twenty-five-year team, and later to the NFL's Fiftieth Anniversary All-Time Team.
- In addition, when the NFL selected its All-Time Team for the league's first seventy-five years in existence, Berry made the team, along with three other greats at his position: Jerry Rice, Lance Alworth, and Don Hutson.
- In 1999, as the twentieth century came to an end, *The Sporting News* came out with their selections for the top one hundred NFL players of all time. Berry was named as the fortieth-greatest player ever. Another NFL survey placed him thirty-sixth.
- Berry, Forrest Gregg, and Mike Ditka share the honor of being the only men included on an NFL all-time greats list of players to have also coached a team to the Super Bowl.

- Five of Berry's lifetime sixty-eight touchdown receptions were on very short throws, from 3 yards out or closer in; eighteen from 4 to 9 yards out; eighteen from 10 to 19 yards; ten from 20 to 29 yards; and seventeen from 30-plus yards from the goal line. Thirty of his touchdowns gave the Colts a lead. The team he scored most often against (eleven touchdowns) was Green Bay.
- In 1973 Berry was inducted into the Pro Football Hall of Fame on the first ballot.

Appendix Two

What Others Say about Raymond Berry

by Wayne Stewart

- Writer Jack Mann from the book, *The Way It Was*: Berry "could get free on a subway platform and catch buttered corn."
- Lenny Moore observed, "Raymond Berry was the one who turned all of us around. What a unique individual—he was something else all the way down the line."
- Alan Ameche is quoted in the book, *The Colts' Baltimore*, as saying Berry "was the least likely guy to do what he did. In '55, everybody in camp thought it was a big mistake going with him. He had very limited ability, but he was the hardest-working guy anybody ever saw."
- Gino Marchetti calls Berry the greatest receiver of all-time. "No doubt about it. He would probably be a tight end today, and if they told him to be the tight end, he would gain weight and be a good one. You always want a guy like Raymond on your team."
- Lenny Lyles said, "You know, Berry could look at your shoes and tell exactly where you were going. He could *read* a defensive back. He was a genius."
- In 1966, Vikings defense back Jim Shorter critiqued Berry after he had caught nine passes against Shorter's defense, "I wish he'd

quit tomorrow. Every time I thought I had him covered he'd cut inside or outside, and then he'd have the ball. He always had the ball, didn't he? He's just the best, that's all I can say."

- Author Christopher Price wrote, "Berry was a laid-back coach who knew how to get the most out of his team. By the time he arrived in New England, his resume was unmatched . . . The players knew his background, and they respected his body of works on the field."
- Weeb Ewbank said, ". . . with the great dedication he had, why, he made coaching a joy. He'd eat up anything you said, try everything. Raymond made himself a great receiver . . ."
- Author Ted Patterson wrote, "Berry proved that God-given ability wasn't always a requirement; endless work and sheer strength of will could also play a part."
- When Paul Warfield worked with Berry, who coached Cleveland Browns receivers for two seasons, he observed, "There probably isn't anyone who knows more about a passing attack."
- Dallas Cowboys head coach Tom Landry stated, "Raymond Berry was the guy who started moves in the NFL."
- Author Dave Klein wrote that Berry "did things that no one had ever done on a football field."
- Columnist Jim Murray of the *Los Angeles Times* wrote, "He didn't play a game of football, he engineered it. He checked the temperature, lighting, humidity, even the position of the sun in the sky. He studied the terrain as if he had to putt on it, not run on it, or build a bridge on it, not catch a pass on it. He could catch one in handcuffs. No one remembers Raymond Berry ever dropping a pass if it was in the same area code. He could hold onto a football in an avalanche."
- Murray also wrote that Berry saw "more film than Darryl Zanuck," and that Berry "could run a pattern through a subway rush hour and shake lose."

- Linebacker Mike Lucci recalled, "The first time I was on the field [going against] Unitas, I saw Raymond Berry, and he would go down 10 yards and break out and the ball would be right there. And they would do it over and over and over again. You always thought, '[They're] going to make you pay if you make a mistake.'"
- Gregory Kane of the *Baltimore Sun* wrote, "When I was a kid, it's possible I could have been convinced there were three more sacred words in the English language than 'Unitas to Berry,' but it would have taken brass knuckles brandished by a guy named Bubba the Violator to do it. For me, those were the three most sacred words in the English language, and the four most sacred were 'Unitas to Berry, TOUCHDOWN!'"
- In his book, *The Best Game Ever*, author Mark Bowden wrote, "He was his own man. He was *poised,* as though he had pondered everything a little harder than anyone else . . . Raymond was his own coach. The way you handled him was to leave him alone . . ." Bowden added, "Raymond was entirely cerebral in his approach . . . to his position . . . He was deconstructing and reinventing the position of wide receiver."
- A Pro Football Hall of Fame website points out that Berry overcame a great deal, that his story "is one of determination, dedication and desire."
- Charley Winner, a former coach of the Colts, said, "In practice, Raymond kept John Unitas on the field, running routes until John's arm nearly fell off. Gino Marchetti would say, 'Wouldn't it be awful if the whole team were Raymond Berrys?' The only way to punish them would be to say, 'You have to stop practice and go to the movies tonight.'"
- Mark McGuire of the *Albany News Union* wrote that Berry's "soft hands could catch an egg from a sling shot and not break it."
- "On all the coaching staffs I've been on," said Don Shinnick, who was an assistant coach for Berry in New England, "and I've

been around Don Shula, Chuck Noll, John Madden, George Halas, some of the greats, I have never been around a man who cares less about taking credit for a team's success. He doesn't care if Mickey Mouse gets the credit. It comes from being a humble individual . . ."

- When asked for a comment about Berry, Unitas once succinctly said, "The best."

Acknowledgments

Thanks go out to our agent, Rob Wilson; to John Ziemann of the Sports Legends Museum in Baltimore; and to the Baltimore Colts who were interviewed for this book—Gino Marchetti, Tom Matte, Lenny Moore, Rick Volk, and Andy Nelson. Others who were gracious with their time during interviews include Mike Ditka and Mike Lucci. We also thank our editor, Keith Wallman. Thanks to Tom Benjey of Tuxedo Press for granting permission to use some quotes from the book *America's Cradle of Quarterbacks,* which features a great deal of material about John Unitas. We are also appreciative for the help provided by Avis Roper, Christian Edwards, and Michael DeBates of the Indianapolis Colts; Chris Schmidt, UIL Public Affairs representative; Zachary Balside, who was with SMU's Athletic Public Relations Department; and Ed Sterling, director of member services for the Texas Press Association.

A final thanks goes to John Unitas, my quarterback and my friend.

Sources

Books

America's Cradle of Quarterbacks, by Wayne Stewart
And the Crowd Goes Wild, edited by Joe Garner
The Best Game Ever, by Mark Bowden
The Colts' Baltimore, by Michael Olesker
ESPN College Football Encyclopedia, edited by Michael MacCambridge
The First 50 Years, by the Creative Staff of National Football League Properties, Inc.
Football in Baltimore, Second Edition, by Ted Patterson
The Game of Their Lives, by Dave Klein
Greatest Football Games, by Hank Hersch
New England Patriots: The Complete Illustrated History, by Christopher Price
Johnny U, by Tom Callahan
The Way It Was, edited by George Vecsey

DVD/TV Shows

"There's a Catch to It," with Raymond Berry, copyright Raymond Berry.
"The Way It Was," Dick Enberg, Executive Producer. Gerry Gross Productions, KCET. Distributed by PBS.

Magazines Articles

"The Greatest Game," by Raymond Berry. *Newsweek*, October 25, 1999.
"Johnny Was Good," by Raymond Berry and Dennis Dilon. *Sporting News*, September 23, 2002.
"1958 Baltimore Colts" by Clifton Brown, with a section, "We Changed the Game," by Raymond Berry. *Sporting News*, January 7, 2011.

Websites

http://access.newspaperarchive.com.oh0006.oplin.org/us/california/oakland/oakland-tribune/1976/09-16/page-70?tag=raymond+berry&rtserp=tags/?pep=raymond-berry&pr=30&psb=dateasc&page=9&pd=1&ndt=bd&pe=31&pem=12&py=1976&pm=1&pey=1976

http://access.newspaperarchive.com.oh0006.oplin.org/us/california/oxnard/oxnard-press-courier-oxnard-california/1974/12-09/page-35?tag=raymond+berry&rtserp=tags/?pep=raymond-berry&pr=20&psb=dateasc&page=9&pd=1&ndt=bd&pe=31&pem=12&py=1974&pm=8&pey=1974

http://access.newspaperarchive.com.oh0006.oplin.org/us/california/pasadena/pasadena-independent/1966/10-31/page-15?tag=raymond+berry&rtserp=tags/?pep=raymond-berry&pr=30&psb=dateasc&page=13&pd=1&ndt=bd&pe=31&pem=12&py=1966&pm=9&pey=1966

http://access.newspaperarchive.com.oh0006.oplin.org/us/pennsylvania/altoona/altoona-mirror/1986/01-07/page-41?tag=raymond+berry&rtserp=tags/?pep=raymond-berry&pr=30&psb=dateasc&page=4&pd=1&ndt=bd&pe=27&pem=2&py=1986&pm=1&pey=1986

http://access.newspaperarchive.com.oh0006.oplin.org/us/pennsylvania/altoona/altoona-mirror/1998/10-02/page-23?tag=raymond+berry&rtserp=tags/?pep=raymond-berry&pr=30&psb=dateasc&page=3&pd=1&ndt=bd&pe=31&pem=12&py=1998&pm=1&pey=1998

http://access.newspaperarchive.com.oh0006.oplin.org/us/texas/odessa/odessa-american/1968/08-17/page-15?tag=raymond+berry&rtserp=tags/?pep=raymond-berry&pr=30&psb=dateasc&page=14&pd=10&ndt=bd&pe=31&pem=12&py=1968&pm=3&pey=1968

http://access.newspaperarchive.com.oh0006.oplin.org/us/texas/paris/paris-news/1955/12-24/page-5?tag=Raymond+Berry+raymond+berry&rtserp=tags/?pep=raymond-berry&pf=raymond&pl=berry&page=14&ndt=by&py=1950&pey=1959

http://access.newspaperarchive.com.oh0006.oplin.org/us/utah/provo/provo-herald/1968/03-10/page-14?tag=raymond+berry&rtserp=tags/?pep=raymond-berry&pr=30&psb=dateasc&page=4&pd=1&ndt=bd&pe=31&pem=12&py=1968&pm=1&pey=1968

http://articles.baltimoresun.com/1998-12-27/sports/1998361115_1_marchetti-unitas-colts

http://articles.baltimoresun.com/2008-05-21/news/0805200334_1_john-sandusky-bowden-raymond-berry

http://articles.baltimoresun.com/2012-09-14/sports/bs-sp-colts-raymond-berry-0914-20120913_1_raymond-berry-raymond-emmett-hometown-hall

http://articles.chicagotribune.com/1985-12-20/sports/8503280388_1_raymond-berry-raymond-clayborn-don-shinnick

http://articles.latimes.com/1986-01-23/sports/sp-28009_1_raymond-berry

http://articles.latimes.com/1989-03-19/sports/sp-345_1_raymond-berry

www.baltimoresun.com/sports/bal-sp.unitas21oct21-story.html

www.businessinsider.com/nfl-50s-tim-tebow-would-have-been-an-offensive-lineman-2011-10

http://fifthdown.blogs.nytimes.com/2009/12/22/falling-out-of-the-playoffs-the-biggest-collapses/?_r=0

http://tv.ark.com/transcript/the_way_it_was-(1958_nfl_champ.__colts_giants)/3468/ESPNCL/Tuesday_January_12_2010/163653/

www.indystar.com/story/sports/nfl/colts/2014/01/25/who-was-better-harrison-or-berry/4867367/
www.nytimes.com/2013/08/06/sports/football/art-donovan-a-behemoth-of-modesty-dies-at-89.html
www.pbs.org/wgbh/pages/frontline/sports/concussion-watch/76-of-79-deceased-nfl-players-found-to-have-brain-disease/
www.profootballhof.com
www.profootballhof.com/hof/member.aspx?PlayerId=25&tab=Highlights
www.profootballhof.com/hof/member.aspx?PlayerId=25&tab=Speech
www.profootballhof.com/multimedia/inductions/2010/12/13/raymond-berry-enshrinement-speech/
www.pro-football-reference.com
www.si.com/vault/1959/10/05/598595/pass-catching-is-thinking-study-and-work
www.si.com/vault/1966/11/14/613384/the-vikings-heat-up-the-war
www.washingtonexaminer.com/johnny-u-working-class-hero/article/25610

Index

About the Coauthor

Wayne Stewart was born and raised in Donora, Pennsylvania, and now lives in Amherst, Ohio, with his wife, Nancy (Panich) Stewart. They have two sons and one grandson.

Mr. Stewart has covered the sports world as a writer for nearly forty years. This is his thirty-first book. He has also written over five hundred articles for publications such as *Baseball Digest, USA Today/Baseball Weekly,* and *Boys' Life;* a Baseball Hall of Fame publication; and Beckett Publications (football, baseball, and basketball). He has written for many Major League Baseball official team publications including the Braves, Yankees, White Sox, Orioles, Padres, Twins, Phillies, Red Sox, A's, and Dodgers.

Furthermore, Stewart has appeared as a sports expert/historian on numerous radio and television shows, including an ESPN Classic program on Bob Feller. He also hosted his own radio shows on a small station in Ohio—a call-in sports talk show, a pregame Cleveland Indians report, and a pregame Notre Dame football program.